MAKING PLACE, MAKING SELF

Making Place, Making Self

Travel, Subjectivity and Sexual Difference

INGER BIRKELAND

University of Bergen, Norway

Routledge
Taylor & Francis Group

LONDON AND NEW YORK

First published 2005 by Ashgate Publishing

2 Park Square, Milton Park, Abingdon, Oxon OX14 4RN
711 Third Avenue, New York, NY 10017, USA

Routledge is an imprint of the Taylor & Francis Group, an informa business

First issued in paperback 2016

British Library Cataloguing in Publication Data
Birkeland, Inger
    Making place, making self : travel, subjectivity and sexual
    difference
    1. Travel - Psychological aspects 2. Travel - Psychological
    aspects - Case studies 3. Identity (Psychology) 4. Identity
    (Psychology) - Case studies 5. Feminist theory 6. North Cape
    (Magerøy Island, Norway)
    I. Title
    910'.019

Library of Congress Cataloging-in-Publication Data
Birkeland, Inger J., 1964-
    Making place, making self : travel, subjectivity and sexual difference / by Inger
Birkeland.
        p. cm.
    Includes bibliographical references and index.
    ISBN 0-7546-3929-0
    1. Women travelers--Psychology. 2. Feminist geography. 3. Tourism--Norway--North
Cape (Magerøy Island)--Psychological aspects. 4. North Cape (Magerøy Island, Norway)--
Description and travel. 5. Feminist theory. I. Title.
    G200.B47 2005
    306.4'819--dc22

                                                                            2005021066

ISBN 13: 978-0-7546-3929-9 (hbk)
ISBN 13: 978-1-138-25523-4 (pbk)

Contents

List of Figures

Acknowledgments

This book could not have been accomplished without the contribution, support and assistance of many people. I would like to thank each and every one of the travellers and informants I met during fieldwork in 1996 and 1997 who generously shared their travel experiences with me. Deeply-felt gratitude goes out to Sofia, whose walk has been a great teacher. She suddenly arrived from the south and showed the way towards the north.

I am tremendously grateful and indebted to Kenneth Olwig and Elisabeth L'orange Fürst for their guidance during the project. They provided invaluable discussion, comments and suggestions during their supervision of this research. In addition, my fellow women in geography – Kirsten Simonsen, Gillian Rose, Liz Bondi, Eli Fosso, Nina G. Berg, Bjørg Lien Hanssen and Victoria Ingrid Einagel – all contributed in important ways. Many people both at home and abroad offered encouraging responses after presenting papers at seminars, workshops and conferences. Special thanks go to all those who discussed ideas for revision with me, read versions of chapters or the manuscript in full, or in other ways contributed to the revision process in substantial and technical ways.

This research project was funded by the University of Bergen (1995-1996) and the University of Oslo (1996-2001). The shipowner of *Ofoten and Vesteraalens Dampskibselskab*, the crew on *Lofoten* and *Nord-Norge* and the small but beautiful tour operator *Feriebussen* provided excellent co-operation during the fieldwork. The Norwegian Non-fiction Literature Fund provided financial support in 2004 to bring this work to completion, while Telemark University College offered a quiet place to write. Thomas Cook Archives gave me permission to reprint copyrighted material. The cover illustration, *Neolithic Goddess Dancing* by Lydia Ruyle, is reproduced by courtesy of Lydia Ruyle.

Thanks to my editors at Ashgate for supporting this project and their patience while this book was in the making.

My family, Arild and Aslak, receive my heart-felt gratitude for their patience, encouragement, love and support.

Inger Birkeland
Midsummer 2005,

Chapter 1

Introduction

An extraordinary departure

In the spring of 1997 one Norwegian newspaper wrote about a young woman from Spain who had walked from Oslo to the North Cape. A distance of over 2100 km. She made the headlines not only because she had walked the distance, but because she said she was walking in search of her own, personal north point. Her extraordinary journey caught my curiosity, and when I read about her, I knew I wished to talk to her to find answers to my questions: What is the north? What is so important about the North Cape? The reason for my curiosity was that I was researching the meanings of the North Cape, a place located in the northernmost part of Norway and a popular tourist destination for travellers and holiday-makers from all around the globe. I intuitively felt that there were answers to my questions in this woman's journey, though I did not understand exactly what these might be at that point.

A few months later my wish came true, and we got the opportunity to talk for a few hours before she went back to Spain. Let us call her Sofia. She generously told me about her life, the reasons for her walking and her experiences during her journey which had taken several months. I was impressed by what I experienced as an exceptional sensitivity mixed with a kind assertiveness towards the world around her. I felt I had much to learn about commitment to personal truths and acting responsibly towards oneself and others, both in the human and non-human world. What Sofia told me has guided the research process ever since then, and her departure for the north continues to fascinate, as I feel her story speaks to many people today. I would like to introduce the theme of this book by telling the story of how she came to search for her personal north point by walking to the North Cape.

Sofia grows up in the 1960s in an urban middle-class family in Spain. She has one brother and one sister, a father working abroad while her mother takes care of the family at home. After basic schooling, she studies to become a teacher, but has problems finding work. It is very hard to get a job in Spain because of high unemployment, so she decides to take another college degree in computer science. In the middle of the 1990s, she feels that she is living a very ordinary life, her future secure. She works in a nice office with nice, ordinary people, just like herself. Weekends and holidays are rich in meaning and activity, and she spends her leisure time on voluntary work, books and studies, friends, travel, and mountain climbing in particular. Over time, she realizes little by little how unsatisfied she is with her life, and that something is missing. She does not feel complete. She feels that her life is passing through her hands. She starts to doubt whether the life she lives is the life she wants to live. One day she realizes she is waiting for the weekend to do the things she likes. She realizes that she is waiting for the summer holidays so she can do the things she likes. Sofia tells me that she felt like she was waiting for her life.

Sofia then decides to stop waiting. She makes an extraordinary decision to quit her job, to give away all her belongings and move away from Spain. Sofia tells me that she started to look for new possibilities and research places all over the world where she could do voluntary work. But something calls her to head North. She becomes inspired to move to Norway, a way to the north. The decision to move to Norway does not belong to the logical realm of life, Sofia says. She cannot explain it, but she feels it is right for her. She discusses the decision with her friends and family. There are mixed reactions. Some of them do not exactly understand why she would leave security for an uncertain future. Some tell her that she is crazy, while others think she is doing the right thing. Sofia tells me that her mother thinks she has 'lost her north'. This is a Spanish saying that describes Sofia's situation. You have lost your north when you stop doing what you have always done, when you take a step out of your ordinary life, when you decide to do something that is not normal, outside of the system or a structure of order. Sofia was told that she did not know where she was because she had lost her north, her point of reference or orientation in life. Sofia explains that in our European civilization, the north is the most important point of reference for travellers. When people want to know where they are, they use a compass, since the needle always points to the north. Ever since olden times, travellers have looked to the North Star to give them direction. When you know where the north is, you immediately also know where the south, east and west are. Then you can get your bearings, and you can go where you want to. To have lost your north means, in other words, that you are lost. You do not know where to go.

Sofia decides to look for her personal north in Norway. She leaves Spain in the autumn of 1996 and settles in a small town in eastern Norway. She finds voluntary work there for a few months, but experiences emotional turmoil and severe depression. Then, one winter morning in 1997, she wakes up early and suddenly realises how to find her north. She must make a new departure. She must go further north, and she must walk. She decides to walk to the North Cape since it is the northernmost point of Europe. Sofia senses that she will find her personal north there. She must walk by foot, partly because she has no other choice as she does not have any money. She wants to walk by foot, even if she feels tired and has little energy. Sofia feels that using her body to travel is the most natural thing to do, since nature has given her two legs to use for transport. Rhythmic walking is the body's natural way of moving. Other ways of movement are inventions of culture. People can travel faster by horse, car, train, ship, bicycle or airplane, but legs are the body's natural tool for movement, Sofia says. The legs create a natural and rhythmic movement when walking which is not present when travelling by other means. Sofia's philosophy of walking also included views on ways of learning. To learn while walking is a very embodied way of learning because of the immediacy of sense impressions, Sofia teaches me. She can listen, observe, smell and touch, and be in the middle of her own life and in the middle of the world wherever she walks. She is in it everywhere. To learn by walking takes time since it is a slow way of learning. In Sofia's words:

> To find myself, I had to use my own rhythm, and this is in walking. I walk inside myself to be inside myself, to look for myself, to use my natural rhythm. This is also walking outside of myself. I have to use the physical world because I am here on earth, and I have to use the ground, the water and other physical things that I can touch. To do that – to travel outside – I had to walk. That is a direct expression of my inside walking.

Sofia started walking in early spring 1997. At that time, the North Cape was only a point on the map at the end of Europe. She walked about 30 kilometres a day for about six months with some short breaks along the way. She only had a rucksack with a few clothes and personal items, a tent and a sleeping bag, and only 130 Norwegian kroner (approximately £11). She hardly ever followed the main roads and avoided walking on the asphalt, choosing instead the smaller roads, crossing forests and small mountains. She was advised not to cross vast, uninhabited areas and mountains alone, but she did cross small mountains and spent several nights outdoors alone. She received help of different kinds during the weeks of walking, as well as free meals and accommodation. Each time she encountered a problem, a solution would come to her. Little by little, she realized that her mood was changing. Instead of feeling more and more tired and broken, she started feeling stronger and better, both physically and mentally. Her mood lightened, and her depression started to disappear gradually. She could not easily explain the reasons for this change. She felt that she was on the right track every day.

Sofia spent about six months reaching North Cape. When she reached the northernmost point, it was ice-cold and snowy, even though it was still late summer. She decided to go back south again at once, but the return journey did not take as many weeks since she hitchhiked all the way.

Sofia's walking to the North Cape as a method of finding her personal north point is a good starting point for presenting the main theme for this book. It is not always easy to have a clear idea of where one is heading when embarking on a journey such as a research project. The research questions behind this book have been inspired by Sofia's philosophy of walking. When I started conducting the research, I was aiming at studying how holiday travel generates experiences of self, or rather, how human beings create self through human encounters with places during holiday travel. I had an idea that self was something located "within" or inside the mind, and that places are located "without" or outside in the external world. Sofia's departure taught me to stop thinking about self and place in terms of dualistic ways of thinking. I have then worked on finding alternatives to dualist thinking, which is in itself quite difficult, given the fact that I am a product of a scientific paradigm and a cultural grammar which has its base in Cartesian philosophy and dualist thinking. Academics generally in the western world are also a product of this. I started researching ways of understanding self and place and how they might be interconnected, and ways of seeing self as a place, and place as a self. The concept of place in human geography and in social and cultural theory may then be thought of as a geographical self, a deep, large and vast self. This understanding has arrived gradually over time, and has been facilitated not just by mindful thinking, but has evolved through the research process as an embodied and mindful journey. This embodied journey has also become a journey of discovery in which one can see bodies as places. As bodies are not sexually indifferent, it has been an ongoing project to create a discourse for discussing place and sexual difference. The main topic of this book is thus to argue for the necessity to theorize place in terms of sexual difference, that place is grounded in sexual difference.

A woman-centred perspective

What is the north? What is the North Cape? What is it that makes Sofia's story interesting? For people living on the northern periphery of Europe, the North Cape has been a landmark for sailors, traders and fishermen. It is part of the natural grazing area for the reindeer herds of the indigenous Sami people. People who do not live in the north have known the North Cape for centuries as being the northernmost part of the European continent which has inspired and attracted travellers to travel north, from renaissance explorers to present day tourists. In an ancient myth, the *Ultima Thule* is a name for the farthest north and the limit of any journey, the edge of the northernmost world. The Italian Francesco Negri, who visited the North Cape in 1664, described his arrival in the following way:

> Here I stand at North Cape, at the outermost point of Finnmark and the edge of the world. Here at the edge of the world my curiosity also ends and I return happily back home (Negri 1664, quoted in Skavhaug 1989).

Much has changed since Francesco Negri's first journey to the North Cape in 1663, though some things remain the same. It seems that people are attracted to the north so they can encounter the edge of the world, the edge of the known world, the edge of our European and western world. The fame of the North Cape among visitors rests partly on its physical and visual shape. From far away and from the sea, the North Cape is a striking, vertical cliff that divides the horizontal arctic plateau from the sea. Since the beginning of modern tourism in Europe, the North Cape has been known as a great place from which to view the midnight sun. The British travel pioneer, Thomas Cook & Son, started organised tourism to the North Cape in 1874. Today the North Cape is a commercial tourist destination embedded in a global economy. Nowadays, nearly a quarter of a million visitors from all over the world visit the North Cape each year, and many travel only in order to have their photograph taken in front of the Arctic Ocean or under the bewildering light of the midnight sun.

Today, the Norwegian popular media often depict the North Cape as an example of mass-tourism, which is so often despised. When the summer season starts in late June, newspaper journalists come with reports from the North Cape. We can read about Norwegians travelling with their camper vans to see the midnight sun or we can peruse snapshot images of German bus tourists toasting in champagne on the cliffs. On the evening television news we can catch a glimpse of groups of chuckling Japanese tourists, portrayed as if they were exotic animals coming out of a zoo. Such images and stories do a good job of maintaining the image of modern mass tourists as peculiar-looking others. This results from confusing the social organization of a particular journey with the individual meaning of the journey. The social organization of North Cape tourism does structure parts of the individual meaning of journey, but we cannot read the individual meaning of the journey from the level of social structure and organization.

In some senses there are similarities between Sofia's journey and Fransesco Negri's journey several centuries ago. They both wanted to find the north as an important personal point of orientation. There is, however, one important difference. Sofia is a woman and she travelled all by herself. Several centuries ago, a wandering woman would have been exposed to life-threatening dangers from the human and non-human world. It would have been much more difficult for a woman to make such a journey, because a woman alone, exposed to nature, would have represented wildness or chaos, and would be a threat to culture. This is not present in today's society in the same way. Today, women do travel alone. They do go hiking alone out in the wilderness, and can do so relatively safely. Nonetheless, women and the feminine still represent a threat to western culture, in the sense that women and "the feminine" is the other for a symbolic order constituted by a male, disembodied self.

Sofia's journey to the North Cape is extraordinary compared to many tourists' experiences in the modern world. Her journey takes place as a direct encounter between an embodied person and the human and non-human world beyond the body. I would suggest that such encounters in the sensuous world will provide transformation qualitatively different from encounters mediated by transport technology or other mediating factors associated with mass tourism in late modernity. Modern travellers who use technical means of transport are embedded in a modern and mechanistic worldview that draws on a widely accepted understanding of the external world as an object, as dead and lifeless matter, in which matter either represents a resource to use or abuse, or an obstacle to be overcome through the use of transport technology. This mechanistic worldview is a part of Cartesian dualism that creates absolute and objective distinctions between mind and body, the internal and the external, the subjective and objective, the self and other, and between the mind and body.

The immediate impression from Sofia's story was and is how extraordinary it seems to undertake such a journey nowadays, in our time and in our part of the world. We can gain access to the north in easier ways. We may think of walking as unnecessary and time-consuming. Walking by foot was something that one did when there were no other means of faster transport. Walking is something that one does today only in a leisurely way at weekends, during short holidays, for a few hours or a few days in the summer holidays. Almost nobody today walks thirty kilometres a day for several months willingly, as air transport makes it easy to transcend the distance from Oslo to Finnmark in less than four hours. But Sofia's journey was by foot and was an existential journey with effects of many kinds. We can imagine how far she travelled "within" when she walked this far "without". Sofia's journey has a character particularly suited to the potential for transformation caused by walking a vast distance for many weeks and months. The urge to walk, though perhaps only at weekends, suggests that humans do not only travel to arrive some place, to find their destination, to reach a goal or an objective. The journey may be meaningful in itself and travel may be more than a means to an end. It may involve the making and remaking of places both known and unknown within one's lived world, though one may not have a clear understanding of where one will end up.

The calling of the north may then have such a strong attraction that it draws people to walk long distances, to do the actual work that travel is, to cross the bridge between the known and unknown. The north is perhaps a myth that signifies an important point of reference that exists outside of the immediate, perceived horizon. As Sofia put it, she travelled to find her own personal north point. Walking towards the North Cape, Sofia personifies the work to overcome a situation in which she has lost her north. She had lost the north of herself. She starts searching for her north by making a literal journey to a northern place. In Sofia's perspective, the north represents a particularly feminine territory of meaning. It is an unknown feminine place, a potentially feminine place in the making. In this context, walking was a method which could be used to find, make, create and recreate truth in terms of a more truthful story, a more useful solution to being *her*self, a feminine place.

In as much as a journey is a search for truth in one way or another, Sofia's journey was quite ordinary. A journey is often viewed as a metaphor for individuation, personal development, change and transformation. In general, travel can be characterized as an exemplary case of personal change, a way of becoming whole and the best that one can be – as, for example, in the understanding of individuation as a journey. The personal change which may be performed through therapy is often described in such terms, as a sort of journey. In C.G. Jung's words, self-knowledge is not an intellectual game, but an arduous journey through the four continents, a journey that embraces all aspects of existence (Jung 1955-6 in Schwartz-Salant 1995:102-103). This theme exists in a broad range of cultural fields: in myths, folklore and fairy tales, in arts and music, film, poetry, novels and other literary genres, and in psychological theory and therapy. In literature or the interpretation of dreams, the journey is an image of a personal change. There is a foreign land or a forgotten place that can be discovered or re-discovered through journeying. Sofia here reminds us of the deeper connection between the self and the world.

It is possible to view the north and the North Cape as a particular place in a person's inner geography. This inner geography is, I argue, similar to the idea of the self, which in Jungian terms refers to the totality or ordering principle of human beings' personality including both the conscious and the unconscious, both centre and circumference. I adopt here a loose Jungian understanding of the self as a concept for the psychic totality of a person. In these terms it is appropriate to see the North Cape as an image of an ordering principle or a stable point of reference from where one may get a new sense of direction or meaning. Thus, we may suggest that Sofia's departure symbolizes the search for her self and her place in a feminine sense, for the ordering principle of the totality of her female inner geography.

A preliminary map for the journey

This book takes its outset in Sofia's departure, and continues with theoretically and empirically informed discussions on place and self mediated through the stories of nine individual travellers and their experiences with the north and the North Cape. The empirical work is based on ethnographic fieldwork and participant observation involving travellers who visited the northern parts of Norway and the North Cape in the late 1990s, with whom life-story interviews were conducted. The stories of the nine individuals differ in many ways from Sofia's story if we are only interested in differences within culture in terms of ways of life. As a human geographer, I would like to shift the perspective from differences within culture to the definition of culture itself. The Cartesian and classical way of understanding culture is to see culture as that which is not nature. I propose to search for a concept of culture which does not depend on an opposition to nature, and which, in addition, is able to account for differences within culture. I include nature in my definition of culture (Birkeland 1998). I will argue that the transformations of place and self, and thus culture, in this sense, constitute one of the most important questions for sustainability and well-being for both nature and culture.

A post-Cartesian cultural grammar needs to understand differences in ways other than just through contrasts. This is the challenge for poststructuralist social and cultural theory. It is probably impossible not to think of some differences without making contrasts. I have already done so myself in describing Sofia's departure as extraordinary, as something which is the opposite of presumedly ordinary departures (associated with tourism). When I describe Sofia's departure as extraordinary below, it is not extraordinary in relation to tourism. Her departure is extraordinary in relation to research traditions that take their outset in thinking about selves and places in terms of dualism. Her departure is extraordinary in that she is a woman searching for a feminine place and self. I am therefore seeking to find a meaningful departure for research in non-dualist terms, focusing on that which exceeds or goes beyond dualism, and I am endeavouring to rewrite place and self in "the feminine".

The main questions that this book addresses are thus: how can we understand place in "the feminine", and what are the potential effects of this understanding in terms of sustainability and well-being for both nature and culture?

By place in "the feminine", I generally refer to the project of difference feminism, which is concerned with sexual difference rather than gender difference. The phrase was originally coined by the philosopher Margaret Whitford (1991), who described the French feminist Luce Irigaray's project as a rewriting of philosophy in "the feminine". Irigaray argues that philosophy has always been written in the masculine language. The man in human being has always been masculine. By this she means that, by offering a critique of phallocentric language, meaning is structured through binary oppositions and this results in the repression of feminine difference. Focusing on the feminine difference refers to a difference that exceeds binary opposites and which moves towards non-dualist ideas of difference. Irigaray and the other French feminists, Julia Kristeva and Hélène Cixous, are known for their ideas on *l'ecriture feminine*, which involves writing and speaking about the feminine difference from a feminine position (Irigaray 1985, Kristeva 1984, Cixous 1990). The basic idea of *l'ecriture feminine* is that the non-dualist difference is named "the feminine". The project of *l'ecriture feminine* is important, because it represents a politics of difference from which difference can be a force for change in modern society and culture (Fürst 1998, Birkeland 2000a).

Thinking place in terms of sexual difference means, as I see it, working towards a strategic reorganization of symbolic language where "the feminine" represents a form of difference without defining it as the opposite of "the masculine". Sofia's journey symbolizes such a departure for speaking and writing place in "the feminine", since she travels outside of organized tourism, outside of the structured wholeness of ordinary everyday life, and moves beyond non-dualist experiences of difference and transformation by walking bodily. As a wandering woman, she signifies the feminine difference, moving towards another truth, feminine truths.

This journey draws on the phenomenological making of place and self that stresses the human beings subjective reality in terms of the life-world. Phenomenology's focus on the lived world, the life-world, or the embodied essence of the place-world, makes sense as a starting point for a discussion of place in "the feminine" (Bigwood 1994). The foundation for writing and speaking about place in non-dualist terms is phenomenology, and, in particular, Edmund Husserl, who postulated the existence of the subjective world and the life-world as the ground for knowledge. There is no knowledge without the existence of knowing subjects, Husserl argued. Husserl shows that knowledge, meaning and consciousness are based in the life-world, and stresses the intentional character of consciousness. Phenomenology searches for the essential nature of human beings' dwelling on earth (Buttimer and Seamon 1980). The nature of human dwelling on the earth, the experiential meanings of places, nature and physical environments for people and the extent to which people fail to or succeed in noticing their geographical worlds, are all important topics for geographers working from a phenomenological point of view. Place is basic for human beings' experience of the world. For the geographer Edward Relph, phenomenology is relevant in order to reawaken a sense of wonder about the earth and its places, a sense of wonder about the world (Relph 1976). Geographers should use Husserl's research programme on the life-world to express human curiosity about and towards the world. This sense of wonder is also described as a sense of *geographicality*, originally a term from the French philosopher Eric Dardel. The term refers to an original wondering about the distinctive and essential relationship between human beings and the earth. Relph argues that place is a hundred times more lived than discursive and is thus as such also taken more for granted. In *Place and Placelessness*, Relph (1976) argued that place has a fundamental significance for human beings, and it may be so that people's relationships to places are just as significant as their relationships to other human beings. Place positions human beings in a way which reveals their external conditions of existence and the depth of human beings' freedom and facticity simultaneously. It is genuinely human for people to have and know their places.

It is not only Husserl who has inspired geographers' place writing. Merleau-Ponty inspired David Seamon to recognize that the experience of place is grounded in the experience of the body (Buttimer and Seamon 1980). The *body-subject*, as Seamon defines it, is the origin of everyday movement or habitual movement that was learned in the past and which will have a direction into the future. Body-subject is a totality of integrating force or energy (drives) and the origin for extension of lived space and world horizons. Heidegger's phenomenology on Being and Being-in-the-world, the basic state of human existence, has also been important for geographers. As Being is always in a world, it means that existence has an environment. Being is always Being of and for a individual person (Tilley 1994). Dwelling, as Heidegger understood it, is a process where the space in which human beings live becomes a personal place or a personal world: a home. According to Seamon and Mugerauer (1989), dwelling is not a closed term for Heidegger. Dwelling is an open term which includes that which may exist beyond the immediate horizon of the home. This will make dwelling into a project, with a direction and a path.

The discovery of the life-world in phenomenological philosophy has influenced many geographers in the twentieth century, but the appropriation of phenomenology among human geographers does not necessarily resemble phenomenology in a philosophical sense (Pickles 1985). The interest in the life-world contributed to research on senses of place, placelessness, and place as a lived experience (see Relph 1976, Tuan 1974 and 1977, Ley 1980), but both place and the life-world were treated as gender-neutral phenomena in geography. How does this research on place work for a woman-centred point of view?

I would question gender-neutral understandings of place and the life-world, and ask how these terms can be understood from the perspective of sexual difference (Bigwood 1993, Fürst 1995, Chanter 1995, Holland and Huntington 2001, Heimenaa 2002). How can understandings of place take their outset in the essentially different, lived worlds of men and women? Woman geographers did not necessarily adopt a woman-centred perspective when geographers started working with phenomenology as one reaction of two against the paradigm of scientism and positivist geography in the 1970s. There were not many women in academic geography then, and being a woman geographer did not necessarily mean that the woman in question had an interest in questions concerning gender or sexual difference. The women who then appeared in geography have, on the other hand, been quite influential (Buttimer 1976, Norwood and Monk 1987, Anderson and Gale 1992, Jacobs 1994).

When the discussion on gender emerged in geography in the early 1980s, the focus was at first on representation. It seemed that geographers were concerned with '"man", as though 'women simply (did) not exist in the spatial world' (WGSG 1984 in McDowell and Sharp 1997:20). The WGSG argued for a feminist geography which would account for the socially created gender structure of society to alleviate gender inequality, both in the short and long term. Feminist geographers argued that this did not only concern the adding of women to geographical analysis but also the changing of the theoretical assumptions underlying the analysis. They argued that the assumptions in phenomenology could not account for women's particular experiences of place, since these did not take into account the power relations between women and men. Women performing gender research in geography in the 1980s and 1990s have primarily worked from perspectives other than phenomenology (McDowell and Massey 1984, Massey 1994, McDowell 1992, Bondi 1997, Berg and Forsberg 2003). Many did not see place as relevant to feminist analysis. One explanation is that the concept of place was considered non-political and without a critical potential, connected to essentialist notions of the local, the ground, the home and the feminine. In this way, it seems that the feminist geographers were colluding with Marxist and socialist geographers who were more concerned with capitalism as the source of social injustice for men and women.

Simultaneously, the ideas emerging on postmodernism, poststructuralism and deconstruction created a stimulus for new research. Feminist geographers became concerned with the problem of theory construction and the way power is connected to theory and knowledge in construction of subjectivity. This was based on a growing theoretical interaction between feminists across the academic disciplines (Harding 1986, Christopherson 1989, Bondi 1990, Bondi et al 2002). Ever since Gillian Rose's groundbreaking book *Feminism & Geography* was published, feminist geographers have recognized that close connections between power, knowledge and subjectivity over time have created masculinist geographical discourses (Rose 1993). When Rose criticized geographers for representing place in terms of woman, she demonstrated that geography's subject position is masculine. This laid bare a clear need to rethink geography's geographical imaginations to include more heterogeneous imagery to account for women's experiences of place. By drawing on a range of spatial imagery used by feminist philosophers, Rose argued for a strategy of paradoxical space to articulate a new geographical imagination that opened up for the difference of other others to create new relationships between power, knowledge and subjectivity in geography. This spatial imagery works with heterogeneous, complex and contradictory geometries and spatialities. The aim was to create a new discursive space within which women could sense, feel, write and talk about space without being forced to choose between centre and margin, in both senses caught in oppressive spaces defined by others. One way was to stand in the paradoxical space and occupy both centre and margin and also elsewhere (Rose 1993, Birkeland 2002). Rose argued that paradoxical space should be seen as one empowering strategy among many open for replacement and reconstruction in the future.

To sum up, a masculinist language has dominated historical and current discourse on the concept of place in geography. The question of sexual difference did not appear until the early 1990s, inspired by debates in feminist philosophy, post-Lacanian psychoanalysis and linguistics concerning the relationship between space, woman and language. This work aims to challenge disembodied, dislocated and implicitly sexed kinds of knowledge. On these grounds, I argue that it is necessary to rethink such basic categories as place and time and to discuss lived life and place-worlds as sexed contextualities of time and place. This is important, because social theory very often structures notions of place in opposition to notions of time, where place acquires its meaning from what time is not. In addition, this pair of concepts is also structured along phallocentric modes of thinking, where place is equated with femininity and time with masculinity, and where masculinity is given a positive value compared to femininity. According to the philosopher Luce Irigaray (1993a:7), Western philosophy has internalized time and temporality in the understanding of the human being, while it has externalized body, matter, and place through an abstraction called "space". Instead, Irigaray sees the temporality of the body, matter and place as central to the constitution of human beings, which comes as two, not one.

In this book I shall therefore discuss phallocentric ideas of place, and towards the end suggest an alternative notion (*chora*) on the grounds that it is necessary to develop sustainable human geographies that take their outset in the interdependency of life on earth, both human and non-human. *Chora*, this notion of place, incorporates time, fluidity, and movement as aspects that can disrupt or reshape phallocentric views of place and time. "The feminine" rupture of place is a travelling mobility and heterogeneity that can be identified both in the stories of the travelling human being and in society at large. The theoretical inspiration for this approach are those, feminist and others, who place the status of the human being in social practice as central, and who seek a third alternative, or some kind of mediation between objectivist and subjectivist theoretical approaches.

In the centre of this work is the understanding of the self as embodied, as uniquely place-open and subject to difference, with sexual difference in particular as the constitutive element for the transformations of both self and place. In the following chapters I will discuss various aspects of self and place. To do this, I need a theoretical map for the journey. The discussion above has hopefully created a preliminary version of such a map. As noted, this map draws on phenomenology and post-Lacanian psychoanalytic feminism. However, it will also become clear at the beginning of this journey that these two traditions do not stand in a face-to-face relationship within which they are able to communicate with each other. The following chapters, the theoretical journey, will go back and forth between these two traditions until I have reached the theoretical north point – that point in my discussion where opposites converge, where I have transcended dualism, and where I can conclude that the self is a place, a geographical place, and where place is a self, a geographical self.

The structure of the book

According to the geographer Mike Crang, research on tourism and travel is traditionally concerned with numbers and quantity, rather than phenomenon, practices and quality (Crang 1999). Within the context of tourism research, this book contributes to a broader view of the qualitative meanings that holiday travel produces in cultural and social terms. It builds on the growing body of international research on travel and tourism from wider theoretical perspectives (Cohen 1979 and 1988, Urry 1990, Lanfant et al 1994, Crouch 1999, Aronsson 2000, Coleman and Crang 2002, Bærenholdt and Simonsen 2004, Bærenholdt 2004). I have sought to incorporate theoretical perspectives gathered from philosophy (Casey 1993, Malpas 1994, 1998, Bigwood 1993, Grosz 1995, Irigaray 1993), social anthropology (Weiner 1991, Bender 1993, Tilley 1994, Auge 1995, Hirsch and O'Hanlon 1995, Feld and Basso 1996, Basso 1996, Gray 1999, Low and Lawrence-Zuniga 2003, and post-Lacanian feminist psychoanalysis (Kristeva 1984, Irigaray 1985) to geographical research traditions on place and space. I acknowledge the relevance of a historical perspective, since historical travel to the North Cape informs the representations of the place today. My focus has nevertheless been to understand the phenomenon of North Cape travel from the perspective of the present and from a woman-centred perspective. This does not mean that I find the perspective of men travelling to the North Cape or the people living in the destination area less important. It only means that my orientation is first and foremost on what we can learn about place in "the feminine" by travelling to the North Cape.

In chapter two I situate and explain the methodological and theoretical framework for the book. The chapter discusses in particular knowledge and place-openness, geography after the crisis of metaphysics and the relationship between tourism, geography and observation through a feminist critique of science and knowledge that leads to the adoption of a feminist or woman-centred point of view.

The methodological and theoretical implications are presented in terms of dynamic, situated and embodied objectivity and subjectivity.

Chapter three discusses the close relationships between tourism, subjectivity and constructions of self. It takes its outset in a critical reading of the changes in the historical production of place-myth of the North Cape in organized tourism. The chapter argues that the making of the North Cape place-myth is connected with a western idea of the self. It is argued that the place-myth is associated with two place-images, the vertical and horizontal shape of the North Cape cliffs and the image of the midnight sun. By comparing the historical production of these images in the 1890s and the 1990s, it is argued that the institutionalization of North Cape tourism has changed the overall place-myth of the North Cape from a sublime myth of the self to a domesticated myth where its former sublime powers have been lost. I conclude the chapter with a request for a re-enchantment of the North Cape place-myth, and propose that it may take a woman's perspective to reanimate the wholeness of the North Cape place-myth.

In chapters four to twelve I present the life stories of nine travellers whom I interviewed during fieldwork. These men and women have very different ages and backgrounds. I have attempted to make a shift from time to place as the ordering principle of writing about life, so that each of the chapters starts with the individual meaning of the journey to the north in the travellers' lives. The stories introduce a theoretical discussion of the particular relationship between self and place that unfolds in the stories, based on the particular meanings of the north in each of the people's lives. Even though each of the stories stands for itself and can be read separately, they can also be read together as an answer to the theme and the questions raised in the introduction. This means that, as the journey to the north unfolds, place and self are transformed. In this sense, the journey to the north represents an epiphany, a turning point for a woman's sense of self. The stories together reveal the meaning of sexual difference in relation to both self and place.

Chapter four introduces Johan and Lena, a couple who live separately but who spend a lot of time together travelling. Johan and Lena experience North Cape differently. The North Cape is meaningful, but difficult to put into words. Lena expresses this by her relative lack of voice (and place) in the story compared to her more outspoken companion, Johan. By drawing on Henri Lefebvre's ideas of leisure space as counter-space, the chapter concludes that leisure places are potential counter-spaces. In this light, the North Cape can be seen as a place for social change if one is able to find an appropriate language for the meaning of this counter-space.

Chapter five starts with the story of Bob, who has travelled the world widely. Bob is unmarried, and lives alone in a working class town. Bob's way of travelling is to sense and to see, to collect places in the world as if they were snapshots in a scrap book. The North Cape does not have any special meaning for Bob. This story is a starting point for a discussion on the connections between travel and masculinity, holidaymaking and identity politics, and representation of (tourist) place in relation to sexual difference. Bob's story sheds light on the discursive connection between place and woman/femininity, which can be seen as a hidden discourse linked to a sexual cosmology, regardless of sexual orientation.

Hans is the main character in chapter six. Hans travelled to the North Cape as a birthday present for himself and turned fifty during the journey. This birthday also marks another turning point for him. It represents a departure from a life centred on a career in banking and a journey towards a new way of living where work is second to quality of life. Hans' journey is a change from a previous way of life to a new way of life, and this forms a starting point for a discussion of the relationship between modern holiday travel, pilgrimage and *rites de passage*.

Chapter seven starts with Julia, a middle-aged woman, who travels to the northern parts of Norway with her husband. Julia feels an attachment to the landscapes of north Europe. She likes the dignity and austerity of it, and the northern nature reflects her inner emotional nature. Julia is in the middle of a very difficult period in her life. She has much to reflect on. The discussion which follows on from this focuses on the inner journey to feminine selfhood as a journey without maps, as a travel story in which a woman is an author of her own story, though not with full authority. It is argued that such journeys take place within a lived world, the life-world or place-world.

Chapter eight presents Marie's story. Marie is a retired teacher who has always lived alone and travelled alone. Throughout her life, Marie has travelled extensively in many parts of the world, and travel has become a method of keeping sanity present in her life. The identity of the outsider is the starting point for discussing the outsider's relationship to home and place. A fluid identity is discussed in terms of feminine identity. Fluidity works as a metaphor for the essence of the feminine, which opens up for the possibility to understand place as becoming, and becoming as home in a fluid, non-fixed sense.

Marianne's search for open space is presented in chapter nine. Marianne travels with her husband to the northern parts of Norway, but is not very happy about the sea voyage. She left the ship at the final port on the northbound route. Open space is very important for Marianne; to feel free, safe, comfortable and at home, to have her feet on the ground. Marianne's longing for open space is the starting point for a discussion of place as a metaphor for feminine subjectivity. Different ways of using spatial metaphors in feminist research are discussed. The discussion is extended with a more critical approach to language, representation, and space.

Chapter ten tells Barbara's story and her way of collecting memories through photographs. Barbara is a young woman who has managed well in working life. Barbara travels to the northern parts of Norway to see her fathers' relatives, their places and to find a place for her father in her own life history. She needs these people and places as images of the north to become complete, for an ordered narrative of the self consisting of time, place and images. It is argued that image, through the meaning of photography, is undervalued in order to create self. The north may thus embody a new part of the ongoing narration of self, where the spatiality of the self covers both the interior and the exterior worlds in a way that transcends dualist thinking.

In chapter eleven, we meet Lavinia, who has a very mixed experience of the North Cape. It was a tourist machine full of people and noise, and quite barren. There was, nevertheless, a feeling of walking at the end and on the edge of Europe, which was an aesthetic, spiritual and emotional experience for Lavinia. This story draws attention to the experience and construction of the positive and transformative content of holiday travel, and the meaning of leisure for women in the western world. The chapter discusses a feminine aesthetic of travel, and ends with a revised understanding of the female aesthetic subject and the feminine sublime, made evident to a women through travel.

In chapter twelve we read about Lars who is an elderly man, a farmer and fisherman. His story is about the experience of seeing the midnight sun at the North Cape. Through his story, Lars unveils for us the extraordinary experience of seeing the midnight sun, which involves viewing the dawning of the sun above the horizon. To see the sun descending and then ascending is a spiritual experience that is full of awe and the sublime. Lars' story is full of wonder, of the simultaneous creation of place as dwelling in the world. It brings forth a discussion about the affirmation of life through creation of place in relation to creation myths connected to the sun from the European north. The chapter concludes with a discussion of seeing the dawning of the midnight sun as a participation in female creation.

Then, in chapter thirteen, I draw the theme of this book together through a discussion of a new conceptualization of place. It is argued that place concepts which depend on dualist thinking are harmful since they deprive place of an animated status. Place becomes a feminized object, not subject. Through a sympathetic critique of gender-neutral and essentialist understanding of place, the concept of place is rewritten. I take Gillian Rose's suggestions for paradoxical space as an empowering strategy and simultaneously develop them further into a geographical imagination that affirms place in "the feminine". I argue that any discourse on place is also a discourse on woman. By deliberately equating place with woman, through the story of Sofia and her journey to find her personal north point, I argue that we should start affirming woman as first place. I further argue that if geographers truly wish to understand place, we must appreciate place as embedded in sexual difference. The philosopher Luce Irigaray shows the way to work with female imagery in the making of place and self in "the feminine".

Why is it important and necessary to create female imagery and make feminine geographical imaginations a strategy for geography in "the feminine"? I will argue that this is of the greatest value. Geography must affirm the identity between woman and place in a more critical and substantial way. This involves working with difference thinking and it means taking the relationship between language and sexual difference more seriously. In the final sections, I suggest ways of rethinking and rewriting place in "the feminine". I take the existence of sexed life-worlds as a starting point, explore the possibility of an understanding of place (in terms of *chora*) from a woman-centred point of view, and rewrite the concept of place by drawing on post-Lacanian psychoanalytic feminist perspectives. Finally, I will argue that writing place from a woman-centred point of view can be termed *choragraphy;* the creation and recreation of essentially different places and selves. Place is thus rewritten in terms of sexual difference, with a focus on becoming rather than being. From talking about dwelling in places, we might talk about dwelling-as-path, where place becomes path and the continual becoming of self.

Chapter 2

The Journey to Knowledge: Place-openness

The geographer as traveller: seeing and knowing

This chapter discusses the methodological question: what does a woman-centred perspective imply in terms of new insights about geography and travel? The question will be answered by discussing a feminist theory of knowledge that creates a well-argued connection between female subjectivity and feminist objectivity. To do this, I will analyse two methodological problems in field research that take their outset in a reconstruction of my own subjective experiences from two periods of fieldwork. The first problem concerns the status of observation in objectivity, while the second concerns the relationships between lived life and the textual representation of this. The starting point for field research is that development of knowledge takes place somewhere. This somewhere is a field. A field is not a physical locality or a territorially fixed community, but a field of care for creation and recreation of knowledge. The field encompasses the researcher and the researched and the factual social relations and interaction between these, in addition to the constitution and outcome of these relations.

The first fieldwork period took place in the municipality of North Cape in July 1996. I had three aims with this preparatory fieldwork. Firstly, I wanted to test out some of the choices of method for the primary fieldwork period, and secondly, I wanted to make contact and conduct interviews with key informants. Thirdly – and this is what I want to elaborate on below – I wanted to reflect on my own preoccupations and taken-for-granted meanings concerning the North Cape by putting myself in the position of a tourist. As a researcher studying tourism, it seemed important to turn myself into a reflexive tourist to reflect on both subjectivities. When entering the field, I saw the visitors' experience of the North Cape as based in visual impressions, and identified with this visual mode of perception. As a field worker and tourist, I took pictures of what was meaningful to me, of tourists who took pictures of the place or of each other taking pictures. Tourists took pictures of me. I was a tourist, and I was not, and I could not know whether any of the other tourists were also field workers. In some sense, they were all workers in the field. I was an object of the tourist gaze, just as much as any other tourist. With a more reflexive mode, I tried to experiment with observation. I spent hours observing from morning to midnight. I had the camera in front of me to look like a tourist (or what I expected a tourist to look like). I took a lot of pictures, and saw the difference between these as the difference between an insider and an outsider, a participant and an observer. It is hard to describe the switch between looking as a geographer and looking as a tourist. It may be like a movement in intention or a sudden change in unintended attention towards something that happened in the environment. Other experiments with observation included sitting outside or in the midst of a crowd of tourists taking notes on what I was observing and why.

After returning home, I felt that I had started Real Research, but I did not feel that I had found Truth with a capital T, as if Truth was deep inside the cliffs at the North Cape, waiting for someone to discover it in a visual sense. It felt more like having encountered otherness in a more-than-visual sense, without knowing the deeper layers of these truths. The field gave me an experience of research as a form of conversation with otherness. It felt like crossing a boundary between the known and the unknown with an understanding of the unknown as existing both within my internal world and in the external human and non-human world. It is quite familiar to introduce the journey as a root metaphor for the research process. Mats Alvesson and Kaj Sköldberg (1996) have argued that reflexive empirical research often progresses in much the same way as a journey does. The journey works as a root metaphor for the research process as a particular symbolic form underlying the scientific discourse in terms of a particular philosophical ground. According to Steinar Kvale, the researcher in social research 'wanders through the landscape and enters into conversations with the people encountered' (Kvale 1996:4). I will add that the researcher in geography may also enter into conversation with the places and nature encountered. Kvale compares the view on research as a journey with the previously more familiar root metaphor for research, the mining metaphor, based in realist and objectivist philosophies of science terms. The journey, on the other hand, creates conversations and communication.

Conversation and communication is profoundly human as a dialogue between two persons, beings about a particular topic. As such, it questions the meaning of being and being's meaning in fundamental ways. In this book, I have chosen to work with conversation from hermeneutical, phenomenological and constructivist perspectives. The goal of conversation is understanding, or knowledge, which put hermeneutical interpretation in the centre. Hermeneutics is traditionally a theory of the art of interpretation but is developed in the social sciences for interpretiation of social practices and events as texts. Hermeneutics was from the beginning on a method to reach understanding, illustrated with a hermeneutic circle consiting of parts and wholes. This hermeneutic process of understanding was later illustrated as a spiral movement (Alvesson and Sköldberg 1996). I have taken this a step further in this book by imagining the hermeneutical process as a journey.

Hermeneutical understanding or truth (*aletheia*) elucidates the melting of different horizons of understanding, which includes meaning, prejudice, values and knowledge. Human beings understand the horizons of other human beings through applying their own horizon. The early hermeneutics of the nineteenth century saw hermeneutics as a method to find absolute or objectivist truth, arising from subjective consciousness and the dualistic thinking of rationalism. Twentieth century theorists and philosophers of hermeneutics turned away from the subjectivism of the early hermeneutics and saw intersubjectivity as the starting point for understanding. Understanding of meaning was then not reducible to interpreting conscious meaning. To find the meaning of meaning one had therefore to make a detour from the immediate consciousness of human beings because understanding or truth may be hidden or not directly available for the individual. The hermeneutical method has since been associated with uncovering hidden, unknown or opppressive meaning. It is argued that hidden meaning contributes to the way things are constituted.

Non-subjectivist hermeneutics is, however, not just one tradition of thought. We may distinguish between existential hermeneutics, hermeneutics of suspicion and poetic hermeneutics. Some authors name poetic hermeneutics a hermeneutics of faith or a recovery of tradition (How 1995). The works of Marx, Freud and Nietzsche are central in the hermeneutics of suspicion. Instead of interpreting subjective meaning, these thinkers focus on economic, unconscious and power structures as constitutive for understanding. Martin Heidegger's later works exemplify existential hermeneutics by representing a way back to the origin of hermeneutics: back to being and the conditions for being. The main thing for Heidegger was to seek the concrete facticity of being and to understand this world we are living in, before all abstractions, before rationalization and building of theory (Alvesson and Sköldberg 1996). Compared to Husserl, who would maintain that subjectivity was the first thing to seek, Heidegger sought existence which was already thrown out without warning, so to speak, in an already existing world. Existence for Heidegger was never abstract, it was concrete and particular and individual. Existential hermeneutics brought three ideas from Husserl, according to Alvesson and Sköldberg. Firstly, knowledge is intuitive and incorporates meaning as a criterion of truth. Secondly, the starting point for experience and knowledge is to differentiate between impressions (*Erlebnis*) and experience. Thirdly, intentionality exists as a part of the lifeworld. Being-in-the world was a temporal and spatial being-in-the world, and intentionality forms a part of this temporal-spatial being.

In a more poetic form, the late Heidegger, Ricoeur and Gadamer deal with language as constitutive of meaning. Central is the discovery of an underlying pattern of metaphor or narration. The common thread for the latter is that language is not only instrumental and formal, it is poetic and metaphoric. Hans-Georg Gadamer (1989) is one of the main contributors to the development of poetic hermeneutics, and has had a strong impact in both social science and the arts. Gadamer shows that the task for hermeneutics is not to develop procedures for understanding, but to make clear the conditions which make understanding possible. Gadamer treats understanding as participation in a process of tradition, like a process of transfer where the past and the future constantly move through reinterpretation. Renewal is in this way closely related to language use. Gadamer argues that language is central in hermeneutic pre-understanding and that language

– and thereby understanding and thinking – is profoundly metaphoric and poetic, not logical and formal.

Aesthetics and art are important for the understanding of culture for Gadamer, since art is understood as the capacity to create images or representations of experience (as aesthetic experience). Images are important as representations of experience because image relates to culture and the cultivation of tradition (*Bildung*). The root of *Bildung* is bild, form, image and picture, and cultivation refers to a process of forming one's self in relation to a normative image or picture. Bildung translates thus to culture, or in other words to the human way of developing one's natural talents and capacities (Gadamer 1989:10). Gadamer frees the understanding of aesthetics, culture and meaning from the subjectivism which it had aquired in classical aeshetics and modern philosophy.

Below I draw on hermeneutical interpretation to elucidate one aspect of the research process associated with the construction and reconstruction of subjectivity and objectivity in both tourism and geography. The focus for the discussion is the use of images in tourism and visuality in modern culture in general. It is a historical fact that observation has been, and still is, important for both tourism and geography. There are important similarities, but also critical differences between seeing and knowing, observation and objectivity in both tourism and geography. Observation created feelings of uneasiness for me during fieldwork because it reminded me of geographical and masculinist observation, discussed by Gillian Rose (1993). On the other hand, I experienced in the field that tourists may objectify and invade others, including the researcher, thus blurring the picture of who is objectifying who. The dilemma for me as a geographer was how to use observation and photography as a means of creating knowledge, while deconstructing and reconstructing observation so as not to use it in an objectifying way. As an ethically conscious geographer, there are limits to how I may use the observations, because the contexts for observation are different for researchers than for tourists. I had to take care so that my observations would not lead to unwanted consequences for the observed tourists. These judgments led to philosophical conversations with the deeper layers of the historical relations between observation, subjectivity and objectivity in both tourism and geography.

Observation, subjectivity and objectivity

It can be argued that geographers helped pave the way for the educated tourist (the 'traveller'), and that the sense of seeing has been important for tourists and geographers. There are similarities between the visual logic of the tourist and the geographer historically speaking (Birkeland 1997). To travel and to see with one's own eyes has been one way for people to learn about other places, different landscapes and unknown territories for centuries. Research on tourism often states that the tourist is basically interested in visual impressions or sightseeing (Urry 1990, MacCannell 1976). Sociologist Judith Adler argues, however, that looking has not always been important in historical travel (Adler 1989). From medieval times, European travel represented a conditioning of the privileged male populations, but it was only in the late eighteenth century that sightseeing and observation became important. In one sense, then, the tourist gaze is a particular modern and male gaze. This is a point frequently made by both feminist and non-feminist writers on the modern condition (Lefebvre 1991, Mulvey 1989, Wolff 1994). Many critical theorists argue that the sense of seeing has been dominant in knowledge production in modernity, in a way that has had destructive effects for individual human beings and societies (Lefebvre 1991). According to Henri Lefebvre, an abstract, visual logic and a masculine rationality have abandoned the body and instead found a resting place in pure, abstract thought. The sense of seeing privileges distance rather than relatedness, and I suggest that objectivity thus is essentially a question related to sexual difference.

Geographer Gillian Rose has argued that geographical research, historically speaking, has depended on observation (Rose 1993). She uncovered the inherent masculinism in the construction of geographical knowledge through a deconstruction of the relationship between objectivity and observation. Masculinism refers here to male notions and a male outlook of the world that argues to speak and look on behalf of all, but which, according to Rose, speaks and looks on behalf of men. She shows that being a geographer has been to occupy a masculine subject position constructing feminized objects of study. The masculine subject position implies representation of geographical knowledge by drawing on particular images of 'Woman' (with a capital W), where Woman refers to fantasized images and not historical women. Her analysis shows that, by drawing on post-Lacanian feminist psychoanalysis, knowledge and objectivity are connected to sexuality and visual desire arising from implicit meaning in the geographer's subjectivity. Rose's deconstruction of geographical discourse shows that the geographer projected wanted or unwanted emotions and qualities onto his object of study.

The critique of masculinism in geographical research traditions is important for the understanding of the relationship between observation and truth. As I see it, Gillian Rose has offered a poststructuralist critique of the construction of the subjectivity of the geographer from a particular perspective, where visuality (in terms of projection) is central. There are, however, limits to this analysis, since it does not open for a phenomenological analysis of the relationship between observation and objectivity. A poststructuralist perspective may create a separation between the sense of seeing and other sense impressions, which connects seeing to men and other sense impressions to women, thus essentializing woman and "the feminine" according to a division of labour between the senses. The most important point, however, in Rose's analysis, is the identification of a historical and structural connection between observation and masculinism to represent geographical knowledge objectively, which should be taken seriously in social research based on observational methods.

The historical connection and blurring between seeing and knowing in both tourism and geography is a good starting point for alternative stories on truth and objectivity (Nash 1996, Kirby 1996b, Nast and Kobayashi 1996). I find that it is important to maintain a concept for objectivity to express the radical historical specificity that makes knowledge an object for reinterpretation and negotiation because of the historical and structural connection between masculinism, objectivity and observation. In the following, I will discuss objectivity in a way that is situated in the embodied, situated and dynamic character of subjectivity. Given the need to stress the relationship between subjectivity and truth, the important question is to ask what makes subjective experience objective. The focus, then, is on the context of observation, and the understanding that no sense impressions exist independent of contexts of interpretation and understanding.

The relationship between objectivity and observation is often discussed with reference to psychoanalytical theory, with an identification of the visual logic as a male logic (Keller and Grontkowski 1993). Historian of science Evelyn Fox Keller draws for example on psychoanalytical and psychological theory to understand the gendered character of scientific development (Keller 1985). Keller's argument takes its outset in the physical sciences, but is also relevant for understanding geographical research traditions. Keller argues that there has been a serious ideological problem in the understanding of objectivity as disinterested and autonomous. The cause was a failure to perceive the mother as subject, which affects the understanding of cognitive development. For young children, the external environment consists primarily of the mother. The environment is like an extension of the child. The psychological switch from identification with mother to identification with father partly explains the historical cognitive switch to autonomy and objectivity in the sciences, according to Keller.

Keller places this cognitive switch as the cause for a historical confusion where autonomy and objectivity are associated with separation and independence from others. Instead, Keller argues for another way of viewing autonomy and objectivity. She looks for flexibility in the boundaries between objectivity and subjectivity based on an affirmation of a connection between knowledge and sexuality, power and love. To do this, we must depart from seeing the process towards objectivity as linear, because this is part of the problem. One does not move from A to B, but in complex, interactive and dynamic processes. Keller uses the metaphors of the maternal and the paternal to understand this dynamic process. She says one must not take the maternal and the paternal as fixed points, but instead stress world-openness and movement between the maternal and the paternal in the journey towards objectivity and autonomy. We should preferably work with dynamic objectivity, an understanding where objects and subjects in the world are granted independent integrity, but in a way that relies on connectivity and reciprocity between objectivity and subjectivity.

Donna Haraway also stresses this complex interaction between autonomy and connectivity. She uses vision positively to illustrate a new objectivity, a new objective knowledge which she names situated knowledge (Haraway 1988). Haraway argues for alternative stories. Her alternative stories are, as I see it, connected to individuation, separation, the birth of the self, but not to an alienating autonomy that is all-powerful. The story of individuation and separation is also a story of connectedness and relatedness, just as they also contain the possibility for difference and otherness, individuation and autonomy. Knowledge, as Haraway sees it, is constructed, and is historically and geographically specific and relative connected to the human condition and to human subjectivity. The problem is to stress the plurality of local claims of knowledge and to maintain the view that objective knowledge must be linked with subjective experience. Haraway brings forth vision as a metaphor for a new objectivity, because it is embodied, particular and belonging to somebody. The metaphor reminds us that only a partial perspective is an objective perspective, because specific experience is located somewhere. This means that there are no innocent perspectives. Geographers, tourists and others are in constant movement, but not in a way that implies detachment from the ground or from social contexts of observation. What movement and travel do imply for a geographer, however, is the provision of a privileged position of situational choices in-between detachment and engagement.

In light of a woman-centred perspective, Donna Haraway is more unclear in terms of what a gendered and sexed understanding of subjectivity means for objectivity. Haraway understands subjectivity in terms of the cyborg, a hybrid between organism and machine that goes beyond classic theories of subjectivity, like psychoanalysis. Haraway argues that cyborg subjectivity should follow other routes than those which go through psychoanalysis, the masculine economy and its dependence on the Other as Mother (Haraway 1991). Subjectivity, according to Haraway, goes through other women and people who are illegitimate according to the masculine economy. Haraway comes close to the French feminists' politics of difference with one major exception since Haraway's cyborg subjectivity is unrelated to sexual difference as a lived and embodied difference. The difference of the sexed body is not relevant to Haraway, and the difference of the female body in relation to the male body for subjectivity becomes blurred. Paralleling Luce Irigaray's statement that speaking (as) woman is not identical to speaking about women (Irigaray 1985), it seems to me that knowing, thinking and writing (as) woman does not appear in Haraway's picture.

I find that cyborg subjectivity does not engage properly with phallocentric language. Phallocentrism means the privileging of the phallus as the original and true signifier in language, also named the Father's Law according to the French psychoanalyst Jacques Lacan (Grosz 1990). This means that language refers to male symbolism and imagery, and not to female symbolism and imagery. It is difficult to be a female feminist subject engaging with phallocentrism. Feminists writing on the relationship between feminism and psychoanalysis have discussed ways to engage with phallocentric texts (ibid:167). The two most discussed paths are either to play the role of a dutiful daughter who submits to the Father's Law or to play the role of a defiant and independent woman. This second path may also lead in several directions. Most known is the path of mimicry, where the reader assumes the feminine role deliberately, and converts what seems like subordination into an affirmation, which thus thwarts or jams phallocentrism. Another path for the defiant woman is to speak as a mysteric, which is a word that connects the hysteric and the mystic. The mysteric can be seen an enigmatic figure whose discourse is untouched by phallocentrism. The mysteric speaks through the hysteric's conversion of emotions to bodily symptoms in the language of the female religious mystic, as described by Luce Irigaray (1985).

My own engagement with phallocentrism is that of a defiant woman, but not by exercising mimicry or writing like the mysteric. The reason is that it is too easy to misunderstand these counter-discourses. It is walking on a double-edged sword where one risks assimilation in a phallocentric discourse or where one does not communicate because one speaks in a foreign language. I choose another point of departure. I see Sofia's philosophy of walking as my model, where my position is to speak as a female human, which means speaking as a human with a body that can walk and talk, as most bodies are able to do, but which in addition can birth, something which only female bodies can do. This subject-position emphasizes that humans have been born by a woman and which makes the female human an example of pure difference. It is a position that acknowledges birth as female creation (Battersby 1998). Speaking from this position, I risk being accused of hysterocentrism or gynocentrism. This is a kind of reversal of phallocentrism where the womb, the maternal function, is privileged instead of the phallus. I maintain that it is necessary to remain faithful to the difference of two sexes and that the split between male and female occurs before language in the body as it is created. This does not imply that gynocentrism is a reversal of phallocentrism. The important thing is to think of the difference in ethical terms, and to consider the accessibility of the other in terms of radical alterity, a non-reductionistic difference (Irigaray 1993).

Subjectivity and objectivity both have bodily roots. I would maintain that sexual difference is important for constructions of both subjectivity and objectivity. The different embodied subjectivity of women and men lead to different stories based on the bodily differences that emerge as lived and sensed differences in a phenomenological sense. In order to shed more light on a woman-centred point of view in this, I would like to draw more attention to Luce Irigaray, who shows how woman is both the boundary/the Other against which subjectivity is constructed and that which confuses all boundaries (Battersby 1998). One of Irigaray's paradoxical views is that woman does not exist but may start to speak (Irigaray 1985). Irigaray does not want to make woman subject or object in a discourse. To speak as woman is to be in an impossible position. It is, according to Christine Battersby, to be in the position of an 'object' with a subjectivity that is neither masculine nor Other (Battersby 1998). It is a genuinely creative event since a perpetual creation of subjectivity is in process. Being a woman with a subjectivity that is neither masculine nor Other means, at one level, a continuous crossing of symbolic borders and, at other levels, to move in a terrain where there are no borders, symbolically speaking (Kristeva 1984).

To conclude this section, my subjectivity is as a female, feminist geographer encountering life and place – and their transformations – through travel. This subjectivity is dynamic and not separated from a dynamic sense of objectivity. In the spirit of world-openness, and what I translate to place-openness, I find much value in Max Oelschlaeger's view that geography can speak to philosophy in the context of the crisis in metaphysics (Oelschlaeger 1997). Geographical knowledge evokes the palpably and cosmologically real because it provides a sense of place dependent on other human beings and their relations to nature, land, climate, vegetation, water and mountains. In the modern world, the human being ("man") has been theorized as a man apart, over and above and in control of the land, places and nature, a human being with no home in his or her own body as place. History and geography have become place-less and being has become transcendental, free of becoming, relations or interpretation. What actually exists instead, Oelschlaeger suggests, are living, feeling, embodied, historical and geographical human subjects who have historical and particular knowledge of themselves and the world. An important part of this knowledge, as I see it, is that this human "being" implicates sexual difference. This means that the truth of being, as I have understood it, implies subjectivity in sexed ways and a reconciliation of respect for human beings' plural experiences and, simultaneously, a critical investigation of language's possibility to reconstruct human experience. The key that unlocked the potential for such understanding is the particular association between observation, objectivity and masculinity analysed above, which, in the end, contribute to explaining the use of post-Lacanian feminist psychoanalysis in combination with phenomenology.

Travelling fieldwork

In reflections on the relationship between the cultural and the spatial in fieldwork, anthropologists have voiced a new sensitivity towards investigating what field actually refers to (Okely 1996, Olwig and Hastrup 1997, Gupta and Ferguson 1997). They ask what one can do when the field is no longer stable or territorially fixed. They show that the anthropological field today refers to an interconnected world. People, objects and ideas rapidly move, and refuse to stay in place, like the global, interconnected network of moving subjects, objects and ideas discussed by Lash and Urry (1994).

Travelling human beings, like tourists, do not stay within place, if we by place refer to a territorially fixed locality. When planning for fieldwork among tourists in 1997, I saw human beings as moving places equipped with an idea of travelling fieldwork. This idea was mainly based on process oriented fieldwork in feminist social research (Wolff 1996, Nielsen 1990, Catz 1996) and the reflexive turn in the social sciences (see for example Clifford and Marcus 1996, Bourdieu and Waquant 1992, Fog 1993, Freeman 1993, Kvale 1996). My understanding of fieldwork was further focused on process in various ways inspired by the recent interest in flows, fluent processes, fluidity, change and continuity, trajectories etc, in philosophy and the social sciences. I understand travelling fieldwork simply to refer to the grounding of travelling theory (Clifford 1986, 1992). Central to both travelling theory and travelling fieldwork is the idea of movement from one point of departure to a site of arrival with an accompanying movement of meaning. Social anthropologist James Clifford views the travel metaphor as a tool for cultural comparison in order to gain comparative knowledge (Clifford 1992, 1997). Cultural comparison and communication is cultural translation that quite literally has created cultural movement and mental travel. Clifford shows that travel is a translation term that encourages the blurring, contestation and negotiation of other categories in general, which is useful for cultural critique. Edward Said was the first to discuss the idea of travelling theory as a way to situate and contextualize theory (Said 1984, in Gregory 1994). In geography, Derek Gregory finds travelling theory relevant for the critical project of permanent reflection and self-reflection and the globalization of intellectual cultures (Gregory 1994). Gregory argues that travelling theory does not really redraw the landscape of knowledge as much as call the principle of representation, and mapping in particular, into question. The most important aspect of such movement of meaning in fieldwork is, as I see it, that there are no absolute borders between the known and the unknown, home and away. Fieldwork is like travelling in-between the known and the unknown, in order to facilitate communication and critical reflection. As a travelling fieldworker, I became a wanderer, a pathfinder, an explorer of traces and tracks made by human beings, others as well as myself, in own and other places, both here and there, known and unknown.

For fieldwork in 1997, I decided to join travel parties travelling to and from the north of Norway to understand better the situatedness of the travel experience from a phenomenological point of view. The North Cape was only one stop among many along the tourists' itineraries. This made my field not a small, localized area, but a large and indeterminate field consisting of the actual journeys to and from North Cape. This fieldwork took its outset in one round trip with the coastal steamer *Hurtigruta*, which is the common name for the coastal steamers that regularly go between Bergen and Kirkenes. The fleet at the time of the fieldwork consisted of eleven ships, owned by three different companies who sell passenger and freight transport. The timetables change according to the season, with daily departures both north and southbound at each of the thirty-four stops along the route. It takes eleven days to sail from Bergen to Kirkenes and back to Bergen again, and it is one of the main ways to reach the North Cape, as the ships arrive in Honningsvåg harbour near the North Cape cliffs.

Hurtigruta was an appropriate field as a place for encounters between many different, individual travellers. I had the time, place and flexibility to move around and meet people, in addition to having places to conduct interviews. On the first trip with *Hurtigruta*, I conducted fifteen life history interviews with individuals from the ages of twenty-two to seventy from many countries in the western world, with a bias towards the educated middle class. When I returned home from the fieldwork in June, I felt intuitively that I wanted to get a broader picture of North

Cape travel. I decided on a combination tour in early August 1997 with *Feriebussen*, called 'late summer experiences along the coast' that was promoted in the western parts of Norway. *Feriebussen* is the tour operating activity of a local bus company in Norway and has over thirty-five years of experience selling bus tours for Norwegians. Holiday tours have been their main activity over the years. The itinerary of this trip was by airplane from Oslo Airport to Kirkenes with the *Hurtigruta* from Kirkenes southbound to Bergen. This trip took seven days and the travel party was rather large, consisting of ninety persons. During the voyage from Kirkenes to Bergen, I conducted six interviews with eight individuals in total, all middle-aged and elderly Norwegians mainly with working class backgrounds.

I kept a field diary during fieldwork. The field diary was a tool to help remember situations, events, emotions, discussions, and to corroborate the interpretative work after the fieldwork. I made distinctions between events and acts and my perceptions of these, but I was aware that both realities are constructions and not direct representations of reality.

Life writing

The stories this book is based on refer to the shared creation of knowledge structured by a selection of the life history interviews conducted during the fieldwork. Fieldwork and life story interviews were a tool for learning about transformations of place and self. I chose to work with biographical methods because of the similarities between the making and writing of self. The idea that human beings order events into wholeness through storytelling is a universal fact in humanism. Traditionally, time is seen as the key to wholeness, with the lifetime as the key organizing principle for creation of meaning through storytellling. I wanted to explore place as that structuring principle instead of time. I suggest that place experience and place events work as an ordering principle in terms of being a meaningful field of experience that create change in the life of a human being. The life of a human being is, I find, a place, perhaps more a moving, vertical body-place, than a being defined in terms of the horizon of the lifetime. Thus, place is both the origin and result of human existence, and the process where life unfolds. It is both structured and structuring. I argue that the shift from time to place as an ordering principle represents a shift towards a woman-centred perspective. Below I will discuss this shift further, since it informs my way of working with place in the coming chapters. The consequence of this shift is a greater sensitivity to the relationship between place, language and sexual difference.

What are the relationships between place, language and sexual difference? Here I turn to feminist philosopher Rosi Braidotti who provides some philosophical glue (Braidotti 1991, 1994). She criticizes the gap between thinking and lived life in modern philosophy that is based on the Cartesian division between body and mind. Braidotti says that this gap or this division between thought and lived life cannot be restored by pouring in more knowledge. She finds ways that move beyond

Cartesian dualism and shows the importance of the materiality in-between bodies and places for embodied knowledge. Braidotti formulates the Cartesian dualism as a situation in which we all, both men and women, have become epistemological orphans. This epistemological homelessness has created an unavoidable historical condition characterized by ontological insecurity (Braidotti 1991). Such experience is, however, also the origin of an ontological desire for other truths, other ways of knowing. Braidotti has proposed a way forward and uses the historical condition to write other knowledges that include the body, lived life, the subjective, emotions, irrational ways of behaving and being.

The place of epistemological homelessness can be thought of as the place of the nomadic subject, which is a figuration originally from Donna Haraway which Braidotti uses to refer to ways of expressing feminist forms of knowledge that are not caught in a mimetic relationship to dominant forms of knowledge (Braidotti 1994). Nomadic knowledges, cartographies, are never either good or bad, but always useful, constructive and critical in passionate ways. To Braidotti the nomadic subject is an existential condition that also works as a style of thinking and working. This nomadism is an intellectual landscape, a horizon, a frame of reference, and each text written is like a camp site, that traces places where the nomadic subject has been, like the shifting landscape of her singularity, Braidotti writes (ibid:17). Braidotti's account of nomadism and nomadic subjectivity expresses a situated and localized ethics, a politics of location applied to writing that produces a totemic geography.

This nomadism exemplifies, if we see it metaphorically, metaphor as a method for explaining the unknown through the known. Many cultural theorists have adopted similar strategies in the 1990s as a response to the fall of European rationality where knowledge no longer can claim to speak for everything and everybody (Chambers 1994). It is useful to think of thinking in terms of nomadism because there is a need to think in non-fixed and fluid ways.

Braidotti's vision of nomadic subjectivity and new cartographies is inspiring for place writing. This shift from time to place is now familiar in post-modern research strategies, where place and spatiality have become more important for structuring events and human experience (Gottschalk 1998). The epistemological position that corresponds with this image of knowledge production is the shifting field in-between radical constructionism and feminist critical empiricism (Haraway 1988, Harding 1986). The feminist standpoint is blended here with a post-modern view of plurality and difference, multiplicity, and local knowledge that is particular and contextual. According to psychologist Jane Flax, a post-modern voice is non-authoritarian, open-ended, and process-oriented (Flax 1990). There is an experience that there is no absolute, static or solid ground under one's feet. The ground exists, but it is not absolute, and has shifting meanings. People move on a floating ground and ground things on a moving earth (Clifford and Marcus 1986). Clifford and Marcus' metaphorical use of plate tectonics illustrate the point that truth is contextual and that contexts change. One must constantly refer to the situated character of knowledge and the limitations to what one has to say.

This focus on place as an ordering principle was useful during the life story interviews. Literature on biographical methods focuses most often on the structure of the life in terms of history or temporality, while I wanted to develop a better understanding of the geographical dimensions. There are at least three characteristics of the biographical method (Bertaux 1981) that can be rearranged with a stronger focus on place. The first is the possibility to gain access to social life in a comprehensive way, the second is the focus on subjective experience, and the third is the historical dimension. For this purpose, I have worked with life writing as a way to enunciate life comprehensively, place writing as earth writing, and writing 'the feminine' which includes the temporality of the pre-linguistic body.

The use of experience in the writing of life means that language travels between, discloses, articulates and reveals experience. Life writing would not have existed without the journey-in-language. Rewriting experience is a process that creates new meaning on the places of dwelling over the life course, over the day. Experiences and future intentions are understood in the context of the immediate horizon, while the present dwelling and journeying are only a tiny step in a path of dwelling. A second aspect of life writing concerns writing place, or what geographer Martin Gren denotes as earth writing (Gren 1994, 1996, Karjalainen 2000 and 2003). Geography is literally earth writing, since the etymological root of the word geography is *geo* (earth) and *graphein* (carving, engraving, to write). Martin Gren writes that geography is concerned with matter and meaning and with the possibilities for ontological transformations (Gren 1996). In this respect, the ontological transformations of geography challenge cartographic and phallocentric practices of engraving lines on the earth. Following Luce Irigaray (1985), phallocentric writing implies a separation between the engraver and the engraved in terms of engraving male (subject) and engraved female earth or place (object). My way of writing place is non-phallocentric by stressing place in "the feminine". By drawing on the French feminists' critique of phallocentrism in language and the project of *écriture feminine*, I suggest we should write place through writing the body as place. As I see it, place writing describes a common field between life, earth and the feminine based in the materiality of life, the flesh of both bodies and natures available to humans through the senses and human beings' relations to other human beings and non-human life. This common field refers to the materiality and situated being of a sexed and gendered person who has a geographical, bodily and localized presence in an external world over a life course. This understanding of life writing has, as I see it, much in common with the Greek term *poiesis*, denoting a making, forming and creating which is, according to geographer Anne Buttimer, useful for an evoking of geographic awareness, critical reflection, discovery and creativity (Buttimer 1993).

I have therefore combined biographical life writing, writing "the feminine" with geographical earth writing in the chapters that follow. Every story presented exists because of a particular justification, or a reason for its telling, through the structure of all the different stories put together. The reason for telling the stories is the way the North Cape experience functions as an epiphany. In literature of biographical methods, an epiphany is understood as a moment of revelation in a human being's life or as events and experiences that mark people's lives in profound ways (Denzin 1989:70). The importance lies in the fact that some events alter the fundamental meaning structures in peoples' lives. It has been argued that personal character is manifested in epiphanies since, according to Denzin, they are like moments of crisis since they bear similarities to the liminal phase in a *rite de passage* (Turner 1974). What kind of revelation the North Cape is varies from person to person. The implicit purpose of each story is not to create wholeness as an expression for perfect truth or Grand Narratives but wholeness as indefiniteness and a form of open-ended, local truths, which emphasize pluralism, difference, change and movement in both lives and meaning. The stories are open-ended, reflecting the open-ended character of the journey the informants were making.

The journey to the North and to the North Cape is interpreted as an important event, and an epiphany, in the lives of the persons, though it be in different ways, with different and often contradictory meanings for each person. The journey to the north is, however, seen as a revelation that has the potential to change the individual's meaning structure. The meaning of this event is interpreted in context. I have therefore studied how this event, has come to mean what it means to the persons by placing it in relation to the journey, the person's life history, their everyday life, and the larger cultural, social and economic contexts and processes in modernity.

When I have worked with personal life stories and reconstructed the person's life history, I have consciously and unconsciously worked with the idea of the coherent subject. There is coherence and wholeness in a person's life that can be told and retold by that subject. During the interviews, the informants presented themselves with a form of coherence when they responded to my wish to talk about the journey to the north and to North Cape. I want to rewrite this coherence. In classic narratives, like the literary biography, coherence and wholeness is very important. Today, the new canon of biography is not coherence but splitting, conflicting and plural understandings of the self. There is coherence in the lives that I present. This coherence is based upon a view where the individual is a creator and author of his or her own life, but not the sole creator or author. Authority and creation in a person's life is dependent on many forms and structures in nature, culture and society. The larger contexts that I have focused on include cultural, social and economic aspects of what we call nature.

The stories are creations, not discoveries of absolute truths. These stories are also a product of our interaction together in the interview situation. We might see these persons as others not only for you and me, but also for themselves. To see the human being as other for himself or herself is one of the key characteristics of poststructuralist empirical research, but we might also see it as a continuation of the project of hermeneutics and the art of interpretation. The story describes the world in new ways, and in this way narration has similarities to the way metaphor works. Narratives do not describe the world directly, but re-scribe and re-tell the world. The important point when using narrative analysis is not to remember to list events after each other in the right way, but to be sensitive to the configurational qualities of a story, or how one explains an event by another. It is the emplotment which is the tool to order experience, in a process of re-scription of events in a structured whole and from which the events are given their meaning. The configurative quality is central to re-scribing of events because it orders events in a plot. Narratives are therefore not copies of the world, they rather construct an as-if-world (Entrikin 1991). The stories I have written are thus truthful fictions (Denzin 1989). The stories are true because readers believe them to be true, and because they are meaningful to the producers in the way the stories were told in the interview situation. Therefore, the production of truth relies not only on the rhetorical devices I as a writer have used to make the stories true, but on facts and facticities, i.e. the events that have occurred and the truthful reconstructions of these events. In both senses, this means that there are only incomplete stories. They are written in process, and read in process, and never fixed.

To conclude this chapter, travelling fieldwork and theory imply not only the symbolic movement of creation of meaning but the embodied, situated and dynamic movement of woman-centred creation of meaning in a cultural landscape that is wo/man-made. This further means to move continuously beyond the borders of meaning in a refusal to fix meaning into the logic of the Same, and to work and write within the endless excess of what I have previously described as the logic of the umbilical cord (Irigaray 1993, Birkeland 2000, see also chapter thirteen). Travelling fieldwork and theory question also the difference(s) between a woman-centred research process and a man-centred research process. One of these differences, I will argue, concerns how the open and non-fixed character of travelling fieldwork evokes understandings of place that are open and non-fixed, and that this further stresses the research process as open and non-fixed.

Chapter 3

Tourism, Subjectivity and Self: The North Cape

Mythic place and myths of the self

This chapter focuses on the phenomenon of travel to find, create and remake western selves. The relationship between tourism, subjectivity and self will be discussed by exploring the North Cape place myths. There are close relations between tourism and constructions of self. Sociologist Dean MacCannell has argued that the tourist is one of the best models that exists of the modern self, and that the most typical experience of the modern and western self happens through tourist experiences (MacCannell 1976). With reference to Claude Lévi-Strauss and Emile Durkheim, MacCannell has analyzed the structural similarities between religious and touristic symbols. MacCannell shows that the deep structure of modern society consists of one common theme, precondition or experience: self-discovery through a search for an absolute other. The deep structure of modern society consists of a self constructed in relation to its other: one's own past and pre-modern societies. Sightseeing is particularly important in the modern experience, according to MacCannell, because the tourist attempts to integrate unconnected experiences into wholeness. The value of sightseeing represents a ceremonial legitimation of the sighted, namely the self. The cultural elite in modern society reproduces this distinction between self and other through travel for the sake of cultural pursuits, but never for pleasure and never admitting to buying a package trip to a tourist destination. The paradox comprises, MacCannell argues, the tourist denying being a tourist. The tourist is always the other one, which means that the tourist nevertheless is fixed in a paradoxical bond to its other.

There are problems with MacCannell's argument both from feminist and humanist points of view, but I would nevertheless follow his main argument that focuses on the relationship between visuality, construction of self, and the institutionalization of sightseeing. I will relate MacCannell's idea of sightseeing as a ceremonial legitimation of the self to the concrete production of place images that together form the North Cape place myth. In this reading, I will look at the production of romanticized place-myths in particular since romanticism has been important for tourism development in many parts of the western world. Sociologists Scott Lash and John Urry write with reference to the growth of British tourism that the development of particular, romanticized place-myths has been important in the production of all travel destinations in Britain (Lash and Urry

1994). Place-myths refer here to a collective set of place-images associated with a particular locality (Shields 1991). Such place-images may be accurate or inaccurate, more or less partial or exaggerated, but result from a stereotyping of place, from prejudice or belief. The images often carry unconscious meaning and communicate beliefs and ideas which are taken for granted. A set of place-images together forms a place-myth. Some core images are common and endure over time while other images may be more ephemeral and transitory. A place-myth is thus both relatively stable and flexible because it results from place-images that have been widely disseminated and collectively held as images of a locality for a long time.

Place-myths are important for human beings because they are elements in complex systems of belief (Tuan 1977). Geographer Yi-Fu Tuan argues that mythic place is connected to ideas of the human being's place in nature in a holistic way and the idea of a terrestrial paradise as half-known areas. According to Tuan, there are two persisting ways of understanding mythic place in modernity. The first is to understand mythic place as opposite to truth or true knowledge, as an area outside of what is known. Mythic place is like a hazy field beyond the field of perception or the immediately visible horizon. Mythic place is non-perceivable place and works as a precondition for the known world. In this sense, mythic place is associated with the hidden or the unknown, the repressed or forgotten and the unconscious in a collective sense.

The second way to conceive of mythical place is to see it as a component in worldview or cosmology, according to Tuan. A worldview is the attempt to make sense of environment as answers to human beings' questions of their place in nature. Mythic place is both material and divine. There are two typical answers to this question, according to Tuan. One way is to treat the human body as an image of cosmos, while the other is to treat the human being as the centre of cosmos oriented from the cardinal points and the vertical axis. In the first view there is a parallel between microcosm and macrocosm. In the second view, the human being is in the centre of the world. The interest in mythic place stems from a genuinely human need for feeling whole, for synthesis, and for introducing a cosmic frame of reference to human life, Tuan writes. Mythic place moves beyond rationalist views of place, dualism, and the logic of exclusion and contradiction, and this makes, I claim, the idea of mythic place useful for understanding the extraordinary dimensions of place. I argue that mythic place is very important for an understanding of the relationship between place-making and self-making. A meaningful synthesis of place and self integrates knowledge of both perceivable and non-perceivable place and draws attention to the way unconscious processes unfolds in the constitution of mythic place. An exploration of mythic place may further facilitate growth in self-understanding in a broader and more cosmological sense.

Through a critical reading of change and continuity in the production of North Cape place-images, I will argue that the making of the North Cape place-myth is connected to a central western idea of the self. I will show that the dominant images of modern holiday travel to the North Cape are associated with the cliffs' vertical and horizontal shape and the midnight sun. These place-images together form the totality of the North Cape place-myth that has, I claim, its psychological counterpart in an archetypal image of the self. In Jungian psychology the *imago dei* or the *mandala* are found in the form of a square or cross and the circle (Jung 1995, Schwartz-Salant 1995). The self is here an archetypal image for wholeness and totality that unites opposites and integrates the whole of the personality of a human being.

In the following, I will discuss to what degree the institutionalization of North Cape tourism over time has created changes in the meaning of the place-images and how these have changed the overall North Cape place-myth. I will show that, over time, there has been a shift in the production of place images from poetic and sublime images to prosaic and profane images, and that this shift is a result of the institutionalization of North Cape travel and changes in transport technology. I will further argue that this domestication of the North Cape is a result of a masculinist, disembodied, and visual logic that has consequences for the way tourists and travellers find, create and remake self through the meeting with the North Cape place-myth. The question is whether it is possible to look beyond the domesticated place-myth and whether a woman-centred perspective on the place-myth will enable a look beyond and a different story of the making and remaking of self.

The North Cape place-myth

The British tour operator Thomas Cook & Son initiated modern tourism to North Cape by arranging tours to Scandinavia and the North Cape as early as 1875 (Birkeland 2000b). The eighteenth century editions of Cook's Excursionist and Tourist Adviser show that the North Cape was an important attraction to visit when travelling to Scandinavia as early as 1866. On June 29 1875, the Excursionist reported that Thomas Cook & Son would send a small group to visit the North Cape and the regions of the midnight sun that was to depart from London in the middle of July. In December 1875, the Excursionist reported about the great expectations people had and the many delays. When the travel party reached the North Cape ('the extreme point'), the weather was cloudy which meant that they did not see the midnight sun as anticipated (Excursionist 9 December 1875).

It is interesting that North Cape represents an extreme point and that seeing the midnight sun is the destination or goal of the tour. This means, first of all, that the rationalization processes in British society at that time had filtered into the leisure and holiday sphere. An application of an instrumental rationality in the holiday sphere means that tourists have an idea that they can find or arrive at their self at some particular locality in the exterior world. Visual images are useful for this purpose by helping frame the destination for the tourists, and this is a typical feature of modern tourism, sociologist Judith Adler argues (1989). The production and consumption of visual images was not important before the onset of modern tourism. Visual images of the North Cape, or of other attractions for the tourists, were not prominent in the material from Thomas Cook & Son to the public during the first years of organized tourism to Scandinavia. It did not take long before the image of the North Cape as a destination, or ultimate goal, found its way through their brochures and handbooks. A brochure from 1892 entitled 'Cook's Tours in Norway, Sweden and Denmark' presents pictures on the front of the sights of the Scandinavian landscape (Figure 3.1).

The North Cape is pictured in the centre of the image with the characteristic profile of the North Cape cliffs with the midnight sun depicted behind the cliffs. The perspective of the view is from the sea, which at that time was the position from which the visitors would see the North Cape for the first time. The images of the vertical profile of the cliffs in relation to the horizontal arctic mountain tops and the midnight sun were used in several ways over the following years. The front page of the brochure from 1892 portrays only pictures from Norway, even though the brochure covers travels throughout Scandinavia. The images together form a peculiar combination of experiences of wild nature and religious places. Images of fjords, ice, water and mountains are combined with images of churches, which point at a connection between sublime nature and religious feeling in the production of the North Cape as the ultimate goal of the journey.

Over time, visual images institutionalized sightseeing, sightseeing subjects and sighted objects in organized travel with Thomas Cook & Son. Sociologist Judith Adler confirms that sightseeing was institutionalized in the nineteenth century through the production of brochures and handbooks (Adler 1989). This implied a conditioning of the travellers in terms of what was important to see. From this, I conclude that Thomas Cook & Son created the North Cape place-myth as a collectively held myth of the North Cape based on the place-images of the cliffs and the sun, and in the following, I will trace the change and continuity in these place-images through a period of hundred years of modern tourism to the North Cape.

In the early twentieth century, there was no road to North Cape, and all visitors had to arrive by ships which were anchored in Hornvika (Horn Bay) (Figure 3.2). We can imagine that the traffic was lively when the cruise ships arrived. The passengers boarded smaller boats that carried them to the rocky beach. There they climbed one thousand feet up a steep zigzag track for about thirty minutes, before making the final steps to the edge of the North Cape (Figure 3.3). Climbing must have been hard work, but also very satisfactory in an empowering sense, because climbing provided a direct bodily encounter with the verticality and horizontality of the North Cape. The ultimate experience must, however, have been to catch a glimpse of the sun at midnight from the point of view of the North Cape.

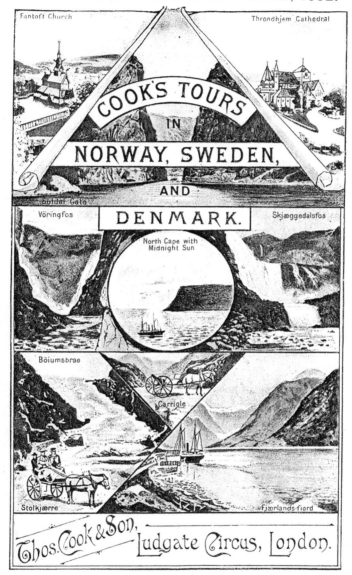

Figure 3.1 The North Cape on the front of a brochure, 1892
Source: Thomas Cook Archives and used with permission.

Figure 3.2 The Horn Bay
Source: Unknown.

Figure 3.3 View of the cliffs from the sea
Source: Unknown.

What was the most important impression gained when being at the top of the North Cape? In the brochure from 1892 by Thomas Cook & Son the reflections of a so-called well-known writer are used to illustrate the sublime feelings of fear and awe associated with the midnight sun:

> The effect of the Midnight Sun has been variously described. Carlyle revels in the idea that while all the nations of the earth are sleeping, you here stand in the presence of the great power which will wake them all; Bayard Taylor delights in the gorgeous colouring; and each traveller has some new poetic thought to register. For myself, the Midnight Sun has a solemnity which nothing else in Nature has. Midnight is solemn in the darkness; it is a hundredfold more solemn than the glare of sunlight; richer than ever it is seen under tropical skies. It is 'silence as of death'; not the hum of a bird, not the buzz of an insect, not the distant voice of a human being. Silence palpable. You do not feel drowsy, though it is midnight; you feel a strange fear creep over you as if in a nightmare, and dare not speak; you think what if it should be true that the world is its last sleep, and you are the living last ones, yourselves on the verge of the Eternal Ocean?
>
> (Cook's Tours in Norway, Sweden and Denmark, 1892:8).

In the last decade of the nineteenth century substantial new travel literature on the North Cape appeared, including travel handbooks and more or less auto-biographical travel stories (Schiøtz 1971). In 1895 geologist Hans Reusch published a book on the people and nature in Finnmark where he depicted the North Cape as a poetic place created in contrast to the neighbouring headland, associated with prosaic place:

> On the road from Hammerfest eastwards the steamer took a turn out from North Cape. This mountain which is flat on top and which has steep walls has so often been described that I need not mention it further. The fame of North Cape is a peculiar proof of the role the aesthetic plays for human beings. North Cape is in fact, as has been shown a long time ago, not the northernmost point of our continent. Knivskjellodden just west of North Cape stretches farther north into the sea, but since this point is low-lying and not much to look at, nobody takes notice of the correct measures and observations. North Cape attracts everybody both because of its appearance and its telling name. North Cape is poetry, while Knivskjellodden is prose. The latter, prose, we have enough of in daily life, which is why so many champagne toasts have been drunk at North Cape, but not one at the other point with the long name
>
> (Reusch, 1895:16, my translation).

We find here an explicit celebration of the aesthetic qualities of the North Cape. This aesthetic experience is associated with Reusch's description of the poetic North Cape distinguished from the prosaic Knivskjellodden. North Cape is poetry while Knivskjellodden is prose. These meanings form a spatial dualism that is also hierarchically organized. This makes the experience of the North Cape more valuable than Knivskjellodden. The aesthetics of the North Cape in Reusch's description rest thus on its undervalued other, which is associated with a low-lying and flat landscape.

Experience and representations of places like the North Cape are cultural and social products and not a matter of fact of nature itself (Olwig 1996, Cronon 1996). The poetic and sublime North Cape is a quality of human communities whose meanings depend on historical and geographical contexts. In the following, I will argue that the production of the place-images of the North Cape in the 1890s reflect romanticist ideas of nature and place transferred to the area of tourism and travel and to the making of self through travel.

The Canadian historian Patricia Jasen points to the development of romanticism in Europe as an important factor for the growth of interest in the scenery of the Canadian wilderness between 1790 and 1914 (Jasen 1995). Jasen argues that there are interconnected, close and persistent relations between romanticism and tourism. Romanticism can be understood as the tendency among the middle and upper classes to value feeling, imagination and sensibility far more than before. Romanticism created associations between images, commodities, emotions and personal fulfilment, Jasen argues, which contributed to shaping consumer capitalism and the development of a tourism industry. Tourism begins in this way with an interest in wild places, with the picturesque and the sublime, with landscape as an expression for style and taste, a growing co-thinking of landscape, nationalism and history and a concern for ethnic and indigenous difference.

Jasen argues that these themes predated romanticism in tourism because they reflect changing notions of the good and wild aspects of nature, and how these were expressed in relations between culture, society and nature. Seeing nature as sublime was particularly important because it dealt with experiences that sometimes created an enhanced state of being, wonder and beauty, and sometimes anxiety and terror, which left people speechless with awe (Figure 3.4). The sublime was an important category of romanticist mentality generally. Jasen points to Edmund Burke, who established the relationships between landscape, emotion, joy and pleasure, as one important reason for the development of the romanticist movement during the nineteenth century (Burke 1957). Jasen explains that before Burke, the sublime referred to the quality of literature and art as an expression of awe or a throw of emotions produced by a piece of art. The new development in the nineteenth century transferred to the experience of nature.

The development of tourism formed an important part of the romanticist movement. Views of nature as wild, extreme, dangerous, magnificent and overwhelmingly beautiful are found in early modern travel in various areas of the Northern Hemisphere. Tourists started to travel to the Alps, Wales, the Scottish Highlands and Niagara Falls to experience the intensity of sublime nature. Jasen claims that such feelings can be understood as substitutes for religious experience, which in the nineteenth century were transferred to the area of tourism and leisure.

Figure 3.4　The sublime North Cape
Source: Mittet & Co.

Environmental historian William Cronon agrees that the sublime is one important expression of romanticism (Cronon 1996). The sublime was, according to Cronon, connected to those rare places where one had a chance to experience the divine, and where the proof of a sublime experience was the emotion evoked. For the early romantics, the sublime was not pleasurable. According to Cronon it was rather more feeling closer to terror and dismay. This feeling, as an experience of the presence of the divine, could best be found on top of a mountain, in waterfalls, thunderclouds, rainbows and at sunset. In this respect, the North Cape would be a likely place to experience the sublime, since the climbing of the steep hill and the midnight sunset could evoke sublime emotions in the visitor.

The romanticist views of nature were over time institutionalized, framed, commodified and represented in many different ways. A secularization of the views of nature took place during the twentieth century, when the meanings of the sublime changed from being bad to good. Cronon argues that the late twentieth century watered down the sublime through commercial hype and tourist advertising. Little of the sublime's former power remained. Patricia Jasen argues in a similar fashion, and presents a linear development in which the romantic and sublime view of nature changed into an ironic and distancing gaze. Cronon argues that the awesome power of the sublime was tamed over time. The sublime experiences were transformed into more comfortable and sentimental feelings. Tourism contributed greatly to this transformation of the sublime.

How is the situation today regarding the particular historical and geographical framing of nature in the Nordic countries? Geographer Ari Lehtinen argues that the nature of the northern peripheries of Europe has become institutionalized (Lehtinen 1991). Nature is institutionalized as parts of nature, national parks and regions of wilderness, and according to Lehtinen, this means that nature is in danger of being framed to death. What would seem to be the root of this development is a two-way construction bound to Christian dualism based on wild and divine places and modern polarization where nature is an obstacle to overcome and an idealized memory of indigenous or pure natures. The idea of wilderness is particularly important here, Lehtinen argues, since this is a biblical projection of nature modernized through the lenses of modern cultural and economic development.

My argument is that this projection has affected the production of the North Cape place-images, and that a polarization of nature was at work in the institutionalization of modern tourism to the North Cape in the twentieth century. The North Cape nature today is a part of a globalized world where nature is, basically, an obstacle to overcome with picturesque traces of first, or pure, natures. To an outsider the North Cape might look more like a machine for mass tourism than a locality infused with mythic and sublime images. The contemporary production of the North Cape place-images has been mediated by major changes in transport technology since 1875. The development of new transport technologies in this century, in particular the automobile, has contributed to a major increase in the number of travellers going to North Cape. Organized travel to the North Cape can be roughly divided into three periods since 1875. The first period comprises travel conducted on ordinary steam ships, while the second period is characterized by the establishment of frequent steamship routes, the *Hurtigruta*, which organized scheduled arrivals between the north and the west of the Norwegian coastline. The third period was brought about by the improvement of roads in northern Norway.

A road connecting the mainland with the North Cape was opened in 1956 (though with a ferry ride to the Magerøy island). Since then, visitors have arrived by both car and ship, and the overall result has been large growth in the traffic to the North Cape (Figure 3.5).

Figure 3.5 The road to the North Cape was built in 1956
Source: Andersen.

Even though the form of travel to North Cape has changed over time, certain images have been reproduced so many times that they would seem to be taken for granted in the 1990s. There are two main trends in the historical development of place-images of the North Cape. Firstly, the present vertical and horizontal shape of the cliffs is an important image associated with the North Cape in the 1990s. Secondly, the place-image of the midnight sun has almost disappeared in the institutionalized production of the North Cape as a tourist destination.

The image of the vertical cliffs dividing horizontal plains from the Arctic Ocean was reproduced in many contexts in the 1990s: in brochures and postcards, images, signs and artefacts, architecture and works of art. This place-image exists

Figure 3.6 The Globe Sculpture
Source: The author.

in material from tour operators and agents promoting tourism to the Nordic north and in private travelogues created by visitors to the North Cape. If we take a look at a brochure produced by *Nordkapp Reiseliv A/S* from 1997, the North Cape is described as the point which marks Europe's northernmost corner. We are told that the cliffs at North Cape have imposing or majestic forms, being the last terrestrial frontier before the Arctic Ocean. The overall impression is, however, that the brochure focuses on the built environment at the North Cape and not the experiences of nature available there.

The brochure presents infrastructural improvements and new facilities indoors and outdoors. Indoors, there are a cafe and restaurant, a souvenir shop, snack bar and post office, movie theatre, exhibitions of historical travel, a small chapel and the Grotto bar underneath ground level from which one can 'see' the north through a large glass window facing north. References to the Magerøy island and Finnmark are found in the form of local handicraft, art ware, souvenirs and gifts and local specialities on the restaurant menu. We are told that the souvenir shop is one of Scandinavia's largest, that the restaurant *The Compass* is described as a good place to eat while holidaymakers can celebrate their arrival north down in the *Grotto Bar*. Of the new outdoor facilities, the most important is the globe sculpture (Figure 3.6), a monument said to be an important point of reference and a reminder of the closeness of the locality to the North Pole, a point of orientation and knowledge, and a sculptural representation of the cardinal point of the north. The brochure states quite simply that the proof of having been at the North Cape is to have one's photograph taken at the globe sculpture, perhaps with the midnight sun in the background. The focus is on the visual framing of the North Cape experience within which visitors are being 'helped' to place themselves in the context of the north. We are also informed that the experience of the midnight sun is not guaranteed to the visitor, though nothing of the former splendour and awe associated with the midnight sun seems present. It is clear that this brochure is focused on economic revenue from visitors to the North Cape. Each economic unit of the building at North Cape is presented.

The place-image of the cliff, with its vertical and horizontal lines, is framed in new ways in connection to the built environment. The main building is low-lying and made in stone and glass with a façade facing the north that has incorporated the theme of verticality and horizontality (Figure 3.7). The building has facilities above and below ground, which creates a nearness to the elements and a humble response to the natural environment. This is where nature reigns. The entrance area has been developed to take care of quite a few busloads of tourists (Figure 3.8). It was necessary to make investments to care for the growing numbers of visitors who just kept coming. This growth is planned and unplanned and results partly from the promotion of the North Cape but also from the improvements in access created by development in transport and car technology and the general economic growth in Europe in the twentieth century. Until 1987, the facilities at the North Cape were fairly basic (Figure 3.9). Large investment at the North Cape is a recent phenomenon. This development reflects the changing conditions for tourism enterprise that have taken place world wide. Through this investment, the North Cape has been transformed into an interesting object of investment and the accumulation of capital, with little or no local influence, and dependent on attracting an ever larger number of visitors each year.

Figure 3.7   Verticality and horizontality
Source: The author.

Figure 3.8 Entrance area with buses
Source: The author.

Figure 3.9 Facilities at the North Cape in the 1930s
Source: Mittet & Co.

From the presentation above, I argue that the image of verticality and horizontality dominates the overall place-myth of North Cape in the 1990s. The experience is domesticated so that very little of its sublime meaning remains. The North Cape place-myth is in danger of being framed to death. In a long term perspective, it is clear that the place-image associated with the midnight sun has disappeared. There is actually very little to read about the midnight sun. What has caused this silencing of the place-image of the sun?

One explanation may be found in the changes in access to the North Cape which have changed the context for experiencing the place-images. Sociologist Jens Kr. Steen Jacobsen has argued that easing access changed the experience of North Cape which correspondingly became less elevated and impressive (Jacobsen 1997). The change in access to North Cape has, however, also changed the experience of the verticality and horizontality. The vertical element experienced by the bodily encounter with the movement upwards has been lost in favour of a horizontal framing. Since, 1956, verticality has been experienced only visually by those who arrive by car or by bus. Most visitors today experience verticality by looking down while standing still, sitting in a car or a bus. A total aerial view appears only when standing on the top of the cliffs. An individual traveller arriving by car has no embodied experience of verticality achieved by climbing.

Developments in transport technology have contributed to a reduction in the bodily encounter with the sublime experience of horizontality and verticality and the midnight sun. Additionally, the experience of North Cape as an encounter with the element of verticality in a deeper perceptual and aesthetic way has been lost. The place-image of verticality and horizontality at North Cape has caused a loss of integration between the bodily and the mental experience of the North Cape place-myth. It is tempting to describe this development as a domestication of the sublime in terms of a secularization of a site/sight to a mere tourist attraction, a disenchantment that is a product of the institutionalization of tourism itself. This influences the experience of the midnight sun as well, since the experience of verticality by seeing the sun exists without a connection to the bodily experience of verticality through climbing. Verticality has become disembodied.

The place-myth in subjective experience

In the following, I will search for a conclusion to the discussion on the phenomenon of travelling to find, create and remake western selves. So far, I have uncovered change and continuity in the production of the place-images in historical and present travel to the North Cape. I relate this change in the North Cape place-myth to the possibilities for a re-enchantment of western images of the self and a participatory consciousness where body and mind again are integrated (Berman 1981). Such integration implies a connection between the meaning attached to a particular locality in the external world and the meaning attached to a particular part of the subjective world of a person. I thus turn the attention to the subjective experience of the self through the North Cape place-myth as a mirror of the self. Above I have suggested that the project of finding, creating and remaking self through travel comes through the experience of images, myths and symbols connected to the North Cape. Here, I will discuss to what degree these have, or do not have, a healing quality in relation to a human being's individual journey. I will focus on images of the cliffs and the midnight sun in order to discuss the qualities of these images by attending to the images of the circle and the square, the meaning of the relationship between the circle and the square, and the consequences of the changes in this relationship.

I locate place-myth and place-images in cultural history and historical conceptions of the self. The images of verticality and horizontality are among the most common symbols in cultural history with a rich variety in symbolic meaning connected to ideas of the self. The vertical and the horizontal dimensions are sometimes given meaning in terms of the square (Becker 2000). In encyclopaedias of symbols, the square is associated with the cross, beauty, with the number four (as in the four cardinal directions), with ground, earth, flesh, matter and the body, which further refer to the feminine and the masculine principles. In Jungian thought the square is associated with the quaternary, which refers to wholeness or completeness, the individuated self. Wholeness would thus include a masculine and a feminine aspect of the element of earth. Images, myths and symbols that unite the horizontal and the vertical dimensions thus carry qualities of wholeness, integration and completion of differences. In Christian discourse, the square is given meaning as earth in contrast to heaven, but the square can also be a sign for a crossroads where two paths cross one another.

In architecture, the vertical and the horizontal are among the elementary signs as well as the circle. The philosopher Edward Casey has discussed verticality and horizontality in terms of architectural tendencies and ways of dwelling (Casey 1993). From ancient times, the horizontal and the vertical have been associated with the relationship between Hermetical and Hestial dwelling. Casey shows that vertical and horizontal dimensions of dwelling must undergo conjunctions to become partners, just as Hermes and Hestia were partners in ancient mythology, guarding the family's fertility and the household. These gods in ancient Greek mythology represent two ways of dwelling in place, Casey argues. Hermes, in being the winged god of travellers, represents the horizontal principle, while Hestia represents the vertical principle by being the goddess of the household, the hearth and the fireplace. The Hestial hearth implies verticality through the upward movement of smoke. An association between the vertical principle and the feminine principle can be found in the mythologies of cultures in many parts of the world, and it stands in direct opposition to modern interpretations of verticality. The French philosopher, Henri Lefebvre, has discussed verticality in terms of the dominance of a masculine principle in modern society (Lefebvre 1991, see chapter four). Lefebvre shows that, at one point of time, there was a shift from a maternal to a paternal principle regarding the production of social space. Lefebvre writes that ever since early times, the development of society has repressed the feminine principle which is associated with an original feminine verticality and the realm of the household, the shrine or hearth, the fireplace, the omphalos and the circular, closed and fixed space.

From what we have seen above, there is substantial but contradictory meaning afforded to verticality and horizontality. It is clear that the meaning of verticality and horizontality at North Cape depends on the context. If we apply a modern and secularized interpretative frame, the meaning of verticality exists without a bodily reference and a complementary connection to the feminine principle. If we apply a mythic and cosmic interpretative frame, the meaning of verticality arises with a bodily encounter with verticality. Only the mythic and cosmic interpretive frame places the human being as a terrestrial, embodied and living being who integrates body and mind, the material and the spiritual. Below, I will show that the modern domestication of the North Cape place-myth is harmful since it has lost its grounding in an embodied verticality.

The sun is a circular image, and the circle is one of the strongest symbols there is. The circle is a direct image of the sun, while it also has meaning as one of the four elements as the fluid element (water). The circle is directly related to the form of the sun and the moon. The circle has a whole array of symbolic meanings but is often seen in relation (and contrast) to the square. The square stands for earth, while the circle stands for water. The circle is associated with unity, perfection and the absolute, heaven and the divine. It is also associated with the wheel, the ring, protection, healing and enlightenment. As the circle has neither beginning nor end, it is related to oneness, eternity and infinity, which in turn are also close to the meanings associated with the feminine principle. It is further associated with the end of dualism since all opposites are enclosed within the circle. In the Jungian tradition, the circle (and the sun) is seen as a psychological archetype and a symbol of the psyche (or soul). In cultures all over the world, the circle is seen as having healing qualities with transcendental potential. It is found in native American culture in the medicine wheel as an image of balance and the repetitive cycle of nature, while in cultures from the east the circle is the model for mandala images in Buddhism and Hinduism. The basic foundation for a mandala is a squared circle.

When the circle and the square are seen together, we get a powerful image of wholeness and the transcendence of opposites and dualisms, for example in terms of a unity between heaven and earth and the spiritual and the material, the masculine and the feminine, body and mind, the immanent and the transcendent. The circle inscribed within the square is a Cabalist symbol for the spark of divine fire that lies hidden within the flesh and the body, the material and the land. The circle and the square symbolize human beings' ascending journey to the divine and the struggle to create heaven on earth or the descent of heaven on earth (Figure 3.10).

Nordkap, Midnatssol.
G .K. A. 11

Figure 3.10 The midnight sun
Source: Unknown.

We have seen that the development of North Cape tourism over time has created a gradual change in the meaning of the North Cape place-myth. This is a change from experiences of verticality based on first-hand (bodily) experiences to non-bodily experience and a change where the image of the sun has gradually disappeared. The North Cape is no longer sublime, but has transformed into a picturesque and domesticated North Cape. Despite these changes, however, it seems that the place-myths of North Cape reflect romanticism in a particular way. There can be no doubt that romanticism is present in the early representations of North Cape nature, and that this has informed the overall place-myth of North Cape. The place-images of North Cape reflect a way of dealing with particular aesthetic emotions or values in western culture. The meaning of the north in this context is that it is possible to put the north and North Cape into circulation for economic purposes. I will argue that this has serious implications for the possibilities for providing the traveller to the north with viable myths and images for finding, creating and remaking self. I will argue that without the place-image of the circle, found, for example, in the midnight sun, the path to individuation seems to be blocked or unfinished. The reason for this development, I claim, is due to institutional changes and general economic growth that has turned focus away from the sublime nature of the North Cape to a profane or prosaic cultural landscape. The question that I will explore in the forthcoming chapters is, thus, to what degree a female traveller and the woman's perspective can lead to a rediscovery of the sun and a re-enchantment of the healing aspects of the place-images of the North Cape.

Chapter 4

Tourism and the Transformation
of Everyday Life

Changes over the lifetime

Johan and Lena come from one of the northernmost countries in Europe and they have lived and worked there all their lives. They met a few years ago and have spent much time travelling together since then. Both are now retired and have been married before. Johan and Lena have separate households and visit each other and spend a lot of time together. Johan remembers many things from his life and tells me about his experiences in an enthusiastic way. Lena's focus is mainly on the experiences from the journey to North Cape, which she had dreamt about visiting for a long time. When they first met, Johan had recently arrived from a motor bike trip to the North Cape and he talked about all the wonderful things he had seen all the time. As Lena had always wanted to go to the North Cape, she was fascinated by what Johan told her, and his story-telling made them decide to travel to the north together.

The *Hurtigruta* has taken the place of the motor bike on the trip to the north this time. Johan contemplates northern ways of life, and he is very impressed by the northerners, who care for all soil available to cultivate the earth. Johan is also interested in the wide variety of nationalities that comprise the passengers onboard the *Hurtigruta*. He expresses a general appetite for difference in all colours and variations, and takes pleasure in the many different languages spoken even though he cannot speak them. Lena is particularly amazed by northern nature, but it is difficult for Lena to talk about her experiences. Words matter so little, she says, since the north is an experience hard to express in words. She finds, however, that northern nature overflows with awe. The north is strong and powerful. Lena says that she sees and feels northern nature and just absorbs it all. This comes first, she says. She experiences northern nature as very barren with a crisp and cool air, which was familiar to her from the island of Gotland of the coast of Sweden and from the mountains of Nepal, but even barrenness has something to offer her, Lena continues. Nature does not always have to be bright, light and warm, she says, because the snatching wind and the sense of coldness are also gifts of northern nature. The experience of the north is definitely not like being in the warm sun.

Lena was born to a working class family in a small town. After her father's death, Lena's mother moved to their grandparents' home which was a farm. Both Lena and her mother were housewives for most of their adult lives. Lena married quite early, and worked in the home for many years before she started looking after children at a nursery school. She has three children of her own with her estranged husband. Lena does not talk much about this as her attention seems mainly focused on the present.

Johan was born in the countryside near an industrial town where his mother was a housewife and his father worked in road maintenance. Johan lives in an apartment in the town where he grew up, and has moved twice within the same building. Johan worked with heavy industrial work for many years. His first workplace was at a mechanic shop right after the War (WWII). He then changed jobs rather often until he got a job in the iron and steel industry. He says that he worked at an iron foundry for twenty-five years until the factory closed and he returned to mechanics and manufacturing before retiring.

Going abroad on holiday was not something that Johan and Lena did when they were young. When Lena was a child, they never went on holidays because they did not have the time or opportunity to travel, she says. Johan's childhood was the same. Perhaps there would be a short visit to relatives during the school holidays in the summer, Johan remembers, but nothing more than that. After marrying, Lena did not travel much either. Johan, on the other hand, has travelled widely. He developed a taste for travel after he started working. He went on his first summer holiday after he had been in work for three years. He and a friend took their motorbikes and went camping in a neighbouring country. This was his way of holidaying for several summers. During the fifties Johan was very interested in motor bikes, he remembers. He stopped travelling with his motor bike after getting married, but began his second period of motorcycling some years ago.

Johan explains that marriage changed his travel pattern. Johan has one daughter with his first wife. The family went camping each summer throughout the 1960s. In the beginning they travelled south in their own country to the coast, to soak up the warmth of the sun. He remembers they were not happy when the weather was bad, and they subsequently joined travel parties to the Mediterranean countries at the beginning of the 1970s. They visited Bulgaria first and continued to visit different countries in the Mediterranean area. Since his divorce, he went there at least once a year during the summer, sometimes several times a year, and overall the break up of his marriage altered his general travel pattern in that he began visiting new parts of the world.

Johan has travelled with the Trans-Siberian Railway and has travelled extensively by himself using a bicycle and a motor bike. He has seen almost every European country from his bicycle, at least ten different countries, he continues. Seeing the former Eastern European countries made a great impression on him, he said, as did learning about the differences in the standard of living. Every time he returned, he was amazed to see how well off he and his countrymen were. He is happy to have a home to return to, but he never longs for home when he is out travelling. He wishes the journeys would last much longer: just one more week, please. Every journey must end, though. He would rather continue travelling than go home. Johan would rather spend his money on travel than on any other thing.

He would rather travel than have a car, he contends. When Johan and Lena met a few years ago, Johan's travel pattern changed once more. They have travelled much together, both near and far. Johan explains that they have been on holiday in the neighbouring countries on his motor bike, sleeping in a tent and touring around. They have also travelled to India and Nepal together. They enjoy visiting festivals and walking in areas of wilderness in their own country and travel to Lena's summerhouse by the sea, where they spend much time together.

Holiday travel and social change

Quite a few people today spend a lot of time travelling over a year. People travel more and more on holiday, and those who do travel, go further than before. When Johan and Lena were children, holiday travel did not exist in the sense that it does today. Their stories are good examples of the changes in holiday making that have taken place during the twentieth century. Modern people are, to a great extent, travelling human beings, and modern societies are increasingly mobile ones (Lash and Urry 1994). Modern ways of living divide time between work and time for leisure, and people spend increasingly more time on journeys. People spend more time on the move to reach some place far away or to get away from home for longer periods. The time spent outside home and work has increased over the decades, both daily and over the year, and within this picture place has become important.

In recent years we have seen a restructuring of the economy which has been characterized by a shift from organized to disorganized capitalism, from modern to post-modern consumption cultures, from industrial to post-industrial capitalism, from Fordist to post-Fordist accumulation, and a move towards risk society and reflexive organization (Lash and Urry 1994). The recent changes in the economy have brought forward processes of globalization, localization and new patterns of social differentiation. For example, the stretching out of social and economic relations have not only led to increased similarity in lifestyles and consumption patterns, but to increasing inequalities in material and cultural capital such as differences in control of mobility between different groups of people (Massey 1994). I would like to point to two consequences that affect the production and consumption of the North Cape.

One consequence is that place becomes assimilated in the world economy by becoming a resource for commodification for the tourism industry and an item for consumption by tourists and travellers. Scott Lash and John Urry claim that the transformation of time and place as resource and a means for gaining power are defining characters of modern societies (Lash and Urry 1994). There is an increasing movement of subjects and objects and a growing flow of non-material objects whereby the image or sign value of these objects gain particular importance. In the tourism industry, the commodification of place is often expressed in the circulation and commodification of visual images and signs connected to particular localities. It is easy to imagine that particular images and myths connected to localities such as the North Cape can play an important role here (see chapter three).

Another consequence is the tourists and travellers' experience of these changes. Commodification of place has consequences for the ordinary consumer, traveller or tourist. Some argue that the changes lead to placelessness or a global place-less space (Relph 1976, De Certeau 1984, Massey 1994) while others paint a two-sided or more differentiated picture (Lash and Urry 1994). Lash and Urry argue that the changes lead to increasing meaninglessness, homogenization, abstraction, anomie and the destruction of the subject, but also to a recasting of meaning for modern human beings because of the turn to reflexivity. In the age of disorganized capitalism, late modernity or post-modernity, leisure travel is a part of an overall reflexive turn. A new focus on human subjectivity and reflexivity offers new opportunities for human beings to reconstruct the meaning of work and leisure, community and subjectivity and create heterogeneous and complex understandings of both place and time. According to Lash and Urry, reflexivity is important not only because of its cognitive aspects (the self-monitoring of an expert system), but for its aesthetic aspects connected to interpretation of self and personal life history. Aesthetic reflexivity represents a heightened awareness of the experience of time and place where human beings reflect and gain understanding of places outside everyday life in a sudden and expanded sense. Daily and annual leisure in this sense is still time and place outside of wage labour but the meaning of leisure is changing. The new meanings of leisure will be relative to many things, but the changes in the world economy and technological development are of utmost importance (Rojek 1985, 1995). Tourists, travellers and consumers engage in reflexive practices, and grounded in aesthetic reflexivity de- and reconstruct place-images and place-myths, and experiences of time and place that lead to re-interpretation of selves.

As Lash and Urry show, aesthetic reflexivity embodies a particular refusal of clock time and an instrumental value of time. It seems obvious that this also implies a refusal of an instrumental and utilitarian value of place. Will we see an appreciation of other senses of place? Will we see a making of other stories of place and new geographies of the self? One indication from this re-writing is a renewed focus on non-instrumental values of the journey itself. There is more concern about why people actually travel other than merely saving time and covering space. As Lash and Urry indicate, physical movement in time and space is meaningful. Travelling is more than simply crossing and transcending distance, and journeys made on holiday are not mere necessities to reach some place, a destination, but a way of being and living in itself.

As we have seen, Johan and Lena have given voice to some of these changing experiences of place. They have experienced how changing family patterns create changing travel patterns, and they have learned how economic growth and public welfare in their home country have created more opportunities to travel and a household economy that allows for travel further away from home. Johan and Lena have learned about how people in other places live, and they have seen that the standard of living in their home country has become superior to the countries they have visited. They have seen that they recognize aspects of place far away relative to their experiences of place at home. Their growing experience of travel over the years that has taken them further away from their home, represents a socialization into a shrinking world. The globe is getting smaller but the life stories are getting larger, creating structures of experience that form an enlarging interpretative horizon and changing views of their selves and their home countries. To travel is thus a way to create society and become a member of a society (Berger and Luckmann 2000). Travellers and tourists create and recreate society by travelling and travel represents a socialization into modern and late modern ways of living. This changing and expanding geography of life outside of everyday life at home offers opportunities for new experiences for individuals and groups and for the production of new popular or vernacular geographies. The stretching out of the daily activity spheres has created changing experiences of time and place for modern human beings that embody possibilities for social change.

The French philosopher Henri Lefebvre provides perspectives for a discussion of the role of tourism and leisure for social change (Lefebvre 1991). Lefebvre's psychoanalytic perspective on social change (Gregory 1995, Pile 1996, Nast and Blum 1998, 2000) are also relevant for a post-Lacanian feminist psychoanalytic perspective. In focus is the possibility for a restoration of a feminine principle. Lefebvre acknowledges that, at one point of time, there was a shift from a maternal to a paternal principle regarding the production of social space, and that it is necessary to liberate social space through a recovery of the feminine principle. Lefebvre searches for the possibility of a differential space, or a utopian idea of a future society, where leisure and holiday travel plays an important role for the recovery of the feminine principle. Lefebvre argues that holiday travel is an arena for the development of a differential space that may transform society and culture. I would like to take up Lefebvre's call for a psychoanalysis of space to explore differential space based on an identification of particular relations between production of place, the living body and the unconscious.

Drawing on Lefebvre's ideas, geographer Steve Pile argues that modern space is phallic and abstract, based upon relationships between verticality, horizontality, and the social relations of production (Pile 1996). Lefebvre argues that modern societies are characterized by repression of meaning, which takes form as taboos or prohibitions. Lefebvre connects the historical development of urbanization to the masculine principle and to the Phallus as an organising principle, and thus uses a male morphology to ascribe meaning to society (Lefebvre 1991). Phallic verticality is in desperate need of explanation and critique, Lefebvre says, as this simultaneously represents a potential for a restoration of a new and meaningful space, called differential space. The critique of abstract and modern space takes its outset in the repression of difference in symbolic terms. Each society has an underground or repressed life, he continues, and the psychoanalysis of space would be a proper method to uncover the repressed content of space. The repressed content of modern space relates to pre-Oedipal space and the female principle. In the history of the production of space since ancient times, Lefebvre sees the beginning of time as a feminine space, cradle or origin. This space refers to the early societies of agro-pastoral people, nomadic and semi-nomadic pastoralists. This is the mother of social space. A harmony existed there between a nucleus and its surroundings, in which the nucleus grew into a town and later into urban space nourished by its surroundings through a symbiotic relationship. Surroundings are thus similar to rural space, a mother space, or feminine space.

Since early times the development of society with its ever-growing urbanization has brought forth a repression of the feminine principle which is associated with an original feminine verticality and the realm of the household, the shrine or hearth, the fireplace, the omphalos, the circular, closed and fixed space. A shift from maternal to paternal rule regarding the production of social space came at some time. Lefebvre argues that modern society has removed itself far from its space of origin. Over time, urbanization has grown further and further based on a repression of the feminine principle, where verticality is associated with the masculine principle instead of being associated with the feminine principle.

The social space of modernity is abstract, geometric, visual and phallic, which means that it is norm-bound, coercive and rationalized. Space is the medium of the national state, its power and strategies, Lefebvre argues. Verticality and horizontality are spatial expressions of the logic of abstraction and visualization. This is a repressive space because nothing avoids visual control and surveillance in modernity. Abstract space is characterized by being quantifiable in terms of geometrical space, and by a widening gap between the qualitative and the quantitative. The logic of abstraction implies a symbolic violence of the totality of the lived life of human beings because abstract, symbolic form continues to erase distinction and difference. This reduces differences between and within human beings in terms of age, class, gender, ethnicity and sexuality. It means we are left with a figure which is neutral and bodiless, without flesh, blood or organs, and thus without life process. Lefebvre argues that a growing abstraction from life process has led to a built environment where dominance means vertical power. He adds that verticality is thus identical with power over horizontality, it expresses a monumental and phallic arrogance with skyscrapers as a good example.

I find Lefebvre's critique of abstract space very compatible with the project of difference thinking. There is a potential in Lefebvre's writing that is underestimated, I will argue, and it is connected to a restoration of meaning in space related to a restoration of the feminine principle. Today, the female principle has diminished in western societies, while space has become phallic space. Lefebvre discusses the possibilities of a symbolic revenge arising from the awakening of the female principle, but says further that he hopes the revenge will not reverse the problem by creating repression. A gynocentric view of social space, or a uterine space as Lefebvre calls it, would not solve the problem if continues to work from within the dualist and either-or logic of abstract space. Lefebvre holds this as a possibility, while addressing the prospect for differential space. Lefebvre does argue that the reorganization of the use and meaning of social space should come from women or through a revaluation of the feminine principle and that men should give way to another way of producing space associated with a revalorization of the feminine principle.

A re-appraisal of the female principle in social space will create a qualitatively different space. Differential space is related to the female principle, and as Lefebvre has argued, it is about to emerge in the repressed areas of everyday life. The leisure and holiday sphere is one important area where differential space emerges. Leisure space may thus work as a counter-space, and could very well form the starting point of a politics of difference where the qualitative, the non-singular, the sensual, and "the feminine" may work together to form a counter-strategy for differential space. The qualitative may re-emerge in consumption of place in tourism and leisure, Lefebvre argues, in terms of sensuous immersion of bodies with the elements of nature, with the perception of sun, snow, grass, sand, sea, mountains and flowers. The qualitative thus refers to aesthetic reflexivity in general, to the awakening of sense impressions and sensual enjoyment of the body experienced as a total or whole body. A new pedagogy – and therapy – of time and place is beginning to take shape. Differential space is a concrete and subjective space, with an origin, a history and geography of lived life. Differential space is dynamic, semi-private or semi-public, meeting-places, paths, itineraries or gateways and pulsating life process.

In this chapter, I have discussed the modern development of travel and tourism in the perspective of the many changes that have taken place in the world economy in the twentieth century, and in terms of characteristics of modernity's abstract and phallic space. Johan and Lena's story has features which can be told by many of their generation. People like Johan and Lena did not have money or opportunities to travel when they were children. As members of their generation Johan and Lena have been shaped by the dreams of sun, sea and sand offered by the tourist industry and the growing need for more sun, more warmth and more of the best in life. Going to places like North Cape formed a part of the dreams people like them used to have. Today, such dreams have come true. The sun, sand, and the sea were part of Johan and Lena's dreams, and formed part of a future, a utopian place where everything would be all right. The meaning of the north in the context of Johan and Lena's story is that North Cape represents a particular counter-space. The northern periphery is a place for the origin of change, not only in the individual perspective but also for groups and generations of people in the western world. The division of labour between places for work and places for leisure is interesting in this respect. North Cape reflects not only the production of verticality and horizontality, but also production of a differential space, a counter-space.

Chapter 5

Travel, Masculinity and Femininity

Sensing, seeing, collecting the north

Bob has lived in an industrial city in North America all his life. He was an accountant at an industrial plant. Bob is very eager to tell me about his life and travels, and becomes almost fervent when he starts telling about the way he usually plans his vacations, as this is very important to Bob. Bob decided to visit the north of Norway a long time ago. Fifteen years ago, he saw a movie from Norway taken by an American professional group of people, and he thought that the scenery was so beautiful that he decided that he would like to travel along the Norwegian coast on the *Hurtigruta* some day. The time had now come to visit this part of the world.

Bob travels in the north to experience the nature there. He does not like doing things outdoors in his natural surroundings such as mountain climbing, skiing, or other kind of sports. He prefers to gain sense impressions of nature by looking. Nature is an item through which one can collect experiences. Even though Bob has travelled extensively around the world and seen great variations in nature, nature does not have any special meanings other than being something to enjoy watching. Bob says that nature is just something that is there, it has always existed and will always exist, whether he does anything about it or not. Mother Nature is powerful, he says, but she is just a part of the environment. Nature does not really touch him unless she spoils his holiday. Bob gets mad at Mother Nature when it rains. Nature can provoke him into anger, but he cannot really change nature nor do anything that moves nature. He does not really care very much about nature. She is just there.

Bob finds the days in the northern parts of Norway fantastic since he appreciates the many things there are to look at. Watching and looking are particularly important to him, and this is connected to an appreciation, an attraction or high regard for what he is looking at that confirms his own place in nature as human. For example, he enjoys the natural world as a fact. He enjoys thinking about the effects of natural and human processes upon nature. He appreciates the difference between humans and nature. He thinks of what nature can do and what she cannot do. Nature can make large glaciers grow and warm summers, but she cannot grow a boat or a bridge, Bob argues. In a similar vein, the North Cape did not impress Bob particularly. The word 'north' in itself does not have any meaning to him either, other than the fact that it shows the direction on the compass, he tells me.

Bob collects experiences of other places by doing a lot of photography. He has many reflections on photography and is aware of the limitations of photography. He does not like taking photographs the way most tourists do in a new setting, although he did start out doing this. Bob explains that photos will never explain how nice it actually is to feel and sense a particular place. Looking at a photo of a certain natural phenomenon is not similar to the sense impressions that particular phenomenon provokes in the observer. Bob cannot take a photograph of the experience of seeing the sun shining warmly and brightly on the horizon at two o'clock in the morning. It is fantastic to see the sun like that, Bob says.

Bob is unmarried and lives with his mother. He has never moved. When he was young, his mother was a schoolteacher while his father worked at a steel plant. The family travelled during the summer holidays to see ordinary tourist places, staying at motels. They also visited his grandmother who lived in another part of the country. After finishing high school, Bob started working at the plant where his father was employed. He has worked there for a very long time – thirty-seven years. He gradually worked himself up through the ranks until managing to become an accountant. It is four years since he retired. Nowadays his days go and he keeps himself occupied by doing the small, routine, everyday things, like sleeping, eating, drinking, mowing the lawn, painting the house, growing tomatoes and so on. He does not do anything in particular at the weekends, because the days do not differ very much. Saturdays are much like any other day of the week.

Work has been important to Bob but it has not been the main thing in his adult life. Bob feels a strong sense of belonging to his hometown. All his friends live there. It is a small community where people live and from which people commute to work elsewhere. It is a town where people like similar things, where people visit the same places and talk about similar topics. Even though this is one part of Bob's life, he is very different from his friends and neighbours. When he started earning money, he got the opportunity to travel more by himself. The first trip he made was to Florida. He had saved money, and was very lucky to be able to make the trip, he remembers. After this he began travelling extensively on the North American continent, crossing the United States and journeying all over Canada. He travelled by car and stayed at motels or slept outdoors in a tent, and he always travelled with a fellow, he explains.

Bob mentioned indirectly that he was gay. On this trip on the *Hurtigruta* he also travelled with a fellow. It seems that his vacations create both time and space for being gay in a way which life in his hometown cannot where he lives with his mother. Since the first trip his vacations have got bigger. He got bigger dreams, he explains. He then branched out. After seeing North America from coast to coast, he travelled to Egypt and Israel, the eastern parts of Africa, the Galapagos Islands, Peru, Australia and India. Bob has travelled because he wanted to see what the world looked like in a visual context. He does not feel that the travelling he does has made him smarter than his neighbours. His friends and neighbours envy him, but Bob usually answers that he envies them as well. Bob takes a trip, while they have a wife and kids, a mortgage on the house and a car to pay for.

Even though Bob has travelled very much in his life, he still thinks of himself as a small town guy. He has developed his own method and philosophy of travel, which includes ways of planning and relating to the places he visits. He tries to get into the right frame of mind so he can enjoy the state of being present at the place he is visiting, which maximizes his enjoyment of it. He has learned many things, but one impression remains the same. He has learned that the world is one 'helluva big place' and that it is human to want to reach beyond the horizon. Bob shows me a piece of paper where he has written about his philosophy of travel:

I always liked travelling to faraway places. These places can be anything important, historically, religious sites, archaeological sites, and anything or everything in-between. To actually stand in any of the above mentioned places will forever leave you with an experience that goes beyond what any picture or words will ever convey to you. You will find that mankind has always wanted to see beyond the next corner. It is human nature to do so. To go the furthest, travel the fastest, be the "firstest", is the little thing in all of us.

Travel, masculinity and femininity

Bob expresses an urge to expand outwards, travel to faraway places and a desire to go furthest and fastest. Is it human to travel, to see beyond the next corner, to go further, always further and further? Or could it be that this is masculine? I will focus on two aspects in Bob's story that may support a line of reasoning underlining that travel may be an expression of masculine subjectivity. The first aspect concerns linearity while the second concerns visuality. Both aspects can be associated with modern theories of identity formation. Below I will show how linearity and visuality relate to representations of masculinity and femininity correspondingly.

Linearity concerns a tendency to think and act in a linear way, to follow a straight line, e.g. from A to B. In modernity, linear logic is the dominant mode of thinking and found in many areas of life. As we saw in chapter two, linear logic exists in theories of knowledge and in psychological and psychoanalytical theories of individuation and separation (Keller 1985). It is also argued that linear logic is associated with masculine pursuits and the paternal principle. In these theories, knowledge, truth and autonomy are represented as absolute and universal. Linear logic is also found in lay and scientific discourse on modern tourism and holiday travel, and expresses a tendency or desire to travel from A to B, from home to a destination, and increasingly further to a new destination in a straight line. In this frame of thinking, the destination represents an ultimate goal with absolute qualities. Bob's story illustrates this point in his philosophy of travel, where he argues that going the furthest and the fastest is the main point for mankind. He talks about a linear logic of travel in a way that presents it as relevant for men and women, in all parts of the world and at all times, but which, however, is situated in the particularity of his embodied and masculine way of understanding the logic of travel.

It is, therefore, not strange that travel is represented as intrinsically masculine (Wolff 1994). However, this statement is rather problematic according to sociologist Janet Wolff, who argues both for and against this view. If we look at historical travel, there is nothing intrinsically masculine about travel since both men and women have travelled historically. Feminist researchers have developed a substantial critique that questions the masculinization of travel (see for example Mills 1991, Ryall and Veiteberg 1991, Morris 1993, Frawley 1994, Robinson 1994, Veijola and Jokinen 1994, Hall and Kinnaird 1994a, Blunt 1994, Blunt and Rose 1994, Squire 1994, Norris and Wall 1994, Richter 1994, Swayn 1997). They have put women travellers on the map and showed that the picture of historical travel has not been as one-sided as one might think. They show that the history of who travels where is a product of discourse, about men who have put men on the map, and social conditions and capital that produced male travellers rather than female travellers. This makes it reasonable to distinguish between travel as something both men and women do and have done, and travel as intrinsically masculine. On the level of social and historical reality, there is nothing intrinsically masculine about travel.

On the other hand, Wolff also argues that there is reason to take the statement more seriously. There is something inherently masculine about travel if one by this means that travel or mobility are central for the development of subjectivity and identity. We are speaking here about travel as a process creating individuation and autonomy, and identity formation, where the process of gaining an identity is like a journey within the psyche or in the psychic reality. Since Freud, identity development is seen as a masculine quest, and in classic theories of gender identity only one difference exists, the masculine difference. Luce Irigaray argues that the journey towards gender and sexual identity has been represented as a masculine journey (Irigaray 1985). This journey is also represented as a journey away from the mother and the maternal, and a journey to the father and the paternal, in the psyche, Irigaray argues. Identity emerges through a break from the mother and the feminine world of childhood. Such theories have been criticized for their inherent masculinism and for failing to consider the other difference, the feminine difference. The reason is that the forefathers of psychoanalysis saw the development of gender identity from the perspective of father-son relations, where both boys and girls were treated like boys, and where the father was the model for the mature human being. The child's relationship to his or her mother was not seen as relevant for development of identity. The early relationship to the mother was seen as a source for non-identity.

The French feminist and psychoanalyst Luce Irigaray has criticized such masculinist views of identity formation. These views fail to consider the difference it makes to have a sexed body. Irigaray has opened up possibilities for understanding the development of femininity through a negotiation of the relationship between mother and daughter (Irigaray 1985). If travel is supposed to have anything to do with development of identity and subjectivity, then travel would be a particularly important strategy both metaphorically and practically for women. This would further mean that women have more of an investment in travel, and thus in discovery of self, because of the need to focus on feminine ways of identity formation that may work in both linear and non-linear ways. Thus, there is nothing intrinsically masculine about travel since travel may express both masculine and feminine ways of identity development.

Bob's story sheds light on the relationship between travel and masculine identity in other ways as well. Mobility and travel are one area where issues of identity are contested (Schurmer-Smith and Hannam 1994). Not only heterosexual variants of masculine and feminine identities have been contested, but also homosexual and lesbian identities. Geographical studies of homosexuality have consisted mostly of questions of social segregation, for example on the existence of gay ghettos in urban and metropolitan areas (Jackson 1989) and the way location plays a role in how sexualities are lived (Bell and Valentine 1995). Travel and mobility can be seen as an ambiguous and contested resistance to or affirmation of particular ways of being and living that are dominant or normalized. In this respect all holidaymaking can be seen as a manifestation of who one wants to be, including the how and when. Travel is a part of identity politics which always implies a politics of location. Bell and Valentine point to the everyday spatial strategies or time-space strategies used by gay men and lesbians. Segregation is a strategy where one establishes geographical boundaries between past and present identities (Bell and Valentine 1995). Bob, on the other hand, establishes geographical boundaries between different forms of identities in the present. Bob at home and Bob taking a vacation are two different kinds of Bob, and holidaymaking thus forms part of his overall individual identity project.

The model of the human being for at least a couple of thousand years is the homosexual, masculine man, according to Luce Irigaray (Irigaray 1985). For a very, very long time western society has recognized only one sexual difference, the male difference. Irigaray argues that western society has been, and still is, a monosexual or homosexual society, which reproduces this understanding through negating the mother and the maternal principle. Western society continues to travel away from its maternal foundation, as a society that operates within the logic of the same. In this respect, Bob's story illustrates this point, as an adult male living together with his mother, but continually moving away from her. Bob's way of being a masculine man is partial and situated from the point of having a male body and a life history and geography that is particular, not universal. With reference to Dorothy Dinnerstein's discussion on masculinity as a solution of the problem of the child's separation from the mother (Dinnerstein 1977), it seems reasonable to conclude that masculinity here is associated with linearity and reached when one travels the furthest and the fastest away from the mother.

The discussion above talked through travel as intrinsically masculine and addressed travel as a departure and a continuing separation from femininity. I will now discuss how visuality interferes with travel in the construction of masculinity and ask if and how visuality represents a means to maintain a separation between masculinity and femininity while travelling. This could manifest in a construction of a masculine observer separated from a feminized observed object, which means that ideas of masculinity depend on a continuing separation from femininity for their existence (Rose 1993).

In this respect, we may ask to what degree northern nature presents itself as feminine nature for Bob. Bob has a cool and detached view of nature. His travels are visually oriented, and the world is his for his visual consumption. Bob simply wants to see what nature looks like in a visual context, he says. His interest in observation and photography stresses detachment. Bob collects images of nature because of an intellectual desire for knowledge. He wants to see what the world and nature look like. This is a classic way of viewing nature because it detaches him as an observer from the object he is watching. However, his story sheds light on those small glimpses of experience that makes him lose sight of the intellectual collection of northern nature. This happens when he expresses his strong fascination with certain natural phenomena and when he mentions that he gets mad at Mother Nature. Bob's interest in the visual impressions of nature expresses a construction of both social-scientific and aesthetic masculinity, to use Gillian Rose's words. Social-scientific masculinity claims access to the world and represses references to femininity in order to gain knowledge and understanding, while aesthetic masculinity admits the existence of feminized nature but only in order to allow for a masculine subject position.

Bob did not create any references to masculine observation in his ways of seeing nature, but he did explicitly view nature as feminine. From a discussion of the connections between travel and masculinity, I will continue with the connections between travel and femininity and discuss how a view of nature, such as that present in Bob's story, forms part of a hidden discourse on "the feminine" in society and culture. According to Kenneth Olwig, the hidden discourse reveals itself in descriptions of places on the surface of the earth through employing metaphors from the female body (Olwig 1993). Olwig interprets this as an expression of a horizontal sexual cosmology that has been fundamental to the notion of legitimacy in the development of modern society. It works as a hidden discourse because it formed part of the emerging discourses on territorial identity, national borders and national identity. The meaning of nature, landscape and place is saturated with ideological power that is useful for underwriting the legitimacy of those who exercise power, and in this sense, a horizontal sexual cosmology was effective.

Olwig (1993) argues that the union of the masculine and the feminine in sexual cosmology is part of how the natural world develops. That there are connections between the sky and the earth is apparent in agriculture, where the fertility of the soil fluctuates over the year dependent on the changing positions of the earth in relation to the sun. Olwig shows that the meaning of the natural process of creation emerges in ancient mythic material through the myth of an intercourse between a celestial male principle and a terrestrial female principle. In a cultural sense, sexual cosmology represents a bridge that unites oppositions between human beings and society. It works just like the image of the *hieros gamos*, or the sacred marriage between opposites, found in various forms in cultures all over the world. In this way, a sexual cosmology was very useful to bridge the opposition between heaven and earth, masculine and feminine. It would seem, however, that what was a solution to the opposition in classic times has become a colonization of nature by culture, according to Olwig, where nature is represented with both feminine and masculine poles present, but where only the feminine is made visible and connected to the terrestrial realm. This shift is found in landscape painting. A horizontal sexual cosmology replaced an earlier vertical sexual cosmology that resulted in an intellectually and physically distanced perception of nature. Nature was transformed into scenery for a detached observer, Olwig argues. The masculine was still present but took the position of being an invisible, structuring principle behind the organization of the world.

Human beings tend to deal with sexual cosmology in many ways, through myths, rituals, or by creating art and poetry. Modern science deals with it, however, through reductionism in many ways. Even Freud was not a stranger to sexual cosmology, Olwig writes (1993). He tried to take possession of it while being influenced by it himself when he described the tendency to represent landscapes, either real or dream landscapes, by employing metaphors from the topography of women's sexual organs. It is, according to Olwig, not necessary to construct it as a primitive, subliminal, psychological fixation on the mother. Freud interprets sexual cosmology in an entirely psychic or psychological sense (as sublimation), but one should not reduce sexual cosmology to mere psychological functions as Freud did, because the malformed sexual cosmology has ideological aspects with cultural, social and political consequences.

Olwig uncovers the shift that leaves sexual cosmology to a unity of a masculine sky and a feminine earth, and shows that one consequence of this shift is a colonization of nature by culture. In the movement away from a libidinal reduction of the meaning of a sexual cosmology, I will argue that the culturalist switch easy switches into a masculinist reduction. I would like to focus on how the shift has contributed to a legitimation not only of colonization of nature but to a colonization of women in modern society. I will show that this colonization exiled women even further to the terrestrial realm while depriving them of a connection to the celestial sphere and the vertical principle, which was not granted women even in the vertical sexual cosmology (in the version of sexual cosmology presented by Olwig).

I will argue that this horizontal sexual cosmology is evident in geographical discourse on the concepts of place and space. According to Gillian Rose and Doreen Massey, geographers have constructed place and space in opposition to time based on a conceptual association between place and the feminine, time and the masculine (Rose 1993, Massey 1994). Gillian Rose argues that masculinist constructions of place and space are characteristic and widespread. Space was either transparent or real, but in both cases only as a medium for social life. Space was infinite and absolute, like an empty container waiting to be filled with meaning, social fields empty of lived and sexed bodies. It is a space covered with non-specified bodies, although with ideas of human agency inhabited by masculine subjects. In contrast to space, place was described in ways that were full of interpretation, meaning and context. Through representations of experience of place, geographers created associations between place, home, and mother. Place was not seen as transparent; it was filled with meaning, passion, and emotion, but was not theorized in relation to relations of power and ideology. Through the concept of place, women and the feminine were made invisible though not by ignoring them, but by engendering place as an other and an object for constructions that confirmed the masculine self, Rose argues (1993).

Doreen Massey draws on Rose's critique of masculinism in geography when she writes that social theory has represented the development of society by drawing on notions of space as time's other: the space taken for granted as place, the home, the familiar, roots and identity, reproduction, emotions, the body, the feminine. Space as place is in this way constructed as the opposite of real life, of history, progress, civilization, science, politics, reason and order; the orderly dynamics of social life. Space may thus represent threat and chaos in relation to development and order. The meaning of space and place was thus coded female and denigrated, either as stasis or chaos (Massey 1994).

It is obvious that a sexual cosmology works as a hidden discourse where control over nature, matter and place is central. If we relate this discussion on the construction of space and place in geographical discourse to the sexual cosmology discussed by Kenneth Olwig, it seems clear that modern society is reproducing a dualist and hierarchical picture of the relationship between the heavenly and terrestrial bodies. The malformed sexual cosmology is represented today in popular terms like Sky Father and Mother Earth (with different meanings in a western, modernized context than in indigenous cultures). It is evident that in western culture's understanding of the creative process of nature women are given the role as a passive, receiving principle (nature, space, place), while men are given the role of expressing the active and creative principle. I find problems with a cosmology within which the feminine principle becomes synonymous with the terrestrial realm and not with the celestial. The reason is that it contributes to a reproduction of the body and the earth as soulless and dead. As I see it, a deconstruction of the hidden discourse on nature, landscape and related concepts such as place is useful since it shows what is missing. A way of seeing both the masculine and the feminine as connected to the terrestrial and the celestial sphere in a balanced sexual cosmology is needed. Men need to discover their connection to the terrestrial sphere, while women need to learn their connection to the celestial sphere. In this respect, women have, perhaps, a much tougher task since they to a greater extent than men have unlearnt that they have a natural connection to the celestial sphere.

Chapter 6

Travel as *Rite de Passage*

Turning fifty

Hans lives in a large city by the North Sea. The sea and the northern landscapes are important to Hans. The fact that he has got the chance to take the *Hurtigruta* is one of his dreams come true. He has wanted to travel for ten years, but never did so because his wife could not travel by ship. Hans has recently got divorced after a long marriage. Two years ago he decided that he would treat himself to a trip on the *Hurtigruta* for his fiftieth birthday, wanting it to be something special. The kitchen crew surprises him during dinner on the evening he turns fifty. Hans is very surprised when he is brought a birthday cake complete with candles while the crew and his fellow passengers sing out their congratulations. Hans is happy to the point of embarrassment that he is the centre of attention.

Hans did plan to visit the North Cape while travelling on the *Hurtigruta*, but it was not his main reason for travelling north. In fact, Hans discovered that the North Cape was not at all interesting. He finds it curious that tourist brochures describe the North Cape as the northernmost part of the world as though it were something interesting. Hans did not like being at the North Cape. There were too many people there. He seems to loathe the other tourists who go to the North Cape simply to have been there. Hans explains that there are many buses going to the North Cape every summer from his home country. The buses have but one sign on them: North Cape and they move straight to their destination.

However, when I start asking questions about his personal experiences of the North Cape, Hans talks only about the other tourists' experiences. Hans claims to know a great deal about what everyone else experiences at the North Cape, but he does not know much about his own experiences. Hans says that he visited the North Cape because it was one part of the voyage with the *Hurtigruta*. He laughs quietly at my questions, as if the North Cape were just a joke and nothing much to talk about. When I continue to ask him whether he has had any experiences that are hard to express in words, he quickly responds and says yes, he has a very special feeling for the landscape. There is a feeling that makes a huge impression on him. Watching the nature of the north makes him himself feel very small and that humans are very small compared to nature. He feels that working life is insignificant in relation to nature.

We continue to talk about the experiences of northern nature, and Hans really enjoys talking about his other sense impressions. He remembers being absolutely fascinated by the glacier he saw and remembers the smell at the fishing villages:

the fish, the pier and the oil. The sea and the mountains are impressive because of the visual contrasts. Hans tells me that he can just stand on deck and look into the water for minute after minute and nothing happens. Time could just go on forever. Hans immerses himself in northern nature and feels at home there.

He explains that he really dislikes the south of Europe. When he was married, he and his wife used to travel to the Mediterranean every other year, alternating with vacations in the northern parts of Europe. Hans' wife enjoyed the south, while he enjoyed the north. They were very different when it came to their holiday preferences. He has come to dislike the hot southern sun and the noisy atmosphere of the southern social climate more and more. When he was a young man, he used to spend the summers going on vacation to Spain and Italy, as many young people do. The north is slow and peaceful, which is what he prefers. Hans has always liked the northern coast of his own country. He has always lived close to water, where he could feel the wind and the sea. When he was a child, his parents took him on summer holidays to the coast where they spent some very pleasant days, he remembers. Hans has good memories from these summers. They did not have much money, but they continued to visit the same family of fisher folk by the sea for several years, he says. Hans learned to fish. He would go out with the fisher folk in the middle of the night to the open sea.

The more we talk, the more Hans opens up. The journey to the north seems to mirror a turn towards a new way of living and being for Hans. He wishes to change the way he lives his everyday life. The divorce made him realize the need for change. For many years, work was the centre of his life, he explains. Hans worked in a bank, and it was as if he was married to the bank and not his wife. It was not good. His wife was at home and Hans was at work. He feels sad that his marriage ended, but he knows that it was his fault. He now tries to put his friends first, and work second. He works fewer hours and no Saturdays. Though he now works less than he did before, he still works more than many people do. An ordinary day at work is very busy and sometimes he has to bring work home with him in the evenings. Because his work is exhausting, he needs rest and vacations to cope with working. Nevertheless, he does now have more time for leisure and spends a lot of time with friends, doing sports (in particular bowling and bicycling) and spends time by himself travelling. Hans compares the experience of the north to the south, and he likes the north much better. The north and the south seem to be important for Hans as a structure of experience that has shaped, and continues to shape, his present situation.

Hans is living with an opposition that practically and metaphorically connects his life to the European north and south. It may be so that we might see the north and the south as parts of his internal geography. The south is full of life, of noise and rushing. The north is more restful and nicer, because all things take much longer to do in the north. The north has become more important to Hans in his adult years, and it is as if he wants to develop the northern parts of himself more. In some way, the north is more compatible with a mature stage of life, Hans thinks. Perhaps the north has come to Hans as a slow move towards himself.

A pilgrimage and a *rite de passage*

The trip to North Cape is something special for Hans. It is a gift to himself to mark his fiftieth birthday. Turning fifty is a special crossing in an individual's life in that it marks the end of the first half of life. Hans is now on his move towards the second half of his life, but he is not there yet. He is in a transition period and searching for new meaning and a restoration of being. In the following, I want to discuss Hans' journey as a particular form of modern pilgrimage. Hans probably would not like to be called a pilgrim because the word is so historically tainted. Historians writing about pilgrimage do see a connection between travel and pilgrimage, but are mostly interested in historical travel, not modern pilgrimage (Blom 1992). There is one obvious similarity between pilgrimage and travel. The precursor of what we today call travel diaries, travelogues and travel handbooks was a range of travel stories and travel literature aimed at pilgrims. According to the historian, Grethe Blom, these suggested where pilgrims could travel safely, where they could eat and sleep, distances between places, places to see, famous churches and places of worship (Blom 1992).

Victor Turner, a social anthropologist, writes that there are particular connections between pilgrimage and holiday travel in the modern age since large numbers of tourists visit pilgrim destinations (Turner 1974). On the other hand, Turner shows that modern pilgrimage is not as integrated into a wider socio-cultural system as it was in medieval Europe and Asia. Some of these older cultural forms are now being reactivated within modern society. Turner shows that these forms are being mixed with the forms of today's society, which he describes as a transitional period of history. Historically speaking, pilgrimage has surfaced in periods of destructuration and rapid social change as a form of liminal or underground manifestation of the religious, Turner argues.

Sociologist Zygmont Bauman argues that while the pilgrim is a good figuration of the human being in modernity, the tourist has replaced the pilgrim in postmodernity (Bauman 1996). For Bauman the world is not for pilgrims anymore. Modern human beings sought to build and construct identity, Bauman argues, while in postmodernity human beings try to avoid fixed and absolute identity. The social anthropologist, Valene Smith, argues that there has been a tendency to polarize the experiences of the tourist and the pilgrim in tourism research (Smith 1992). This polarization is not necessarily easily justified, partly because the words are etymologically related. Generally, in popular discourse, the pilgrim is a religious traveller, but the Latin meaning conveys a much broader perspective of travel experience. A pilgrim can be a traveller, a foreigner, a wanderer or an exile, in addition to being a newcomer and a stranger. In Latin the word *peregrinus* means stranger or foreigner (Blom 1992). The origin of the pilgrimage is old, and the meaning of pilgrimage is familiar in all the major religions in both east and west. In European countries, the social significance of the pilgrimage is connected with the Christian medieval pilgrimages. Julia Kristeva argues that the pilgrim, the *civitas peregrina*, appeared with Christianity (Kristeva 1991). The meaning of a stranger as pilgrim in medieval times was double, however, since it was both Christian and political in terms of incorporating the stranger into the local political powers and the feudal state in terms of economic and political meaning.

The word pilgrimage is more restricted in meaning, and refers to a journey which implies a hope for something better, something good, a kind of purification or therapeutic work on pain, sorrow or loss, according to Valene Smith (1992). During the medieval ages, pilgrimage referred to a religious search for relics of saints and persons or the burial places of saints. Pilgrimage focuses on experiences of a different or strange place away from the ordinary place of home. It requires work of some kind to reach that other place. Hope, goodness, knowledge and promise are sought in another place. The pilgrim acts on the basis of devotion, hope and belief towards a strong wish, intention or understanding, which creates a longing for another life, another place. The belief in the good after much effort is central to the experiences of the pilgrim. Meaning comes through travel, as project, and the goal is to overcome the distance between emptiness and meaning, Bauman writes (1996). I will add: to overcome the distance between placelessness and place. The classic view of pilgrimage is that it aims at something beyond or outside the ordinary and secular that is found in places, sites, and nature, which represent the source of some sort of miraculous experience. The theme of pilgrimage is, however, also connected to quests or wayfaring tales, e.g. in literature where a hero or heroine tries to find out who he or she is outside the structure of everyday life (Turner 1981). Enlightenment or revelation comes from the outside or from extraordinary or non-ordinary reality, which is not outside of structure, but within a different structure.

It is reasonable to argue that being a holiday traveller is, in many ways, an expression of a pilgrim's wish and desire to settle new land or a new place in one's own self. This place is not a physical setting or locality, but a restoration of an internal place of the self. In the pilgrimage, the desire for new land might be an expression of a place that is missing or lost – or it may be the discovery of a mythic place never experienced. This search may take on a particular meaning in late modern holiday travel. I suggest a connection between late modern travel and pilgrimage where the central experience of healing emerges through the making of place as the simultaneous making of self. In addition, I suggest that the road towards change goes through mythic place and the ideas of the human being's place in nature in a holistic way. In Hans' story, the search for wholeness comes through work with the internal north through his experience of northern nature.

If the human being is the centre of cosmos oriented from the cardinal points and the vertical axis (see chapter three), I would like to focus on the north-south axis in cosmology. Yi-Fu Tuan writes that a mythic ordering of the world in terms of a binary opposition is usual, as in the north-south axis (Tuan 1974). Such binary oppositions depend on an idea of centre, which seems to be crucial in the cosmological ordering of the world. Tuan argues that mythic place concerns the whole but in all ideas of cosmos the centre for this wholeness is very important. Though centre is important, it does not exist in a fixed or absolute sense, since any movement of the axis' polar opposites distorts or changes the centre. Hans' story suggests that the centre of his cosmology is undergoing change but it seems that his movement refers to a restoration rather than a distortion of wholeness. The new centre is necessary for the expression of a new wholeness. I suggest that change of the centre towards the north, in terms of mythic place, is a move towards something better, given a view of western cosmology that does not express a harmonious connection between the north and the south.

The new centre may be a middle place, in-between the north-south axis, the east-west axes, and the vertical axis. That the centre may move means that one side of one of the axes has been able to draw the centre closer to its periphery. Notions of centre and periphery have been present in European worldviews since the medieval age. Europe stood in the centre between the northern and southern peripheries of the continent, both seen as uninhabitable, unknown and dangerous regions. Europe was delimited to the east due to the mountains that blocked the way to the east, while the sea represented the border to the west. At that time the north-south axis of Europe meant the area between Trondheim in Norway and Cádiz in Spain, according to Tuan (1974). Today, in popular speech, North Cape is represented as the northernmost part of the European continent. The North Cape was first marked on a map from 1553 by the British navigator Richard Chancellor, who was a participant on the Willoughby expedition that set out to find the northern passage to China (Skavhaug 1990, Jacobsen 1997). The association of the North Cape as the outermost point of the European north was also made by the Italian Francesco Negri, who described the experience of visiting North Cape as being at the edge of the world (see chapter one). The North Cape was the edge of the world to him because there were no places further north populated by human beings.

Through travel as place-making, human beings bring peripheral, mythic place into their lived world as a part of their life-world, in a newly found wholeness, where the result is the creation of a new centre for being. In this way, the pilgrimage to the north has qualities of the *rite de passage*. The term *rite de passage* traditionally refers to rites undertaken when individuals and groups are going through a change in state or status, according to the social anthropologist, Victor Turner (Turner 1967, 1974). Rites are performed when the individual changes in life-cycle status (birth, initiation, marriage, death), and also when the individual crosses seasonal, temporal or spatial boundaries. Such rites do not only refer to ascribed statuses but also to achieved statuses, Turner writes. In this process of change in status or state, change in spatial position or spatial movement is very important. All societies have such rites, while they are more explicitly expressed in societies where change or transition is bound up in natural rhythms rather than technological innovation. This does not mean, however, that modern societies are without such rites (Salomonsen 1999). Therefore, a transitional period of human beings' life may be expressed in holiday travel when this functions as a *rite de passage* that changes a person's state of being. The transition rite takes place in another place and time, and not in the ordinary reality or in everyday life.

Many rites have a particular form or structure comprised of three temporal stages separated spatially. Turner understands the rite as including three stages: a preliminal, a liminal and a postliminal stage. The liminal stage can be compared with the actual journey on a pilgrimage, or holiday travel, and is characterized as a stage of reflection. Liminality implies a certain freedom that comes from simultaneous being and non-being. One is betwixt and between, like a traveller who has left home and not yet returned. Liminality is therefore both a negation of one social order, and an affirmation of another order.

According to Victor Turner, there is a *rite de passage* in pilgrimage, which works like an initiatory ritual (Turner 1974). The liminal state in pilgrimage is characterized by participation in the divine, and not by looking at it. The pilgrim becomes a symbol of totality or wholeness. Turner shows that there is a striking simplicity in the exhibited, acted or presented in a rite. The outward form of a *rite de passage* in pilgrimage may be simple, but the interpretation may be complex. Even though visible expressions of ritual may be lacking, this does not mean that there is a lack of rituals per se. There may be a wealth of ritual meaning in individual holiday making that is unavailable for those who do not make the same journey because it cannot be seen directly (see also Barth 1961).

The liminal state is interesting in the context of holiday travel because it represents a threshold for a human being. Victor Turner argues that modern human beings are given several possibilities to walk in and out of liminality. Modern human beings are liminoid, he says. How the liminal phase stands in relation to the ordinary reality, however, does not always occur through inversion. Inversion implies opposition. An oppositional conflict may be articulated through the liminal phase, even if this is not always the case. There are different ways of conceiving this opposition or the movement in and out of ordinary reality. Below I will discuss a few aspects that connect the liminal phase to extra-ordinary or non-ordinary place.

The first is that liminal or non-ordinary place in western culture is often thought as a sacred place (Graburn 1976). Social anthropologist Nelson Graburn suggests that sacred-profane alterations are important markers in social life that mark the passage of time. Each year is marked by a shift between ordinary life and non-ordinary life, such as a holiday, Christmas or a festival, and Graburn suggests that annual holiday travel is an important marker of the passage of modern human life. Yi-Fu Tuan has described these two dimensions by using two roles played by the human being, the social-profane and the mythical-sacred (Tuan 1977). The human being is thus polarized in two temporalities, one cyclical and vertical, the other linear and horizontal. The horizontal state of the human being is connected to the secularization and modernising processes and the accompanying concept of linear time. Tuan argues that the modern human being is not purely secularized, but is kept within the polarization of the mythical-sacred and the social-profane.

The second is that the liminal phase in tourism gives possibilities for ludic behaviour and play. Geographer Berit K. Svanquist argues that nature can be viewed as a play ground for human beings during holiday travel, with nature acting like an object of transition that helps people to handle the lack of trust they feel towards modern society and its institutions (Svanquist 2000 a and b). Social anthropologist Runar Døving sees the element of play in tourism in a different way, and writes that holidays in the Mediterranean countries seem to represent a dream world, with an underlying myth of paradise, both in public opinion and in the information provided by the tour organizers (Døving 1993). The myth of 'the south' is that of a Paradise on earth, a dream world with peace and harmony, love and freedom and lack of conflicts among human beings (Døving 1993). Words like warmth, beauty, peace and quiet are found everywhere, as is the ubiquitous suffix 'paradise' (golf paradise, surf paradise, love paradise). The original myth of paradise tells of reunion with the divine, but this southern tourist paradise is not this kind of paradise. The rite legitimates a life without conflicts, but it does not feel right to live in such harmony all the time. The mythic south in a tourist cosmology is, however, a place with no connection to its polar opposite, the mythic north.

Døving also notes that the sense of temporality changes in the south, which is the third aspect of liminal place. In the Mediterranean countries, tourists take off their watches. Clock time is, in other words, out. The experience of time in holiday travel is connected to the yearly rhythm and alteration between work and leisure, the profane and the sacred. The year as a unit of time is an old invention. The year is like all other natural markers (such as the sun, the moon, and the tides) an expression of rhythm and recurring time. It is different from clock time, which is a conception of time necessary in industrial societies, where time is a resource to use and allocate (Adam 1990). Clock time is irreversible time, connected to a mechanistic view of nature and the machine as root metaphor for modern society. This means that the journey to a different place is also a journey to another time.

What place and time does the north have in Hans' life? What other aspects of liminality does his journey to the north have in relation to his ordinary life at home? If the south is paradise, what is then the north? Hans seems to be telling two stories about the meaning of the north. He really enjoys the peace and solemn qualities of the north all by himself, and he expresses real disgust at mass travel to the north. What Hans wants to see is a result of his imagination and experiences, and not a direct reflection of what travel agents want him to see. Perhaps Hans wants his own experiences to be his alone, true and authentic, and perhaps these experiences are not possible to express in words. Perhaps they are experiences that should be left unarticulated. Many people that I spoke to, not only Hans, are more articulate about the representations of the north in mass tourism rather than the making of the North Cape as a subjectively meaningful place for them. For example, the name North Cape is represented as a place where tourists are promised experiences of change. But none of the travellers wants these experiences or the kind of change represented by the tourism agents. All the other tourists may have these experiences, but not the ones telling me why they travelled north. Their experiences may be extraordinary or perhaps sublime, since they lacked words or language. Perhaps there is a second poetic layer of geography being made at the

North Cape, one which takes time to see and hear, and which takes time to become animated in the verbal paths of travellers.

This is a point also made by the social anthropologist Edward Bruner, who argues that tourists are promised a transformation through a *rite de passage* (Bruner 1991). That tourists will be changed is a claim repeated in tourist brochures all over the world. You will become a different person! Bruner says this is rather sad given the fact that the same tourist brochures also stress that the natives never change, they are unchangeable, they are the exotic and fixed others. This is in many senses an overestimated value, according to Edward Bruner's experiences from fieldwork in Indonesia. Quite the opposite was found, since natives may gain more and change more than the tourists do, and these changes in local culture are not necessarily positive.

The distinction between tourists and travellers is often found in tourism research. These were also classificatory concepts among the travellers I spoke with to the North Cape. They present themselves as travellers rather than as tourists. Nobody sees themselves as tourists. One reason may be scientific and popular discourse on modern tourism itself, which is full of negative and derogatory representations of tourists. There is an idea that is repeated rather often that tourists are in some sense living less authentic lives on holiday than travellers. It is therefore not strange that 'tourist' and 'traveller' are conceptualized as opposites, as James Buzard does in a view on modern culture built on a structure comprising tourist and traveller (Buzard 1993, Culler 1981). The tourist experience is expressed in a negative way, as opposed to the travellers' supposedly real, authentic and true experience. Edward Bruner does not distinguish between tourist and traveller in this way (Bruner 1991). He shows that the distinction is difficult to maintain in reality. Human beings do not live in separate worlds. It is not possible to avoid the well-trodden paths of tourists, and tourists are never some sort of object directed by remote control, Bruner shows. The picture is much more complicated if one looks at tourism and travel from an experiential point of view.

As I see it, Hans' way of telling about the experiences of the North Cape reflects this contradiction in meaning. Hans experiences the sacred and the profane, the north and the south and the ordinary and the non-ordinary simultaneously. The north implies a meaningful relationship between human being and place, though in a way different from what is experienced in the south. The north is about the profane but it is also about the sacred. Perhaps every human being has his or her own north and south to get to know. For Hans, the north was associated with a lesson initiated by loss, but with much to gain. The journey for Hans represents a significant *rite de passage*, with the promise of change from within. However, this change does not imply leisure or paradise in the meaning of freedom as in the south, but hard work. The important new element in Hans' life here was that work and banking became less important, and that human relations, friends, family and emotions became a priority. It seems that for Hans, the north is a lesson about the meaning of the feminine principle. Going north for Hans can be seen as a way to unite both the south and the north into an integrated whole. It may be that the south and the north are poles of experience, and that both are necessary to feel whole and have an integrated self. Going north implies a change where the centre moves from a previous location, and Hans' story illustrates a change of centre to a place farther north than before.

Chapter 7

The North as Epiphany

The austerity and dignity of the north

Julia is a middle-aged woman who is travelling on the *Hurtigruta* with her husband. They live in a major European city. The idea of travelling to the northern parts of Norway came when they read a newspaper article about the *Hurtigruta*. Somebody they knew had made the trip, Julia says, and they found it so interesting that they wanted to make the same trip. She is not going to see North Cape, she says, but she just loves the nature in the north. It is not so much about Norway, as it is about the nature of the north.

The north seems to refer more to an internal rather than an external geography because it expresses a state of mind or feeling, as opposed to actual localities. Julia describes the north by talking about her feelings towards Scotland, which is a country she likes visiting very much. The sea and the landscape make her very happy. There is something restful and peaceful in northern nature that makes her calm. The cold weather does not bother her. The cold brings austerity and dignity. Julia feels that the northern landscape is indifferent to her, which is good. This indifference puts things into perspective for Julia. It makes her realize how insignificant and small she is, and how little she matters to the earth. It may sound strange, she says, but that is comforting to her. The north is hard, cool, it is indifferent and does not care, and Julia finds this good. Experiencing northern nature to her is like being in the middle of something that does not care at all. Ideally, she would prefer to be alone in the northern nature, with the scenery, the landscape, the birds and the trees, with no other human beings around. She would like to have things drop away from her emotionally.

The voyage along the coast represents purification to Julia, and she does not want to express or put this process into words. She just wants to absorb it and make the north come to her, which is related to a spiritual experience of nature. What she gets out of northern nature spiritually, she keeps saying, is an absence of emotions. This is not negative at all. Quite the contrary, it is actually very calm and positive. Julia searches for something that she describes as purity and calmness.

Julia was born in a large industrial city in another part of the country. Her parents come from a very poor area of this city. Julia is the only child. During childhood, the family moved twice to different regions in the country. Her father made all the money, while her mother was a housewife. One place she particularly remembers is a town in the northern part of the country located by the North Sea. She spent some very happy years there, though it was a very unhappy time for her mother, partly because she wanted to move to where they had previously lived. Julia often went to see the North Sea, to be near it, because she felt OK there. After some years they moved again to a town in the south, though again by the sea. She thinks that her upbringing was respectable, which was very important because her parents came from poor backgrounds. Money was very important. Materially they had many possessions, but emotionally it was very cold. The family did not travel much during holidays. They went to the seaside in the summer and spent Christmas and Easter with family and relatives.

Julia met her husband early on, and they married at a relatively young age. When she finished college, she started working as a librarian and they both moved to where they live now. She chose to take a vocational education because her father felt it would be a waste to do a degree. At present, she is head of department at one of the university libraries. If she did not have to worry about money, she would choose to write. She does some writing, but has not published anything yet. When Julia started working, her husband was still a student. Now they are both librarians, but they do not work in the same place. Children have never been in the picture because she has never felt particularly maternal. Neither of them expressed an interest, so they ran out of time. They have travelled much together, many times to Scotland. Julia loves the islands in the west in particular; Mulden and Skye are very beautiful, austere, perfect, small and peaceful. And then there is the sea of course, Julia continues.

Julia fondly describes her vacations as lapses of time when she has the opportunity to think. Whenever she goes on holiday, she says that she tries to use the holiday to do a lot of thinking. This holiday is different, however. She feels that she has even more time to think while being on the *Hurtigruta* than she normally does. Everything is taken care of. She is free to look around, sit down, take a walk, read, or just relax.

Julia has many things to think through, she says. The time on the ship is very intense and she would have preferred being on her own on vacation this year. At this point of our conversation, Julia asks whether we can move to a more private part of the ship to continue. We do so and she then says that her life is very stressful due to a crisis that she does not know how to handle. The coldness of the northern landscape is a great contrast to her emotions. Northern nature gives her peace and rest to compensate for a stressed mind. Julia knew that these emotions would come on this trip along the Norwegian coast. Julia feels she has to explain more about her need to reflect and think. She starts telling me, with a long introduction, about her relationship with her husband. The time has come to decide what to do about the future. Something strange happened some months ago which is connected to the north, she says. Julia met a man and they have some sort of relationship. He is from a country in the north of Europe, and is a very different person from Julia. He goes out on the glaciers in the mountains, and is a kind of force of nature himself, she explains. This man has changed the way she thinks about things, she says, because everything seems to come together. She has realized that she has not really had a chance to be young. She does not feel happy in her marriage. We are very different, she says. Her husband thinks that the man is more important but neither of them is equal, Julia feels. Leaving her husband would cause a lot of trouble, but she feels that staying with him would not give her a life where she can do things for herself. Julia has always envied people who just walk out and never go back, but she also feels it is expected of her to be with someone. She does not know what the answers to her dilemmas and problems might be. The journey to the north seems to provide time and place for new thoughts and reflections but she does not yet know what to do.

Creating a new map

The coming together of things in Julia's life is difficult. Julia does not have any ready-made maps to help her on this journey of discovery. Her journey does have a trajectory, however, just as the *Hurtigruta* is slowly but surely taking her north, and past the north point, and south again. Solutions will surface when the time is right, and when her internal journey has taken her north, and then south, she will perhaps have made a new map for her life.

Michel De Certeau has a way of thinking about the need for maps and itineraries that illuminates Julia's journey (De Certeau 1984). Discovering and learning take the form of the travel story according to De Certeau. To make a travel story, one must travel, walk and move. A travel story takes its outset in a traveller who follows the logic of the itinerary characterized by the absence of a map. De Certeau writes that the problem of meaningful practices, as in Julia's journey of self-discovery, is not to become an expert, not to go too far, not to talk in another field and not to talk in another's place. Julia's truths can never be an object in any discourse because she can never get an overall view of the meaning of her life. She has to live with it from within, since there is no total aerial view that can offer solutions. It is impossible to make any shortcuts to authority because there is no way one can have full information on the possibilities. There is no privileged position from which to speak. One is a stranger within familiar territory, or, as De Certeau writes, a savage in one's own house.

This distinction between map and itinerary also has relevance in a wider perspective. De Certeau uses the distinction between itinerary and map in a cultural critique of modern forms of reason for the past five hundred years. The gap between the map and the itinerary has increased over the centuries, De Certeau argues. In the development of modern scientific discourse, map making has gradually disengaged itself from the traces and tracks made by human beings. The earliest medieval maps were drawings of actual itineraries, with special information for travellers, such as places passed on the journey or localities to spend the night, with distance measured in hours and days of walking. The maps were memories transcribed into a visual schemata of action, like a visual grammar for movement. These maps did not assume the position of the neutral and all-seeing eye. Over time, however, the map has become a theatre, or a representation, containing two types of knowledge. The first type of knowledge reflects Ptolemy's geography, while the second type of knowledge draws on the traditional knowledge of navigators, sailors, and travellers on land. The renaissance-map expresses knowledge based on both observation and tradition. The great shift in the modern map is that the storyteller and tour describer have disappeared. The itinerary is lost in favour of an abstract view from above. The map authorizes legitimate and dominant knowledge in modernity, and mapping relates to power over place, to dominant technologies in a society and imperialism, in which knowledge is power.

This is a point also made by Kathleen Kirby, who suggests that cartographic practice is the key to the interrelationships between the subject, imperialism and science (Kirby 1996a). Mapping, she argues, comes to reflect and reinforce a new way of seeing both subjectivity and space. The spatial format of the mapping subject has coherence and consistency, and is comparable with a rational space within a stable and organized environment. In other words, cartography is both an expression of enlightenment subjectivity and a technology allowing for the new subjectivity, Kirby argues. The emerging image of the subject is the monadic self, which is dependent on its other, i.e. space or land. The monadic self reflects the ideas of the eighteenth century philosopher Leibniz, and describes a self that is an indivisible individual, with a clear and constant boundary between the inside and the outside. Kirby argues that the ideas of the individual and the land developed at the same time. The human being separates from his environment for the first time, and the sovereign self depends on sovereignty over land.

De Certeau criticizes this form of reasoning. He presents an alternative to modern strategic rationality through a way of operating called tactics. Strategic rationality or ways of operating refer to a particular place which works as a basis for manipulation of the environment. A strategy means that one has delimited and claimed sovereignty over a place called one's own, which is the foundation for power over external places conceived either as targets or threats. A proper place is constructed in opposition to another place. This dualist construction of place, one's own or the other place, has three characteristics according to De Certeau. The first is that place takes priority over time. The second characteristic is that mastery of place depends on visual control over the environment. To see means to foresee and to be in front of time by reading a place. The third characteristic is that this mastery of place depends on a relationship between power and knowledge, whereby unknown places and territories translate into readable places. Language becomes a means to appropriate and colonize place, which gains ontological status through linguistic practices.

A tactic, on the other hand, differs from strategy because it lacks the presence of people with power and will, and thus a proper place. A tactic is a calculated action without power over the external environment. Place is never one's own for somebody acting tactically. A tactic has to work within and on place owned and controlled by somebody else. One is like a traveller in a foreign land. A tactic is thus the art of the weak and those without authority or power. Even though tactical ways of operating seem to be without power, they are not powerless. Tactics constitute practices that re-appropriate place in a collective and individual sense. Tactical ways of operating are empowering, but work with a concept of power that differs from strategic power. The resource for tactics is time. Since strategy takes time for granted, tactics use time creatively and grasp opportunities that exist in the present. De Certeau uses reading to illustrate the creation and re-creation of place through tactics. The production of a story in reading is just like making a journey to a foreign country or unknown place. De Certeau argues that these travel stories are necessary to have a personal place in the world. He argues that when human beings deprive themselves of making travel stories, a loss of place will also occur, within which regression and a fatalistic experience of a formless totality will prevail. When one moves within time, place will appear or re-appear; not because it was a target in itself, but only because it was part of a tactic, as an emerging or potential place. Place will appear in time and with time.

A short summary of the difference between strategy and tactics is that strategy takes place for granted in a way that tactics never can do. Tactics, on the other hand, control time rather than place. Strategy controls place, while tactics work with time. What relevance do De Certeau's ideas have for Julia's story? The distinction between strategy and tactics has something to tell about the differences in the status of the masculine and the feminine principle in western societies. It means that the feminine principle, or the difference of "the feminine", is characterized by a lack of a proper place from which to operate from a woman's point of view. The masculine principle compares to strategy, while the feminine principle compares to tactics. As the masculine controls place, the feminine works with time. It follows here that place is divided according to dualist thinking, either as a target for control or threat to one's existing control. It is obvious that place, within strategic ways of operating, never exists as pure difference, but exists only within the logics of either-or, as target or threat. It is equally obvious that in tactical ways of operating place in "the feminine" may appear in time and not as part of a feminine or feminist strategy, but because of tactics that re-appropriate time through the creation of place in travel stories.

Julia's story shows the necessity of her coming to terms with her crisis and her creating a new and personal map for her life. In this work towards change, tactic is a provisional way of operating until the appropriation has taken place. Julia is a tour describer of her own life, where sovereignty over land is non-present. She is an author of her own story, but not with full authority. What connects De Certeau's understanding of the itinerary to Julia's travel story is that an itinerary for the journey towards selfhood is necessary. The logic of Julia's journey resembles the logic of the itinerary. To be a traveller, like Julia, is to be a creator of place through a spatial logic named tactic. De Certeau says that every story is also a travel story and a spatial practice (De Certeau 1984), as is Julia's story.

Julia has realized that she needs to create her own place in the world. She does not need to live in a world where place is not her own. I will call this realization the epiphany of the north. An epiphany is an extraordinary event and experience that brings forth sudden realizations of truth, which provide the opportunity to change a human being's structure of experience and meaning. An epiphany represents a sudden manifestation of the essence or meaning of something, a truth or something divine, or a comprehension or perception of reality through an intuitive realization (Eliade 1987). It is a profound and subjective experience. In Julia's case, the epiphany is symbolized by Julia's meeting with the man from the north. Julia has realized, to use Michel De Certeau's words, that she is not living and making her place. Julia says that she has always liked the north, but a new experience or meaning of the north appeared after meeting this man. He represents not only a real presence in her life, but their meeting has made her realize that the place she has been is not the place that she would like to be. The meaning of this meeting will unfold over time, since she does not yet know what to do. In the meantime, as a provisional interpretation, the epiphany of the north implies a truth strong enough to bring forth change not only in thinking about place and self, but also in living and making place.

The profound truth takes place within Julia's lived world. The meeting of difference is not imposed from the outside. There is no overall plan or map for Julia's self. I would like to connect Michel De Certeau's ideas on the differences between maps and itineraries to social anthropologist Tim Ingold's discussion of topological metaphors in environmental discourse. I will discuss these in the following as metaphors for making new maps of the self in terms of their appropriateness for women's making of self. Tim Ingold discusses the image of the globe in contemporary debates about the environment (Ingold 1993 and 2000). He writes that the image of the globe is familiar to westerners who have been socialized into models of the world in terms of a globe. The globe offers a view of human life where the world is an object, a thing to contemplate detached from lived experience, simply because it is only a model of the world and not the world itself. The globe is a world apart from life, Ingold argues, and it is not a life-world. It depends on a view from outside and above. The image of the sphere represents a completely different view of the world, which is a view of the world from the inside. According to Ingold, the sphere stresses the horizontal qualities of the cosmos with a particular centre. Tim Ingold argues that human relationships to the world are centrifugal, while the global view would be centripetal. These two images are two ways of representing cosmos according to Ingold. Whenever we have a cosmology that takes its outset in a globe, the environment is divorced from life. Knowledge gained by participation and action in relation to the lived world is not valued in global imagery.

Over time, there has been a movement from spherical imagery to global imagery, Ingold (1993, 2000) argues, and current debates on globalization and localization reflect this global imagery. The idea of globalization seems to take its outset in an ontology that stresses detachment and the view from outside. Ingold shows that sometimes even the discussion on the local and localization will stress engagement, world-openness and the lived world from within, but with a meaning of the local that is non-spherical. This happens when meanings of the local are created from global imagery. As Ingold shows, the global ontology is indifferent to place and context. The local difference is only comprehensible in terms of a discourse on boundaries, co-ordinates, positions and containment. Each local community is confined within itself and represented as limited in relation to the global totality, and will thus have no identity in terms of its own uniqueness, only in relation to the whole picture at large. According to Ingold, the movement to global imagery also contributes in the understanding of the difference between cosmology and technology. Ingold argues that while cosmology provides principles for ways of operating within the world, technology only provides principles for ways of operating upon the world. The shift from spherical imagery to global imagery corresponds with the shift from cosmology to technology, and this is nothing less than a movement from revelation to control, from partial knowledge to calculated risk.

A view of life from the point of view of the sphere is missing in the global perspective. There is a visualist assumption in global discourse that the world becomes nothing more than a *tabula rasa* for the inscription of human history, Ingold writes. He also writes that the philosopher Immanuel Kant was important for explaining the global view. Kant found that the earth was global in form. He recognized the earth as it appeared through the senses, and made the actual slotting of each observation into a position within a complete, unifying spatial framework. Ingold describes how Kant had in mind an image of the globe, or an idea of the surface of the earth, onto which the experiential data could be mapped. This is the origin of the global outlook according to Ingold. For the Kantian, global traveller, the world is a globe, and the traveller moves upon its outer surface. When one travels on the surface, there is no centre. Any point of the surface can be a point of origin or a destination, Ingold explains. From the perspective of the sphere, however, one travels within the sphere that is in some respect a world. When one travels within one's sphere, it has a centre from which the spheres extend but this centre is within, not without. There is no separation between the traveller as subject and world as object. The world is not an object. Humans belong to the world, but the world does not belong to humans. This imagery also concerns human conceptions of change. In the global outlook, change is exogenous to the world, while in the spherical outlook change is endogenous.

I would like to develop the imagery of the sphere a little further, closer to phenomenological ways of thinking. It seems clear that Julia is not a Kantian traveller. Julia travels within the world and she has a centre that is inside. Her journey is away from technology and towards cosmology. There are possibilities for a connection between sphere and the lived world since both presuppose the existence of a centre within a horizontal world. The meaning of centre is important in the worldview of human beings in many areas of the world. The historian A.Ya. Gurevich studied the worldview of the ancient Scandinavian peoples and noted the horizontal quality of this worldview (Gurevich 1969). The geography of this cosmos is complex and undifferentiated, and simultaneously practical, religious and mythological, with a particular centre based in the dwelling-place and the farmstead. The quality of time is also central here, though not in abstract form, but as specific in nature. The meaning of world in this worldview is therefore our age, or the age of the humankind in the Scandinavian part of the world, Gurevich argues, and where the concepts of life, space and time were inseparable. I would like to make an additional point in relation to this northern world. Gurevich stresses that there is no clear separation between the qualities of human beings and the qualities of nature in this understanding of world. The relationship between nature and human beings is organic, and as such, human beings are not able to achieve a detached view of nature through an aesthetic attitude towards nature.

This means that world is perhaps a suitable metaphor to describe the lived world of human beings, and for the making of female selves, compared to sphere. Both globe and sphere are images of a world, but only world is our world or the historical presence of dwelling on earth. I would add that this our world may also refer to the particular northern world, so that the epiphany of the north makes itself heard in this way as well. A similar understanding is found in the national epic of Finland, the Kalevala, as described by the geographer Ari Lehtinen (Lehtinen 1991). There is a particular meaning of northern nature according to Lehtinen, with reference to the meaning of the northern forests in Finland, which presupposes interdependence between different natures, the nature of the human being and the nature of nature. A dualist understanding of the relationship between human beings and nature makes no sense in the lived world of human beings, and is therefore not relevant.

Julia's journey of discovery takes place in a northern world, or Julia's northern world. In this respect, Julia's story illustrates thinking about self without any ready-made maps of the self. As cartography means ways of understanding maps, we may need an epistemological shift in the way maps are understood, as geographer J.B. Harley has argued (Harley 1996). As I see it, this need for an epistemological shift regarding maps is important since it concerns the making of maps for the creating of female selves. We need, in other words, a new map for the female self. A post-strategic and post-modern map for the female self would not be a printed map, detached from its producers. This map is partial and located, with production connected to use and consumption. Such a map would not present an aerial view of one total global space, but would present the subjective and objective world. It is seen from one particular person's point of view, which is not a point, but an itinerary, with existence in time, in flow, as an unfolding life process. Every single human being has his or her own itinerary through life, and such itineraries are not possible to create beforehand – they have to be lived. The self is not a map or a globe – the self is a lived place-world.

Chapter 8

Estrangement, Fluidity and Femininity

My kind of travelling

Marie is sixty-three years old and lives in a small town in the middle of Europe. She joined the *Hurtigruta* in Bergen, having flown in from her home country. She is travelling alone and enjoys spending time alone on deck reading or just relaxing. Marie decided to travel to the north on the *Hurtigruta* several years ago, but not as an ordinary tourist. She is not travelling because of the North Cape. Being an ordinary tourist is not her kind of travelling, Marie claims. She wanted to travel with a postal ship, a historical and authentic ship, not a cruise ship. She distances herself from the tourists she is travelling with, saying they are interested in the wrong things when they travel. Tourists book package tours, she says, and place great value on unimportant details.

Nevertheless, Marie does have an intellectual interest in travelling north, because she agrees that the north is appealing. She reveals many connections to her own life that make the north interesting. She has visited Iceland before, and her family lived in Sweden for some years when she was a child. Subconsciously there is some connection, she continues. Marie enjoys experiencing the nature of the north – the fjords, the ice, the mountains and all that. Marie will not however visit the North Cape. She thinks North Cape might be a positive experience for many, but not for her. Representations of the North Cape in the newspapers had a great impact on her expectations, which were very negative.

During her adult life, Marie has travelled extensively throughout the world, both professionally and personally. She has a university degree in fine arts and she has worked as a teacher for many years. When we met, she had been retired for some years. She has worked in her home country and in different South American countries, teaching arts and language at foreign schools. Marie did not marry and she never had children. She retired earlier than usual, she tells me, because of her health. Her interest in travel has stayed with her since her college days. In the beginning, she did not have much money to do holiday travel because she had to pay back the money for her college studies. The reason she applied for work abroad in South America for the first time was partly that she wanted to travel, and secondly that she did not like the first job she had. While staying in South America, she met many people of her kind, outsiders as she calls them, people who enjoyed travelling and living alone. She realized when living in South America that she would be an outsider all her life. She has cultivated that, was more or less obliged to, during her adult life so that now she is almost unable to join groups.

She usually meets other travelling people, whom she spends time talking to.

The pattern of doing much travel as a necessity for freedom combined with work abroad has created a particular way of living that is continued in her everyday life as a retired person. However, it was not until her mother died that she got the opportunity to travel even more. Her current life consists of spending about two to four weeks in her home country, and then she travels. She is away from home about half the year, but not in one go. After four to eight weeks of travel, she returns to her hometown. She is happy that she now has the freedom to decide where to go when she wants to go somewhere. This made a big difference for her when she retired. After retirement, she has travelled to many places and countries around the world. During the last three years, she has spent many months in countries like Eritrea, Peru, Cuba, the Maldives, Vietnam, Laos, Kampuchea, Thailand, Ethiopia, Syria, Lebanon, Tanzania and other African countries. She explains that she never chooses expensive tours. There are three limits: health, money, and time. She does not have money, she says, so she has to work with health and time. Marie says she does not feel privileged to travel. Travelling feels more like something she needs to do to handle her life. It is like a quest for peace in the soul. Travelling is hard work, Marie explains, and reminds me that in French the word for work is in fact *travail*. Friends have asked her why she does not do things at home, such as nursing or helping in the church, but Marie is not interested in that. Marie travels to heal herself. Marie travels because it is a way to give form and meaning to her life, and to find out about her own life and personality. She travels only for own benefit and not for knowledge. She meets people of her kind when she travels, young people and older people who get out of work to travel for a year, she explains, from whom she learns about herself. The beauty of the scenery and those sorts of things do not teach her much about herself, Marie explains.

Her home lies in a provincial town located by one of the major European rivers. She grew up and went to school in this very small town, though coming back to her home country after many years abroad was not easy for her. It made her feel like an outsider even more, because she had different viewpoints compared to her colleagues there. She feels that she lost her roots in her home country. On the other hand, she never felt at home in her childhood years, since she grew up in an artist's family. It was never possible for her or her family to fit in with the rhythm of ordinary people, Marie tells me. Marie's father was a painter. He was a devoted and accomplished artist most of his life. Marie remembers that he always talked about people who wanted to be artists but who also wanted to have safe money. As he saw it, an artist cannot have both safety and creativity simultaneously. Her father did not earn much money, so they were very poor, Marie says. Although Marie's parents were poor in material terms, they provided other values. Instead of nice toys, they gave the children things that did not cost money, like walks where they learnt about the ways of nature. These are very nice memories for Marie.

From very early on, Marie was interested in becoming a teacher to teach children and young people to appreciate art. She says she inherited some talents from her father and admits that she draws a little, but too little for her satisfaction. Her home is now the basis of security. The English have a saying that goes like this: 'My home is my castle!' Marie has made that saying her own. Her way of living affects her everyday life at home as well. It is almost impossible for her to have a normal life, in terms of stability or concord centred on the home place. Nonetheless, she tries to create some stability in her life, because she has acknowledged that the way she lives creates health problems. She says that she has neglected the need for stability for so long. She is not able to live an ordered life because she enjoys freedom too much. She fights with this every day. Her days at home are spent as unplanned as possible. She says she tries to keep each day a festival day, Marie says laughingly, and she has many interests and activities that keep her busy during the days at home. She enjoys reading very much and she spends time in the garden, which looks just like a jungle each time she returns home.

Fluidity and estrangement

Marie finds authenticity in short-lived social relationships and acquaintances in unfamiliar places, and feels that she has lost her roots to her hometown. Marie's journey to the north and all her other journeys provide form and meaning to her life. Travelling is a way of handling the challenges of her life. Marie seems to be a nomad in a way that creates a feeling of being at home anywhere. She has created a way of life based upon periods of geographical dislocation, combined with periods at home, which together make it possible for her to be herself in familiar and strange places. Home is still her castle and a safe place to seek refuge in from the external world. She feels like a stranger or an outsider at home at the same time. Being at home is not dependent on a particular place, but on travels between home and away. The experience of estrangement is something that exists within. One way of looking at this experience is that human beings may feel at home with one's self as an outsider and traveller. The feeling of being at home, and wholeness for that sake, does not necessarily depend on the absence of estrangement, conflict, or ruptures. I would like to explore the relationship between travel and the feeling of being at home more closely in the following discussion. The connecting points between travel and wholeness, as I see it, are fluidity and estrangement, and first I will start with fluidity or movement.

Fluidity is a metaphor that describes Marie's form of life and the way she lives or acts out her self. In this sense, Marie's story illustrates the tendency in the social sciences and the humanistic disciplines to write about culture and social processes through evoking metaphors of fluids, flow, movement or travel. Often, this flow ontology is connected to women, the female principle, or "the feminine" (see for example Braidotti 1994, Kristeva 1984, 1991, and Smith 1996). There are also the ideas of travelling theory, travelling culture, travelling subjects and studies of tourism, gypsies and nomadic forms of life (Bauman 1996, Bruner 1994, Chambers

1994, Clifford 1986 and 1992, De Certeau 1984, Curtis and Pajaczkowska 1994, Okely 1996, Pile and Thrift 1995), I would like to connect this tendency to the spatial turn and the aesthetic shift in representational strategies, where space is used as a representational strategy in visual and textual media through experiments in form and style (Crang and Thrift 2000). This shift coincides, and partially results from the postmodern and poststructuralist turn.

Movement is a theme that the geographer Anne Buttimer has also explored from a humanistic perspective (Buttimer 1976, 1985, Mels 2004). Buttimer develops a fluid conceptualization of place and a dynamic conception of the life-world when, for example, she stresses rhythm and bodily processes in connection to the life-world. The life-world for Buttimer represents a major scheme or research programme for geographical thinking. As I read Buttimer, the unconscious plays a role in the dynamics of the life-world. She brings the unconscious into the discussion as forces that set the human being's relationship to the world and to place in motion. The living and sensing human body is the starting point for sensing the time-space rhythms (Buttimer 1976). Anne Buttimer has also discussed the lived world in terms of wholeness through the symbolism of a more concrete form of fluid, namely water. In a study of conceptions of nature in western thought, she explored the role of water symbolism as one root metaphor or world hypothesis (Buttimer 1985). The interest in wholeness thus has much in common with Yi-Fu Tuan's discussions on mythic space and place myths. The water symbolism works in different ways, but Buttimer focuses on its characteristics of flow and motion. One of the areas where water symbolism has a great impact is when water works as symbol of personal and social identity. She brings forth examples where place and family names include water symbols. Anne Buttimer notes the relevance of fluidity as an element that not only lubricates, but emancipates, renews and recreates human existence.

The use of fluid metaphors in Buttimer's way of thinking represents, I will argue, an interesting parallel to the French feminists' fluid philosophy (Irigaray 1985, Kristeva 1986a). The common theme is an interest in flow symbolism for creating emancipating and new symbolic language to give expression to more humane ways of life. For the French feminists, flow is a metaphor for "the feminine", while for Buttimer fluid symbolism represents a way of life more in tune with the dynamics of nature and its rhythms, and a more harmonious relationship between human beings and nature (Buttimer 1985). Buttimer has not discussed gendered dwelling or discussions of place from a woman's point of view, yet she connects water with women in her discussion of water in creation myths, where creation is feminine and fluid. The mother's womb is the first element that a human being (the unborn child) experiences, Buttimer argues, and the womb is a fluid element. Buttimer draws on Heidegger's notion of dwelling here, as the gathering of the fourfold: Earth, Heavens, Mortals and Divinities, and focuses on his use of water. Buttimer acknowledges that water strangely does not play an important role in Heidegger. The interesting point is that Buttimer uses the omission of water in Heidegger's thinking to elucidate neglected aspects of human dwelling, and she does this from the point of view of creation. Buttimer focuses attention on wholeness in terms of horizon rather than on destination. To her, water symbolism is a way towards holistic understanding and the improvement of communication. Perhaps one could say that place continually comes into being through water symbolism and metaphors of fluidity and that a viable concept of place needs the fluid element to become an expression for wholeness. As I see it, it is possible to view wholeness not as an essential and unchanging presence, but as a fluid presence in terms of a fluid metaphysics (Battersby 1998).

Julia Kristeva argues that there is a connection between the fluidity of culture and "the feminine" (Kristeva 1986a). There is a concern for flows and fluidity now, at this point in history, when women have gained a position in society which relates to changing conceptions of time and a new interest in feminine temporality rather than masculine temporality. An interest in fluidity is thus related to conceptions of time. Kristeva indicates that the concept of time in modernity expresses a masculine and linear conception of time. Modern temporality is identical to project, teleology and goal-seeking activities. Linear time refers to the time of language and the structuring of words in sequences. Modern temporality is structured like a narrative consisting of stages of departure, progress and arrival. By drawing upon Nietzsche, Kristeva distinguishes linear time from monumental time. A feminine time concept would be cyclical and monumental, and it stresses eternity, recurrence, biological rhythm similar to the rhythms of nature, cosmic time, vertiginous visions and *jouissance* (bodily joy, freedom, happiness, empowerment). This feminine temporality is all encompassing, infinite and monumental. Kristeva connects feminine temporality to the infinity of imaginary space, which means that the central issue is the meaning of space rather than time. Kristeva sees this as having an origin in the matriarchal religions where women are symbolically associated with space rather than time. In modernity, these two temporalities exist together, but it is the masculine time concept that has dominated the development of society. Monumental time does not appear as the opposite of linear time. Kristeva argues that feminine subjectivity contains both cyclical time (repetitive time) and monumental time (eternal time) because both are related to motherhood and the reproduction perspective. Feminine subjectivity is overall characterized as cyclic, repetitive and monumental. Kristeva argues that both conceptions of time, cyclic and monumental, are fundamental dimensions of time in a whole range of civilizations and forms of experiences. Monumental time is repressed, however.

The relationship between feminine temporality and fluidity is also relevant for the experience of estrangement. As we have seen in Marie's story, periodic travel places Marie in a strange, unusual or new situation, in a continuous movement, with or without breaks and tension. We may thus say that Marie makes herself other to herself each time she leaves home. Julia Kristeva has written about the experience of estrangement as interior to being (Kristeva 1991). Human beings are not only others to other human beings, but others to themselves, because the foreigner lives within, as she puts it. Otherness is internal to subjectivity. The identity of the stranger is characterized by a continuing loss. Being a stranger implies that one is never at home any place, that one is never going to an absolute home and that there is no fixed dwelling, as Anna Smith puts it (Smith 1996). To be a stranger is a difficult position, but it also makes one raise other and more critical questions. Being a stranger creates both melancholy and power, Kristeva argues (Kristeva 1996). The ethical responsibility is not only to accept this otherness but also to use it constructively and productively.

Kristeva's understanding suggests the possibility of seeing the self as an other who exists within, or as a strange or unknown region of meaning forming part of a subjective geography. This idea of being other to oneself is also present in Kristeva's theory of signifiance (meaning) based on a dynamic view of the human being, the subject in process/on trial (Kristeva 1984, Smith 1996). Signifiance refers to the result of the heterogeneous forces, both conscious and unconscious, of the human being. Otherness refers to the unconscious, which dynamically interferes with the conscious life of the human. In her understanding of the heterogeneous subject, Kristeva sees construction of meaning as a revolutionary and emancipating practice. Modern society represses the conditions for meaning construction according to Kristeva, who wants to give meaning creation better conditions. Kristeva sees meaning construction as a social process, a material and bodily process, and as a dynamic process in constant movement. The revolutionary force is heterogeneity which creates movement in psychic space, and which brings about revolution and *jouissance*. For Kristeva it is the living body and its drives, energies, flows, conflicts and desires that is both the beginning and the end, the means and destination. The materiality of heterogeneity is Kristeva's focus, since the pulsating drives of the body produce heterogeneity. The movement is not only symbolic or linguistic, but based in the bodily drives.

To Kristeva, meaning creation is an ongoing, unbounded and generating process. It is described as a passage to the outer boundaries of the subject and society. Kristeva creates a spatialized language where meaning construction represents a process of passage, and where the meaning obtained represents an arrival at the border areas of the self and society. There are gaps and lacks that are not produced by the conscious self, but which arise from the hidden areas of the self and the forgotten regions of the time-space of modernity. Kristeva understands construction of meaning as a heterogeneous process, which indicates both a social construction of biological drives and the transformation of biological drives via social and linguistic practices. Meaning thus depends on being given linguistic form through social interaction. Meaning is created by a movement of two sets of dispositions in the subject, semiotic and symbolic dispositions. These two sets of dispositions are drawn from Lacanian psychoanalysis, but Kristeva gives them new meaning and a different function. Semiotic dispositions represent the primary process in psychoanalysis, but this meaning is extended with a linguistic function. In other words, semiotic language is associated with the feminine principle (represented by the mother), while symbolic language is associated with the masculine principle (represented by the father). The relationship between the two sets of dispositions is difficult, but semiotic dispositions can be compared with the presence of the genotext (competence) in the phenotext (performance) (Kristeva 1986b). The semiotic cannot be described since it is manifested in linguistic practices. This means that semiotic language and the feminine principle do not exist in themselves, because they depend on a manifestation through symbolic language and the masculine principle. This further means that we must acknowledge that there are gaps or fractures in meaning construction and language use. The human being is a creator of meaning, but not an author who has full authority over his or her meaning. Kristeva's subject in process is never sovereign, but it seems that the female subject is even less sovereign to Kristeva. The core of heterogeneous production of meaning rests on an asymmetric relation between the feminine and the masculine principle because of their different status in relation to symbolic language. The destiny of the female subject therefore seems to be a life in exile in relation to symbolic language, but this also represents an exit or point of departure. There is a gap resisting transcendence, but still with a potential for processes of change in psychic space.

The philosopher Kelly Oliver has elaborated on Julia Kristeva's ideas on psychic space (Oliver 2004). Psychic space describes the consciousness and subjectivity of marginalized human beings (Kristeva 1995). Psychic space is a free-floating entity, dependent on the movement between affect and language, body and culture, and is thus a space of transformation and an open, productive space. Space refers here to a medium or a process, not a thing or an object. Oliver understands psychic space as a dynamic within the individual connected to the absence and presence of social support. Oppression or lack of social support lead to a colonization of psychic space, Oliver argues. I suggest that it is fruitful to discuss the relations between feeling at home, fluidity and femininity further in terms of psychic space, and that the experience of estrangement may not only be meaningful but also productive within psychic space.

In particular, Julia Kristeva has studied language use by those who struggle with language, i.e. writers, and artists. It seems that her ideas shed light on the experience of female exile/exit. It is clear that Marie has struggled to create form and content in her life. Common to people who struggle is an experience that not everything in the world can have form in symbolic language, according to Kristeva. Literature and journeys may be therapeutic, though in different ways. Kristeva actualizes the ambivalent relation between language and the experienced world as a real possibility, and this relation works by never equating language with experience, and representations with reality.

According to Anna Smith, writers and artists are permanent travellers because travel is a permanent condition in a way where life is an extraordinary existence at the edges of meaning (Smith 1996). It may seem that Marie is a prime example of an estranged or displaced person in the modern world. What can we learn from Marie in this respect? Marie teaches us that symbolic language cannot put everything in place, but she also teaches us how it is possible to transform homelessness through travel. In this way, the world becomes Marie's home, a home that is not a bounded, absolute and permanent place. Marie is constantly living on the edge; in other words, in a world that seems like a border country. Marie thinks she is no artist, but we might say that she is since her struggles resemble the struggles of writers and artists. In this respect, Marie is an artist, but the material that is turned into art is her self and not objects outside of her body. She has turned herself into a piece of art.

Kristeva shows that the foremost model of the stranger is the female traveller (Kristeva 1984). Marie's journey does not have the male traveller as a model and her journey does not appear within a linear temporality. Marie's journey does not have any particular goal. She never buys ordinary package tours, and she does not live an ordinary family life at home. Her days are not like most people's days. She loathes going to particular attractions when she travels. She dislikes the idea that she is supposed to see them. She does not have to, she knows that, and this is the story she tells. She is no ordinary tourist, but a traveller moving between the semiotic and the symbolic, between home and away, between the feminine and the masculine. When Marie switches between home and away in her life, she also switches between different experiences of time. This is the struggle. It seems that she is trying to move between linear time and another time, the experience of eternal time, associated with infinity and imaginary space. Therefore, the location North Cape in the external world is not a goal for Marie. In the light of Marie's story, the North Cape seems like a goal for the modern human being in search of her or his soul, but to Marie such a goal does not exist in the external world. Instead, Marie's journey suggests that we may view the goal, the feeling at home in place, as associated with becoming, and becoming as homecoming in a way where home is fluid and synonymous with journeying. Home and place are not absolute points in the world, instead place becomes potential place and potential home. This understanding of home and place is transitory. All the places Marie visits are important to her. She has seen beyond the North Cape and the linear logic of travel, and she has done so for a long time. She knows that the journey is a game, and that it does not represent absolute truth.

Chapter 9

Femininity and Open Space

Searching for Open Space

Marianne is in her fifties and lives in the countryside outside one of the major European capitals with her husband Peter. She was not very happy about the sea voyage on the *Hurtigruta* since she has always been a little afraid of the sea. Peter had said that it would not be like the sea at all, and this he ought to know as he has been a sailor all his life. Marianne thought they would be going to and fro between small islands, but in her view this is not what they did. Being at sea was not a good experience for her. She had planned to get off the ship in Tromsø because she really was not happy about the experience. Nevertheless, Marianne continued and this surprised her. When we arrived at Kirkenes two days later, the final port on the northbound route, I learned that Marianne had left the ship and taken a plane to Oslo.

Marianne is very articulate about herself and her surroundings. Her impressions of northern nature were just as she expected, she says. She did not expect to see many people. She wanted to see open space and to have peace. Marianne searches for a feeling of open space, and northern nature provides just that. The north is empty or unknown, she says, and it gives her a great sense of peace. She likes to travel to places that make her feel this way. Open space is an expression that Marianne returns to several times during our conversation. Open space is associated with a pull towards going up the mountains, she says, where there is space to go walking out and about. She feels drawn to being out in the open, being close to the open. She does not like buildings, habitation or parks. The experience of open space is peaceful. This was also relevant for the way she sensed nature. She liked looking at mountains and rivers, in fact at anything at all in nature. There is silence and strength in looking. Noises are blocked out, and she stops thinking. She feels the awareness of the world, which is awesome and wonderful simultaneously, and senses that human beings are really nothing in comparison to the world. Marianne uses the words 'awesome' and 'wonderful' to describe the experience of open space, which points to experiences of the sublime. There are spiritual or mystical feelings connected to sensing the north, she says, but these are not only present in the north. Open space is anywhere, and it is both internal and external. Marianne practices T'ai Chi and describes a way of being in the world, in nature, that may look very detached, but which for her is more like forgetting the border between the internal and the external world.

Marianne was born in a small town, where she lived until she was ten years old.

When she was a child, her mother worked as a seamstress while her father worked in an insurance company. Her father contracted an illness from which he later died, and the family moved to a seaside town for the sake of her father's health. Marianne did not want to move there. They lived close to fields and the wood, and she and her brother used to have a lot of freedom to play outdoors. Looking back, she thinks the move probably did her good. Her parents took her on holiday in the summertime. They always went places in the summers with relatives, spending time camping by the coast. The fathers were mostly working, but the home-working mothers were always there. Marianne remembers spending two wonderful months camping at the seaside each summer.

Marianne started working after finishing school and training for secretarial work. She worked as a secretary at a solicitor's office for many years, and after some time advanced to clerical work and later still she became an assistant solicitor. She ended up with a very good job. Though work is important to her, she managed to marry and raise one son. The marriage broke down after a few years. Marianne's mother helped look after her son after the break. However, there have been difficult times, she continues, because she has always felt pulled between job responsibilities and motherly duties. Now Marianne has time and does for her grandchildren what her mother and grandparents have done for her. That has always been the way in the family, she explains. She lived alone for many years. That was easier than having a man in the house, she says. She devoted herself to work and her son. She enjoyed being the one who made all the decisions. She knew that if she made any wrong decisions, she was the one to blame. During this period, she travelled with her son in the summertime. After he had grown up, she could afford to go on her own to foreign countries. She went to evening classes in foreign languages, and has seen most of Europe but has a particular affection for France where she has a summerhouse.

By the time I got to speak to Marianne, she had already been retired for some years. She decided that enough was enough. She had brought up one son and got him through university and could afford not to work any more. Some years ago, she met her present husband Peter, who also spends much time with her family. Their friends seem to think they should not help as much as they do, but Marianne and Peter say that they have committed themselves until the grandchildren have started school. Neither of them is very concerned about keeping the house particularly clean and tidy. Marianne does not think very much about housework. She admits that when she was alone she was very picky about cleaning the house. She now thinks that she was simply imitating her mother's way of keeping the house. Marianne felt that this was what she ought to do, but she did not feel this for very long. Now she enjoys gardening more than housework and prefers being outdoors to being indoors. She goes out in the day, takes a walk, and lives very much in the garden. At the weekends, Marianne and Peter go for walks, and they often take the camping car somewhere and stay for a couple of days. The camping car is really their hobby. They also have an allotment where they grow vegetables. Marianne and Peter travel to France twice a year, once in the spring and once in the autumn. The weather during the spring and autumn is nice in France, they feel, because it is not too hot. While in France, they go and see places, and then they travel for a week in other parts of the country.

They plan their holidays together, and think that they are going to do a lot of travelling in the future. Now they have money to travel far, something they did not have before. Marianne says that she could even be perfectly happy to move to France, but Peter would not be happy there. They have made an agreement which involves her going to France sometimes without Peter, because he does not always want to go there. Marianne feels that she does not have any particular roots anywhere. Marianne uses the expression of a life's journey to explain how she feels about places. Any place can be her place. Place does not mean so much. She feels happy being in any place, and she is happy to move on. She can come and go. She can live anywhere. She does not have any close relatives left now in the town where she was born. You cannot stay in the past, Marianne tells me. There is so much to see and so much to experience, and simultaneously, she admits that she prefers to come home to a place called home. She says that this is a contradiction in terms, but we all have to go back somewhere.

Space as metaphor for feminine subjectivity

Open space is important for Marianne. She feels free, safe, comfortable and at home in open space. Marianne shows a combination of inner calm, control and strength, as well as sensitivity and vulnerability. Marianne seems settled and at home with her life. Marianne's working life, her career, is probably rather unusual for women of her generation. Many of her friends started working life as secretaries and are still doing the same thing. Marianne was the breadwinner and she moved up the career ladder while taking more responsibility and getting more income. Now, she has the opportunity to live comfortably since she has had a well-paid job, even if she had the responsibility of taking care of one child alone. It seems there must be some experiences in Marianne's life that have given her the confidence so that it was possible for her to do this. The uneasiness about being at sea was unexpected and it came as a surprise that she left the ship when she reached the final port on the northbound route. The unbounded feeling of open space is very different from the feeling of being at sea. To have one's feet on solid ground is different from the floating feeling of being on a ship's deck.

Open space can be understood in many ways, but one way is to see it as a metaphor for the feeling of being in control. Being in open space can mean providing support for oneself, materially, socially and emotionally. In the context of Marianne's story, it is relevant to ask in what way the metaphor is connected to feminine subjectivity. It could be argued that there is nothing intrinsically feminine associated with the openness of space. At one level, open space creates association to masculine subjectivity rather than feminine subjectivity. Open space can represent the horizon of visual control, or the landscape conquered visually from an observation post. Open space can be the area one may visually seize and control from the top of a mountain. In addition, it may signal a relationship to the exterior world that takes its outset in the embodied character of this relationship independent of the type of sense impression and sexual difference. On the other hand, however, a different interpretation is also possible. I would like to suggest that open space is essential to feminine subjectivity as a mental image, or a metaphor that is useful in creating a relationship to the interior world of a woman. Open space is thus a metaphor that works to support the growth of feminine psychic space. Below, I would like to discuss open space as a metaphor for empowerment of feminine subjectivity, and I will focus on symbolic language's possibilities and limitations in this respect. One obvious problem concerns the degree to which language may represent what it is supposed to represent. Is feminine, psychic space possible to represent through language? This is a relevant question because the debate on language and reality connected in both feminism and geography has brought forth a new discourse on metaphor and representation in geography. There has been a growing concern about geographical language's ability to represent the reality of women, women's knowledge and experiences.

Since the early 1990s, there has been a growing discourse in geography about spatial metaphors, representation of space, and the spaces of representation (Soja 1989, Ley and Duncan 1993, Keith and Pile 1993, Smith and Catz 1993, Pratt 1993, Massey 1994, Gregory 1994, Pile and Thrift 1995, Simonsen 1996). Nigel Thrift and Mike Crang have named this a spatial turn (Thrift and Crang 2000). There is a new spatial vocabulary used to understand the world with little reflexivity on which conceptions of space are actually used. It has been argued that spatial metaphors express a multitude of meanings and a complexity that is taken-for-granted. Space seems to be a very clear and uncontested term, but its meanings differ much, and may be used to hide meaning rather than express and reveal meaning. Space exists both as a historical set of ideas in social science and a premise for research with consequences that are not necessarily possible to see or know. The geographer Geraldine Pratt shows that metaphors are representational strategies that are used to articulate particular ways of being. Metaphors organize and structure what is possible to think and represent. She shows that there are mainly three types of spatial metaphors used. These are metaphors of mobility (nomadism, travelling, migration, the *flaneur*), metaphors that centre around positions of centre-margin, marginality and exile, and finally, metaphors that are based on space as a border-category (border-land, paradoxical space, heterogeneity) (Pratt 1993).

I want to focus more attention on what kind of space we are talking about with particular focus on the representation of feminine psychic space. This is important because it concerns the presence or absence of reflexivity in representation. To be reflexive about the metaphorical use of space and place in geography is important because of their status as key areas of study in geography. Space and place are not gender-neutral phenomena and concepts. It may seem that there is just as much taken for granted about 'space' as there is with 'woman'. If we look at the history of these constructs, it is obvious that they are linked ontologically. In the history of ideas and philosophy woman is represented in a spatialized language (Irigaray 1985, 1993) while in geography space is represented in masculinist language (Rose 1993). The French feminist Hélène Cixous shows how many fundamental pairs of concepts in western philosophy are structured in the same way and how the meaning of these concepts originates in the pair of concepts Man-Woman (Cixous 1981). Women over time have been associated with the sphere of physicality, materiality and nature, while men have been associated with the sphere of culture and superiority of reason. This is a consequence of Cartesian dualism founded on a separation of mind and body. Other pairs of concepts that are linked to the mind-body dualism are for example activity-passivity, sun-moon, culture-nature, day-night, father-mother, head-heart, intelligible-sensitive, logos-pathos/mythos, form-matter. The philosopher Val Plumwood has deconstructed dualist thinking in philosophies of nature and culture (Plumwood 1993). Dualist thinking is not only structured by opposition, Plumwood argues, but by a hierarchical logic where one term is given a positive value because of an opposite term that is given negative value. A dualism, Plumwood writes, results from a denied dependency on a subordinated other. This means that language never represents reality in a transparent way, nor is it able to represent reality in a gender-neutral way. It is thus important to reflect on how space as metaphor informs, constructs, or deconstructs certain ways of being, doing and knowing in geography.

Metaphor in Greek means *metaphorein*, which in English means 'to transfer' or 'to transport'. Using metaphors means making associations between different semantic fields, and by using metaphors, one understands or explains one thing by invoking something else because it connects two ideas or things in order to construct meaning (Lakoff and Johnson 1980). This happens when words and expressions are used in a transferred way. The significance of metaphors lies not in the literal meaning, but that the meaning extends into another field. Metaphoric association makes it possible to create and express a multitude of meaning by making images or explanations of something unknown or unfamiliar, hidden, strange or different in terms of something known or familiar, present and visible. The historian of literature, Georges Van den Abbeele, argues that metaphor is inherently spatial because it is impossible to think with metaphors without some notions or experience of space (Van den Abbeele 1992). Metaphor is inherently spatial because something unknown or different is explained by invoking something that is known or familiar.

As metaphors are social and cultural products, they represent both possibilities and restrictions. Metaphors are not empty, neutral and value-free words, because language-use is not transparent in the process of creating knowledge and images of the world. Metaphors legitimate or deconstruct existing knowledge, or may change it. A particular way of using metaphor carries with it already existing ideas and values. The travel metaphor is problematic because of the relations between travel, power and knowledge. The sociologist Janet Wolff argues that the travel metaphor has gendered meanings and connotations that for a great part are non-conscious or not reflected on (Wolff 1994). The travel metaphor excludes or pathologizes women, according to Wolff, which reproduces androcentrism and male dominance in academic texts. For Wolff it is not enough to deal with this by studying the different meanings of the travel metaphor because, as she says, the discourse on historical travel is a discourse created by men about men. Caren Kaplan argues that cultural critique should be grounded theoretically and empirically so as to avoid what she calls theoretical tourism, a position whereby a first world subject travels to the margins as a new poetics of the exotic (Kaplan 1987).

Though the ideological dimension should not be forgotten, I will focus on metaphor's creative or constructive dimensions in the following. In the remaining part of this chapter, I will discuss the relevance of the travel metaphor for rewriting feminine psychic space in terms of open space. Here I will stress the critical potential of the travel metaphor, in particular its blurring function in contextualized and sexed theory. This is the obvious connection between the openness in open space and the travel metaphor. The blurring strategy has been important in feminist philosophy. Rosi Braidotti's figuration of nomadic subjectivity and the polyglot (the linguistic nomad) is one example, where the nomadic subject refers to an understanding of a situated, post-modern, culturally differentiated subject (Braidotti 1991, 1994, chapter two).

In the spirit of nomadic thinking, I turn to Gillian Rose who has discussed how spatial metaphors are used in feminist research on feminine subjectivity (Rose 1993). She discusses both works where space and place configure as masculine and works where they actively confirm or create space and place as feminine. In the first place, feminists have described experiences of space and place as defined and controlled by persons other than women. This space gives women experiences of objectification and of space as dangerous and threatening. Space may seem like an enemy by itself (Koskela 1999). Rose shows that these examples reflect the previous role of women in society, where women have a presence not as their own places but in others' spaces. To exist in others' space means that one does not control one's own place linguistically and physically. Space is a masculine construct and women remain invisible. Rose also shows examples of feminist research where spatial metaphors express feminine subjectivity in a way that evades masculine space. These examples take their outset in an affirmation and positive evaluation of female positions primarily through a description of the place of the female body. The metaphors express lived and felt experiences, but also negotiations about power and positions. Often such gynocentric thinking works by creating a female space to gaining control over the other. This means that it operates within the either/or logic by only switching the gender of the person holding the space of control, and not really addressing the real problem, which is dualist thinking and either/or logic based in an absolute border between self and other, the internal and external world.

Against constructions of androcentric and gynocentric space, Gillian Rose draws on the feminist philosopher Teresa de Lauretis to discuss a third strategy to create metaphors for feminine subjectivity. De Lauretis argues for a diverse difference that tries to avoid the exclusions of master subject, according to Rose. This subject is constituted through language and culture, class and ethnicity, gender identity and sexuality, but does not present her self as unified but multiple, not divided but contradicted. Dualist thinking is avoided in this rhetorical strategy. The body as place in this third strategy is just 'different'. The individual human being (both men and women) is a site of difference whose language takes its outset in one's own multiple places. This is the strategy of 'paradoxical space', which refers to an identification with two places at once, both in the centre and on the margin, both inside and outside, and being both a prisoner and in exile. This space is multi-dimensional, shifting and contingent and paradoxical. The paradox refers to spaces that are mutually exclusive if charted on a two-dimensional map. Thus, paradoxical space is not mapable in terms of geometric space. According to Rose, spatial metaphors of this paradoxical kind appear frequently in the works of feminists who share this concern for difference thinking. Such strategies have in common the fact that metaphors of space and the female body as place do make a difference in terms of being woman since they confirm that the female body essentially exists as a part of the world's materiality and life process.

I would like to exemplify this strategy with the metaphor parabolic space, which is from literary theorist Kerstin W. Shands, who stresses the need for a powerful reconceptualizing imagery concerning spatial images in feminist writing (Shands 1998). Through a discussion of different spatial metaphors, she suggests that parabolic space is an eclectic tool. I suggest there is a particular connection between parabolic space, paradoxical space and open space since each of these searches for a new spaciousness for writing feminine subjectivity. The parabola is a spatial form that is both open and embracing, a bowl-shaped or curved space. The image of the parabola unites place and movement, space and curvilinear departure from or within that space according to Shands. Space seems to refer to freedom and independence, action and future, as something one has or has not. Shands wishes to displace this idea of space as frightening and masculine (abstract space) with the concept of parabolic space because it rewrites space as awesome, open and embracing. Parabolic space is a feminine spatial imagery that grows out of an appreciation of the earth's roundness (no finite ends, the roundness of the female body), her curvilinear shape (no linearity, bodily curves rather than even bodily lines). The metaphor signifies a way to relate out from the earth (the arms stretching out from the body by making curvilinear movements) or relating to earth (touching the earth's and the body's curves and roundness), depending on the subject position in relation to the earth. Parabolic space changes the experience of space as frightening and awesome to open and embracing. In Shands' view, the metaphor signifies a way to relate to the world from the position of the earth or the body.

This interpretation has much transformational power. Perhaps this is how Marianne thinks of open space; as a feminine spatial imagery of being woman that grows outwards and which is powerful without being repressive. Kerstin Shands is only one of many feminist thinkers who have found it useful to draw on spatial metaphors to rewrite women, the feminine, feminist theory and practice. Indeed, Shands is confusing the concept of space with the concept of place, but the main point here is the essential qualities of open space (which also are those qualities that turn open space into open place).

To conclude this chapter based on Marianne's life story, I would like to draw attention to the work of the geographer Anne Buttimer, as she reveals the deeper connections between modernity and representations of space and place (Buttimer 1980). Buttimer shows that ideas of space are built in the worldview of every historical period's philosophical and scientific ideas. She says that the notion of place and environment has been extremely important in particular periods in history, characterized by abrupt and strong social changes. The Newtonian idea of space as a container for action suited the political and economical systems of the Enlightenment and Industrialism, while the Romantic literature on place in the late eighteenth century and early nineteenth century represents a reaction against the Newtonian worldview. The industrialization and urbanization in the second half of the twentieth century formed new concerns about space and place. The current focus on place, space and landscape in the media, science and elsewhere, is therefore not a new phenomenon, Buttimer argues, but the context for this focus is always changing. Underlying geographical thinking there are certain views on the world and nature, which Anne Buttimer calls metaphors of world. According to Buttimer, the Green Movement represents one external force for the interest in the local, locality and place as a lived phenomenon. I would add that the Women's Movement plays an equally important role in this interest, but Anne Buttimer does not discuss this. The French feminist Luce Irigaray is perhaps the clearest spokesperson for the relationship between the Women's Movement and feminist philosophy, and argues that a rethinking of the relations between the sexes will require a rethinking of how we think and feel about space and place (Irigaray 1993). The spatial turn described above does take place at a time when the human and social sciences have gained a heightened awareness of the body, sexual difference, nature and the material environment. It will hopefully lead toward the deeper but still dormant layers of modernity's spaces; the place-worlds and their life processes.

Chapter 10

Travelling Internal and External Worlds

A journey in personal history

Barbara is a North-American woman who works as a programmer for a computer company. Barbara was born in a town in the southern part of the continent. She moved a lot when she was a child as her father worked in the Air Force. Her mother was a waitress most all of her adult life, Barbara explains, but after her parents' divorce, her mother went to school to learn accountancy. Europe relates directly to her personal history since her father had Norwegian parents and her mother's family came from Germany. She has never seen her relatives in Norway, and now she wants to explore this side of herself. Barbara did not talk about her expectations concerning visiting her family, but referred to her father as a person she did not like very much, but who was one of the bravest men you could ever want to meet. Barbara is very curious about learning more about her relatives in Norway who are roughly the same age as her. One thing she would like to learn more about is the history of Norway and how Norwegians see themselves, because she has noticed that Norwegians still tell stories connected to World War II. At home, she says she never even heard about World War II. She is sure there is a monument somewhere, but she does not know where.

It is difficult for Barbara to pin down where she feels she belongs, because she has moved around much. After moving to new places, one or two new sisters were born, and her mother gave birth to six girls in total. She considers herself a Californian in spirit, because she spent all her high school years there and then moved out of her parents' home. She worked as a secretary for some years until she decided she wanted to go to college. Barbara did very well, and found out that she wanted to continue. She got a job for an employer who paid for her university tuition, and that is why she could afford to go to a larger university and take a degree. She has advanced at work, moving from secretarial work to programming. At the time of the journey to the North Cape, she is in a situation where she has to decide what to do about her future. She decided that one of the things she wanted to do on the trip to the North Cape was to find out what she wanted to do. She wanted to find direction. She has reached her goal and got a Master's Degree, and now she questions whether she should follow one dream she has. This is to work less hours and start her PhD. It will take her some years, since she has to work to live, but people have asked her why she does not apply for a scholarship. She says she is thinking about it.

Barbara likes to travel around the world, but she had not done much travelling until her company asked her to work in Europe. Since then, Barbara has moved much, including travel outside North America, and she thinks this has made her reflective. She notices other people and places, and thinks that every place has a unique mentality. People are not alike everywhere. She has not always been able to travel as an adult, because she was quite poor. Barbara worked all the time, and she did not take vacation. Now travel is affordable for her and she travels every year. She started with Germany, and went on to visit every country in Europe, except Spain, Portugal and Norway. This year it is Norway, Barbara explains. When she was small, her parents did not take the children on vacation very much. She remembers that they went on three or four vacations to visit relatives and stayed overnight in tents 'roughing it'. Now that she is grown up and has a say in the matter, she is not roughing it, Barbara says, laughing.

Northern nature does not represent anything in particular to Barbara. She just hopes that she will have enough time at the North Cape to see the place in its uniqueness, from every angle, and to be able to have enough time to walk around. To her, the North Cape is like a curiosity, it is 'cool', relaxing and fun. The North Cape seems to be something to have in a visual sense to Barbara, but on the other hand, she finds that nature should be a part of everybody's life. Barbara's life in North America has not made her experience nature in any direct and immediate way. She realizes that she would not have discovered the meaning of nature unless she had direct experience of it. She has started to wonder whether she should move to another state, because the state she lives in is not very pretty, she says. Nature gives her a quiet time and place to cultivate the imagination, and her mother and sisters do not understand that. They talk and make a lot of noise all the time. When she travels, Barbara is able to find peace.

When in a new place, her feet represent her most valuable tool to sense and experience. She is tempted to talk about the eyes, she says, but she does not only want to see, but to get up close to things, go around them, climb them and see what is on the other side. Seeing is important to Barbara, but she is perfectly clear about the difference between seeing places in a book and seeing places through experience. She cannot touch or feel the difference of Europe by reading a book. Barbara has in fact created her own method of travel, which is to see as much as possible and cover as much geography as possible during the vacation. This does not include just setting her feet across some border of a country. While in Norway, it means that Barbara really wants to see as much of the country as she can. She also plans her vacations very systematically because she gathers as much information as she can, and list alternatives of what she wants to see. Then she finds out what kinds of tours are available, and compare the offers, and eventually chooses the tour that suits her interests the best. Travelling on the *Hurtigruta* enables her to see the entire coastline, and that is what Barbara wanted to do. She says she prefers to join an organized travel group before she goes off by herself.

Travel has changed her way of thinking about work and leisure. Having leisure and taking vacations are important for work in many ways. She explains that she comes up with her best ideas and her most creative thinking when she is away from work. She also tries to learn new things, and takes many photographs when travelling. This time she has even brought a video camera. The pictures are most important because they help her remember. She takes pictures of whatever she finds fascinating at any given moment. She has made a photo journal of each trip she has made, only for herself, and she explains that she has created a colour code from her vacations in Europe. Germany is in a green box and Italy in a red one. Norway is associated with a bluish green and bluish grey, because everything she looks at has a bluish or greenish colour. She thinks she will have a couple of hundred pictures taken of the mountains and scenery with the bluish green colour.

Time, space and narratives of the self

There is a saying that when one wants to look forward, one has to look back first. Barbara's journey to the north is partly a journey into her family's history and geography because of her Norwegian relatives. It is possible to interpret her journey as a journey to a wider sense of self, opening up this field to new images, with their own forms, tones and colours. In this respect, Barbara's story shows the importance of images and photography for the narrative of the self. Below I will discuss how photography, or the practice of taking pictures, reinserts not only time and temporality in the narrative of the self, but also space through visual images. This, in turn, will lead to a discussion on the interiorization of the self, which considers the role of time and space in the narratives of the self.

According to Mike Crang, there is a need for a past, which contributes in seeing the self as an accumulatory project (Crang 1999). Photography plays an important role in this project, Crang argues. Photography has an ability to capitalize on experiences that provide opportunities for accumulation of cultural symbols. Tourists are self-knowing and reflexive individuals, and photography plays an important part in the creation of spatial stories. Compared with classical autobiography, which is dominated by linear, chronological form, photographs are popular creations that create spatial stories, Crang argues. The photographs taken and the circulation of images in modernity are not only about loss, but also about connectivity and communication between the times and spaces of the individual. The photograph is an object in itself, not only a pictorial form. Against this background, Crang shows that photography is a spatial and temporal practice in tourism and a form of self-narration suitable for the modern age. Photographs form narratives of the self that are dominated by chorological form. Barbara takes photos only for herself and the 'colour code' that she has can be seen as part of the narration of her self, where countries she has visited have been ordered in photo journals. These are important for the narration of self because different countries become metaphors for her self, while the photo journals together represent a metonymic logic. The photos and the various colours remind us of a larger whole, the self. The metonymic logic of photos is important, according to Crang because of the temporality accorded to them.

Crang argues that it is important to see photography not as simply recording an event but as the creation and making of self. The narrative is important for this self-creation. Narration of social practices is not about representing an external reality as well as possible. Narration is travelling into another landscape of meaning that is fictional. Narratives do not discover something hidden or unknown, but create something new through what they tell, according to Michel de Certeau (De Certeau 1984). Traditionally, a narrative is a form of story based on hermeneutics and on humanistic ideals such as coherence, development and rationality. The interest in narrative in modernity is based on the humanistic idea that human beings create coherence in their lives gained through organization of change over time in a holistic sense. A narrative describes truth in new ways, and thus narration is similar to how metaphor works. Narratives do not describe the world directly, but re-scribe and re-tell the world. Narratives are therefore not copies of the world; they construct rather an as-if world, according to the geographer Nicholas Entrikin (Entrikin 1991).

Narratives in this way can be re-creative and empowering. They are ways of writing oneself in new ways through the wandering lines of tactics (as Michel De Certeau saw it), as acts of self-defence, as a re-appropriation or re-creation of self in terms of a personal internal world. The self is a spatial story. The practices of photography can thus be seen as a way not only to occupy the space and time of the self, but to dwell in it in a self-improving way. The accumulation of pictures into a whole expresses the self in a way where space and not only time are important, both in individual and cultural terms. As pictures are viewed in a serial way, with particular preferred stories to accompany them, the narrative of the self is created and experienced in a temporal and spatial way, linking the exterior world, past and present, to the interior world of the person.

In this chorological project of self-making, other places represent hidden or forgotten areas of memory, or not yet known areas of the self. The past is a foreign country, as the historian and geographer David Lowenthal puts it, invoking a spatial vocabulary to representing lost or forgotten historical meaning (Lowenthal 1985). It is common to represent hidden and lost meaning of the present by evoking spatial metaphors. For example, the unconscious is often thought of in terms of forest, sea. The conscious functions of the ego or the I are thought of as centre in relation to lower functions like bodily drives and higher functions like conscience or higher consciousness. In addition, it is also common to think of the self, subjectivity, or the psyche, as a world with partial unknown areas. In her book on childhood and the idea of human interiority, historian Carolyn Steedman uses the concept of interiority to describe the insideness of the modern self (Steedman 1995 a and b). Steedman studied the interiorized self as the product of a personal and cultural history, where the self in modernity is a construct that articulates inner space or something similar to psychic space. Steedman is inspired by philosopher Charles Taylor who described the development of thinking about the modern self as a historical movement from outside to inside (Taylor 1989). The modern self exists inside or through inwardness, Taylor writes, because humans have inner depths that are partly illuminated, partly existing in the dark. This makes sense in everyday life. It seems strange not to think of our thoughts as something that occur in a particular place, i.e. inside ourselves, and to locate the origin of one's own thoughts and ideas at a placed other than inside is viewed as a pathological sign.

According to Taylor, this division between inside and outside is a product of the modern world, resulting from the gradual self-interpretation that came with the rise of the Cartesian I. This dualism between interiority and exteriority is a modern phenomenon, but in comparison to other cultures and times, this dualism is indeed strange, Taylor argues. The dualism is not a universal phenomenon and no historical law says it must continue to exist in the future. Where is this inside, and what does it look like? For Charles Taylor it is important to show that these questions are inseparable from existing in a moral space. Being a self has to do with identity and how one ought to be, to find a standpoint, to occupy and be a perspective within a moral space.

The constructs self and subjectivity have traces to Cartesian thought, while there is a variety of meaning and usage (Pile and Thrift 1995). Both subjectivity and self are metaphors for subjectivity and psychic space, and I use these terms as signifiers for the interior world of individual human being. The focus here is how experiences and representations of space (and time) play an important role in the constitution of self. It is not new to speak about self, the psyche, identity itself, as a space, and Kathleen Kirby argues that this is one of the most common and truthful representations for the internal world of human beings (Kirby 1996 a and b). The problem arises when we ask what spatial form it has, according to Kirby, who shows that the monadic self in Enlightenment is worldless and non-contextual. This worldless self is further identical to the Cartesian subject, with a corresponding view of the lived world in terms of global imagery. The worldless person is concerned with the outside world only in terms of a globe. As Kirby shows, the problem with the monadic self is its spatial form because the individual is undivided within itself, separate from other subjects and objects (see chapter seven). It is a worldless space without a body, without experience and memory, constituted only through consciousness or thinking, before everything and from itself. The worldless self is even today the normal image of the self, because one is supposed to be self-enclosed, self-determining, and autonomous. Against this worldless self, Kathleen Kirby argues that modernity is experiencing a crisis of subjectivity, connected to the crisis of Cartesian dualism. We now live in post-modern space, and previous models of the self will not do. Kirby paraphrases Frederic Jameson, who argues that being lost in the modern age is now the post-modern experience. There are no structures in post-modern space. It is rather characterized as a derealization of space where space has become synonymous with plasticity and infinite semiosis (Jameson 1984). Space has lost its secure external referent. The post-modern human being, just as post-modern space, has lost its spatial form based on an interior world clearly demarcated from an exterior world.

According to Kirby, to speak of the self as a space is relevant, but the spatial metaphors are not the goal in themselves. It is worthwhile only because space is a medium or a bridge to the real world consisting of other subjects and objects. Space is a medium and a process, not an object, a goal, in itself. In this respect, a spatial representation of the self, dependent on a demarcation from the exterior world, is not very constructive. In other words, we need spatial metaphors that bring together the exterior and the interior world, where communication and exchange can take place.

Can we speak of the self in terms of both interiority and exteriority? This is a relevant question because the meaning of interiority and exteriority does not depend on the border between the inside and the outside of the skin of the body. Consciousness is also a limitless entity because it can take us far away from the body through active imagination. It can spread out almost with no limit and engulf the whole world, and much more beyond it. Kirby shows that any imposition of a boundary between the self and space is a reality already constructed, or in the making (Kirby 1996a and b). The construction of an external or physical world does not exist without an inside world. Continents, places, countries and patches of land are states of mind as much as geographical locations, according to the psychologist Roger Brooke in an analysis of Carl Gustav Jung's deep psychology from the perspective of phenomenology (Brooke 1991). There are even more ways to speak of the non-divided self that bring us closer to a naturalist interpretation of space and place by attaching life process to space and place. As individual human beings live as animated beings (often through the idea of soul or spirit), places in the external world may also have *genius loci* or *anima loci*, an essence of place that expresses meaning beyond the individual self, according to the architect Christian Norberg-Schultz (1980). Here, place gains human, living or animated qualities in a sense where human beings and the more-than-human world form parts of an interconnected world in a deeper sense, as lived place (Norberg-Schultz 1980, Abram 1996, Fisher 2002).

What I propose to do in the following is to speak of subjectivity, or the self, in terms of both interiority and exteriority by trying to go beyond Cartesian dualism. The environmental philosopher Neil Evernden has argued that the self is not identical to something that is inside the surface of the body (Evernden 1985). He finds that the self is more like a field of care. What is the self if it is a field? I suggest that we may talk about the self as something which stretches outside of the body and as something which creates a bridge or connection between the interior and the exterior world. The geographer Anne Buttimer has discussed this by drawing on the ideas of the philosopher Gaston Bachelard (Buttimer 1980, Bachelard 1994). Buttimer's interest in the deeper relationships between the self, space and place draws on Bachelard's idea of analysis of place (topo-analysis). Topo-analysis is an exploration of self-identity through place. Bachelard shows that since place may have many dimensions and meanings ranging from symbolic, emotional, cultural, social, political, economical and biological, it might give more understanding of the self than the psyche and the personality, which is the object of study of psychoanalysis. In topo-analysis one understands place as partly known and partly unknown or unconscious. The object of topo-analysis is psychic place immersed with love (or the lack of love).

This means, quite literally, that we are moving into the spatiality and placiality of the psyche or soul, which is a place for images (Bachelard 1994, Casey 1997). The psyche provides a psychic place with an inward or non-physical extension according to Bachelard, and this stands in contrast to Cartesian Enlightenment, which claimed that human beings had no inward extension. Bachelard provides a language for understanding the human being as situated within, or as interiorized. Casey suggests that Bachelard poses a way of thinking similar to Freud's and Jung's, with the idea of psychic depth and interiority intact. The philosopher Jeff Malpas argues that the interiorization of external space simultaneously represents an exteriorization of inner subjectivity, and that topo-analysis blurs dualist understandings of place and person (Malpas 1994). Any exploration of place will also be an exploration of the unconscious, Malpas writes. The unconscious knows how to find a place, or make itself a home. The unconscious is also a place.

The psyche or the soul is more or less a receptacle for poetic images that are entities with a particular (but not causal) dynamism of their own, referring to the depths of the unconscious, according to Bachelard (1994). This means that psychic space is not chaotic or formless or without content. It has its own order, system, logic or language, and expresses its presence through the poetic imagination. Bachelard wants to uncover the affective meanings of psychic place and explore how poetic images emerge into consciousness as a result of the being of human beings. Bachelard uses the house as a privileged image of the soul, or psychic space, which is a great image for integration of thoughts, memories, and dreams. The house becomes the topography of intimate being, and by remembering all the houses humans have inhabited, they learn to live at home with themselves, and thus the important task is to protect the affective relations between place and human beings. Topophilia is another name for the investigation of the poetic image of the house (see also Tuan 1974).

Bachelard shows that the house or the home is the first place, in opposition to the idea of the universe as the first place. According to philosopher Edward Casey, instead of saying that the world is a house, Bachelard says that the house is a world. The house is a place-world, a world of places (Casey 1997). Bachelard further says that the world outside the house is cosmos. Cosmos is non-house, which is also identical to non-I. In this context, the house is given meaning as mother, where the image of the house is seen through the image of mother. The house is not, however, a closed universe according to Bachelard. The universe is invited in so as to form a flexible understanding of the image of the house. There are no absolute borders between what is inside and what is outside. Good houses are like good psychic states (dynamic, alive and breathing), while bad houses are like bad psychic states (rigid, fixed and motionless). Therefore, place is a living, moving place.

The human being should not only dwell within this house, one should come out and enter life, accept the calling of life and the outside world. Thus Bachelard sees the human being as a being with both interior and exterior being, and the exterior life is given form or tone by the form and tone of inner space or psychic place. Bachelard calls this intimate immensity, which means that one is both inside and outside at the same time, or, it is to experience oneself in a larger world in miniature, according to Casey (Casey 1997). One is not being in a world, but one is being a world. One is in the out, Casey writes, and feels the out in.

With psychic place, the centrality of time, which has been so important in modernity and modern philosophy, is undermined. Instead, the spatiality of interior being becomes more important. Space becomes more the form of inner sense according to Edward Casey (Casey 1997). It emerges as a field of meaning with its own rules and regulations. A topo-analysis thus requires an analysis of the places one has experienced and inhabited throughout life, and a narrative construction of self with a stronger focus on place. In the external world, roads, crossroads, hills and rivers are for every living human being his or her own roads, crossroads, hills and rivers. Every unexplored or unmapped area of the earth is simultaneously his or her unexplored or unmapped area, and by mapping the memories of these areas, humans start abiding the world, Bachelard argues. In this sense, Barbara is mapping the memories of her affectionate past, her family and relations to the north, collecting photographs that together form a particular image for Barbara that is her personal interior house. Through the poetic imagination, earlier indifferent spaces and areas of this house become subject to the reconstruction of a particular and personal narrative in both time and space. Barbara's exploration in personal time and space, and her travel method, seems to illustrate what topo-analysis is really about.

Chapter 11

A Feminine Aesthetics of Travel

In-between worlds

Lavinia is a European working woman in her thirties, who lives and is travelling alone. Our conversation began naturally about the excursion to North Cape, which we had gone on the same morning. She said she had expected it to be a huge tourist machine. However, there were not too many people there when we arrived, as it was early in the day. Lavinia says it was like being on the edge of the world. The land was barren and she felt like she was walking at the end of the earth, or at least at the end of Europe. She tells me this in a more or less matter of fact way, as if it were obvious to everyone and the most natural experience in the world. It did not leave a big impression. I do not know whether she is being ironic or serious. It seems to me that Lavinia is expressing a particular feminine way of experiencing North Cape. I will come back to this later, but first I would like to go into Lavinina's reasons for visiting the north, which did not have much to do with the North Cape in itself.

This year Lavinia was looking for a trip that would not be too exhausting, some place where she could see a lot and stay at the same place at the same time. The travel agent suggested the *Hurtigruta* for her, which she had not heard about before. She laughs and tells me that she wanted to see whales. The north to Lavinia is associated with Scandinavian architecture and interior decorating, but most of all it is an idea of purity, untouched by industry and commerce. For her, northern nature is associated with uncultivated nature and barren land.

Lavinia seems to be a practically oriented person who also enjoys reflecting on and observing her fellow travellers and the travel party. This reflexivity is also turned upon herself, and she has discovered that she is an observer. Normally she is quite a participant. The *Hurtigruta* transforms passengers into (relatively) passive observers since one is bound to stay on the ship for as long as the ship is at sea. Usually, she stays outside looking at something, and participates. She gets a bit tired of sense impressions, and says this is because of the immense quantity of sense impressions associated with numerous attractions, sights, sites and tourist spots in tourist areas. There is something to see everywhere, just like in Athens where there is ruin upon ruin, meaningful and splendid ruins, but Lavinia just felt like getting out. Even though she is very fond of the sea and nature as a whole, it was too much too absorb even on the *Hurtigruta*. However, Lavinia does want to learn something when she travels, and that is the reason for her seeking distance, because she can see better from a distance. Distance provides time and place to get bits and pieces together, in order and in perspective.

She is perfectly clear intellectually about the meaning of nature to her, and yet the emotional response is that it is too much to take. From one point of view, she describes the typical division between reason and sense impressions (and emotion) in western thinking, but from another perspective, her response represents a break with the same division. During our conversation, it dawns on me that she may be a wanderer between these two worlds. She seems overwhelmed by the emotional value of sensing nature, such as when she stays awake during the night to experience the light. She comes back on deck in the middle of the night, at one or two in the morning, and feels that she cannot get a grip on the light. It is light everywhere. Seeing the midnight sun is incomprehensible. It reminds her of a book she had as a child about the northern parts of the world with pictures and stories about the differences in light and darkness. It is an aesthetic, emotional, and spiritual experience. Every day and night there is only light, and no darkness. What language belongs to this unspoken world of meaningful experience? How does Lavinia transcribe this? She uses photography and writes a diary. She writes letters to her sisters but finds it difficult to describe her experiences.

Lavinia was born in a small town in central Europe, and the family moved a lot when she was a child. Every time they moved, she had to start in a new school, and now she does not feel attachment to any particular place. She does not feel settled in one place. She is not like a tree, whose roots go deeper and deeper under the ground. She is reminded of this as an adult when she has to travel a lot in her job. The parents took their children on vacation almost every year, she remembers, mostly camping two or three weeks in the summer. Lavinia went to an art college after secondary school, but had to terminate her studies. Something dramatic happened. Her mother became seriously ill and Lavinia had to return to her parent's home to take care of her family until her mother passed away one half year later. After that, she started to work in a publishing company during the day while replacing her mother in the household at night. This continued for a year until she finally moved out.

Lavinia never got a degree from art college, but she took night classes at law school. She still works in the same publishing company, but now as an editor. Her job is very important to her, and since she lives alone, there is nobody to care for but herself, but she tells me about the difficulties of being the only woman at work. Most men are very nice, but they have treated her differently than their male colleagues. They have questioned her competence and wanted her to do secretarial work. With time, she has learnt to handle it very well and proven her competence so that she has become equal. She showed them that she was not dangerous, because it was obvious that they felt threatened by her. With time, she learned to take advantage of their behaviour towards her. Now she fits in, but Lavinia does not plan her future like her male colleagues. She works hard and takes classes and courses, and does not really have any career plans. On the one hand, she is very career oriented, since she does the right things to get promotion in her company, while on the other hand, she describes her way of managing her career in nonstrategic ways. She manages working life differently, and it works very well for her. It seemed to me that she does not think in a linear way, and at the same time she ends up being a winner.

Since she has worked very much, she has not had much time to take vacations. During those years when she went to law school in the evenings, she never took vacations. She took a week or so off to visit family and relatives, but nothing more. Over the last few years she has taken vacations, and travelled quite a bit. She now takes four or five weeks of summer vacation, and can afford to because of her well-paid job and a generous employer. She has visited Kenya and Tanzania, southern Spain, Ireland, Uzbekistan and Russia several times. She likes to travel to places where she can merge into the crowd, to see while not being noticed as a tourist. She thinks that is the best way of seeing how people really live. In Africa, this was impossible, because she obviously had the wrong colour. Africa was a shocking mirror to her, because it revealed to her who she was and where she came from: white, rich and competent. Lavinia wants to learn from her travel, and the important thing is not exactly what she learns, but the opportunity to meet other people and live in other circumstances. Then she finds time to think. It feels good to create distance and time to get bits and pieces together deliberately.

Living between the ordinary and the extraordinary

Modern, everyday life has become more and more complex. Lavinia knows very well the hardships of modern everyday life. Her story reminds us of the traditional role of women and the new roles many western women take on in working life. But what does leisure and life outside of work mean to workingwomen? What is leisure? What do vacation and holidays mean to someone like Lavinia who has not had much leisure? Work and production is the key defining factor of and for western modern society in twentieth century social theory. Work is central to ideas of a good everyday life, especially in northern Europe (Højrup 1977). There are many theories of leisure, but they all tend to have a common definition drawn from the centrality of work and productive life in modern social life (Rojek 1985, 1995). Understanding work as non-leisure, and leisure as non-work is problematic. This depends on an idea of work as paid work, which further underestimates the dynamic, social forces within the area of leisure itself. Henri Lefebvre argues that holiday travel and leisure comprise one of the key areas for a transformation of everyday life (Lefebvre 1991). Leisure is, however, a modern invention that refers to particular experiences and practices, and sociologist Chris Rojek argues that knowledge of leisure is relative to knowledge of everyday life (Rojek 1995).

Rojek argues that there are two myths of leisure. Firstly, it implies a modern understanding of authenticity, which is problematic, because it has projected authenticity onto the leisure sphere, while emptying the work sphere of any understanding of authenticity. Secondly, leisure is represented as an area for realization of the self, and as a sphere of life where unproblematic satisfaction of desire can take place. This means that leisure is seen as an escape from inauthentic everyday life. Some argue that human being's quest for a place outside of everyday life represents an alternative reality or another place (Cohen and Taylor 1976). Such escape attempts encompass many different things, i.e. activities like hobbies, games, play, sex, and new landscapes and objects of consumption like holidays, mass culture, art, and new so-called mindscapes, drugs and therapies. Escape attempts work as ways out, as exits, in relation to working life. The holiday is meaningful as an escape attempt, Cohen and Taylor argue.

Chris Rojek explains, however, that this way of ascribing meaning to leisure and holidays simply cannot be true because it rests upon taken-for-granted and fixed ideas of work (Rojek 1995). Work and leisure play symbolic roles in structuring identity, Rojek argues, but not with fixed meanings. There are similarities between work and leisure and both have varying, flexible and contextually changing meanings. This brings about a new theoretical problem. It is difficult to understand the nature of the relationship between leisure and work, and the nature of the difference between leisure and work. This is because leisure and holiday stand in a relationship to work and everyday life, but in ways other than through opposition and hierarchy. Holiday and leisure represent practices related to many social processes. Leisure practices, in my opinion, are like the backstage of everyday life, but not as the opposite of everyday life. Work and leisure do not have meaning in an individual's life as opposites, but as differences within lived life as a whole. This is related to life history, everyday life as it is lived and differences in life projects and planning. Men and women, for example, interpret leisure differently because they live different everyday lives and because they have different life histories. In addition, leisure will have different meanings for different groups of women, and even within individual women. As Lavinia has particular experiences with homemaking and being a substitute mother for her family, her intentions and aspirations for both work and leisure will differ very much from what many other women may want to do.

I would suggest that work and leisure are key concepts that inform the meaning of holiday travel. Nevertheless, leisure differs from holiday travel. Leisure is often defined in terms of clock time, daily leisure, weekly leisure and longer periods of annual leisure. This implies a geometric spatiality or placiality. I would suggest that we can think of leisure as difference, as a form of otherness concerned with a different form of temporality and a different form of placiality. Most research on everyday life in modern societies has focused on life centred on the spatial axis between home place and work place. Modern holiday travel, I would suggest, goes beyond what we mean by both leisure and everyday life. Vacation and holiday travel imply a different experience of being than the being of everyday life. In addition, leisure concerns place just as much as time, but we need other conceptualizations of the placiality and temporality of leisure than clock time and geometric space can provide.

Lavinia's story illustrates this problem by describing her summer vacations as time to get bits and pieces together. Lavinia missed the word place in this picture.

Her story shows that there is a tendency to think about social life in terms of time and forget about place, but she opens up for a different place when she tells me about the aesthetic experience of seeing the northern nature. This does not aim at perfection but at being complete. In the remaining part of this chapter, I will interpret Lavinia's story in terms of extraordinary experience and aesthetic experience from the point of view of a female traveller. When Lavinia described her journey, she expressed paradoxical experiences. North Cape was barren land, and it was also the end of Europe and the end of the earth. She knew that North Cape was a tourist machine, but she also felt it was a part of Europe that was saturated with purity and untouched by commerce and culture. The midnight sun was a big surprise to her, it was something different that she had not expected and which was not comprehensible for anyone who had not seen it. It was an aesthetic experience, she says.

The aesthetic is a concept that originates in the Enlightenment project, and feminist historians and critics have discussed the degree to which this category takes into consideration women's experiences of the aesthetic. Below I would like to discuss Lavinia's story from this perspective. This discussion will focus in particular on the possibility for a feminine aesthetics, and the woman as an aesthetic subject. In a study of women travel writers in the eighteenth century, literary theorist Elizabeth Bohls argues that the place of aesthetics in modern society has become a distinct sphere (Bohls 1995). Bohls' intention is to re-invent the sublime as a new way of reading feminine experience, and she identifies the enlightenment of women by asking what happens when women start speaking as aesthetic subjects. Bohls understands aesthetics discursively, as an open discourse about topics within aesthetics and a language to speak about these topics. The aesthetic discourse, as Bohls understands it, deals with understandings of art, beauty, taste and judgement, and more generally on pleasures gained from sense perception and the experience of perception. Bohls' analysis of women's travel writing shows that a disconnection between aesthetics and other spheres in society is harmful to human beings. Women travel writers tell different stories about the relations between the aesthetics and the visual sense and challenge the understanding of the disembodied aesthetic subject, which characterizes Enlightenment aesthetics. Bohls' analysis shows that the feminine aesthetics do not reproduce the separation between aesthetic and other experience as Enlightenment thinking presupposes. The feminine aesthetics actually breaks down experiential borders and distinctions in a way that works as a fundamental critique of modern aesthetics.

Elizabeth Bohls has studied a selection of travel stories written by women in the period between 1716 and 1818. She shows that these women writers strived for the authority and prestige of aesthetics, but they did this in ways that challenged the fundamental premises of aesthetics. The position of these women in relation to men's hegemonic discourse on aesthetics was marginal. For example, they used literary genres that were better suited to women, and their aesthetic language expressed non-rational argumentation. The feminine aesthetics grew in more or less subtle, indirect or unconventional ways. The romanticist movement, for example, had a strong impact on the possibilities for feminine aesthetics during the nineteenth century. Bohls agrees with literary theorist Mary Louise Pratt, who has argued that romanticism may have originated in the contact zones of culture, the Americas, North Africa and the South Seas (Pratt 1992). Contact zones are social spaces with a heightened cultural communication, often within highly asymmetrical relations between cultural groups. Bohls suggests that a similar structuring of romanticism took place in British society in the nineteenth century. The vulgar, women and non-Europeans were constructed against the male aesthetic subject on the basis of a disembodiment of vision, and a distancing of what is seen from the viewer. Scenic tourism and gardening exemplify this. The distance between the aesthetic and the vulgar was reinforced.

The construction of the male aesthetic subject presented problems for the female aesthetic subject, Bohls argues. The problem for women was of course their ambivalent position in relation to constructions of beauty. The category beautiful had connotations to weakness and timidity and particular versions of femininity, and instead of using this category, women travel used the picturesque and sublime. Bohls shows that Mary Wollstonecraft in particular developed a whole register of meanings of the sublime in her published letters from a journey to Scandinavia in 1795 (Bohls 1995, Wollstonecraft 1987). The affections connected to the sublime range from gentle melancholy to daring transcendence, Bohls shows. Wollstonecraft transforms the categories of the picturesque and the sublime in this travel account through her contemplation of Scandinavian nature, grounded in a concern for the needs of people who live off the land. Bohls argues that Wollstonecraft experimentally poses a feminine, embodied and non-distanced version of the aesthetic subject, and concludes that Wollstonecraft exposes what great a risk a society takes when the aesthetic, as a category of value, separates the body and materiality from human life.

Bohls shows that Wollstonecraft's aesthetics and politics are closely interconnected. Wollstonecraft rewrites aesthetic experience as sensuous pleasure that arises from the daily practices of human beings related to wider social processes and power relations in society. Aesthetics is related to a corporeal, practical and political way of being. Wollstonecraft writes from a female middle-class background on behalf of the working classes and women, and from a position of critique of essentialist notions of aesthetic experience, the aristocratic ideology of the beautiful and the accompanying ideology of the vulgar. Her aesthetics are anti-aesthetics, according to Bohls, which is a continuation of her critique of masculinist aesthetics. Wollstonecraft wrote *Vindication of the Rights of Men* a few years earlier as a critique of Edmund Burke's views on aesthetics, attacking his conception of landscape aesthetics because it separates the viewers from the users of a landscape. In *Letters* she confronts this further and develops a new way of understanding the relation between the aesthetic object and the perceiving, aesthetic subject. The Scandinavian journey had healing qualities for Wollstonecraft. Scandinavian nature represents a vision and a positive attitude towards the future for her, and during this trip, she recovered from a depressive mode of being. She sailed in dangerous waters because of wartime to a country that was practically speaking *terra incognita* searching for treasure, which gave it a kind of supernatural or magical, glow of being really out of this world. It was a mysterious, urgent and almost nightmarish pursuit to do this journey, and while in Norway, Wollstonecraft had an urge to travel farther north to seek exile from her life's disappointments and sorrows.

Mary Wollstonecraft is different from most women travellers of her time, since she was a well-known writer, though controversial and radical. Writing letters was a familiar genre for woman travellers of her generation, and Bohls shows that this gave Wollstonecraft freedom to switch back and forth between narrative, anecdote, social commitment and personal reverie. The storyteller in her book is cast differently from the norm of contemporary travel writers. The norm was an impersonal voice, while Wollstonecraft uses the episodic structure of the travel narrative. It represents a symbolic re-arrangement of the perceived object and perceiving subject, gendering and embodying both subject and object. In this respect, it seems that "the difference" of a Scandinavian relationship to nature influenced her. She saw nature differently than her fellow middle class and male travellers did who viewed nature through the distancing gaze of the Grand Tour. In Letter 19, she writes that the experiences of the Scandinavian countries represent a new way of seeing the world's improvement, as she calls it (Wollstonecraft 1987). She constructs the beauty of nature closely to the use of land and nature, which Bohls argues was an aesthetic heresy (Bohls 1995).

According to Bohls, Wollstonecraft uses a broad range of strategies to achieve this anti-aesthetics: she stresses senses other than sight (e.g. smell), she avoids a literary framing of the land by stressing active verbs which makes the land present itself as open and non-composed, in constant motion and change. The relationship between human beings and nature is described as a practical one, and she refuses to separate the aesthetic dimension from the practical relationship. These strategies work to focus on the material conditions for human life in nature, and the aesthetics is deeply embedded in everyday life, not separated from it.

Bohls concludes that Wollstonecraft redefines aesthetics in terms of making it more humane, inclusive or focused on corporeal attachment rather than separation because of her feminine gender and because she is a mother. Mary Wollstonecraft brought her daughter with her on this journey. This must have had an impact on how she saw nature, because she brings forth perspectives on the relationship between the human being and nature in terms of mother-child relations. This approach is familiar in women's writing about nature both in geography and ecofeminist discourse (Semple 1911 in Åquist 1994, Nesmith and Radcliffe 1993, Braidotti et al 1994, Warren 1997). Elizabeth Bohls suggests that Wollstonecraft's experience of motherhood changed her attitude towards nature. The trip to Scandinavia gave Wollstonecraft an opportunity to seek and interpret the pleasure of nature in terms of mother-child relations. In addition, Bohls identifies a connection between aesthetic pleasure and erotic pleasure. Wollstonecraft uses here a remarkably direct voice that is unfamiliar to contemporary women writers. The common ground is the relations between the well-being of the body, described in terms of motherhood, aesthetics and erotic pleasure, which suggests that transcendence can be grounded in the sensual body, according to Bohls. I find this connection between the body and the mind and the corporeal and the reflexive in Wollstonecraft's letters relevant in relation to Lavinia's story. This connection is particularly relevant for an understanding of the feminine aesthetics in travel, which I will name the female sublime.

Women writers have in recent decades written in the sublime mode, which is a writing mode that has been the domain of male writers, according to the sociologist Patricia Yaeger (Yaeger 1995). Drawing on the French feminists' concern for difference in writing, Yaeger equates women's writing with a release of what she calls geothermal energies. Yaeger characterizes the masculinist language of aesthetics as an old-fashioned regime of domination associated with a vertical sublime, where the masculine self insists on superiority in relation to a horizontal other. The feminine sublime, Yaeger argues, moves instead through a horizontal sublime, towards sovereignty or expenditure in a way that expands and spreads outwards in multiplicity in a refusal of an Oedipal and phallic fight. This female sublime represents on one side what Patricia Yaeger has described as the sublime of nearness (Yaeger 1995). It does not represent what she calls a failed sublime, that is, experiences of unexpected empowerment that are snatched away by a masculine counter-sublime. Neither does it represent a sovereign sublime, which consists of the appropriation of a masculine genre by women in a very straightforward way, thus reinforcing the regime of domination. The sublime of nearness is not only a revision of a masculine sublime, but is a pre-Oedipal sublime that presents a more genuine alternative, Yaeger argues. This interpretation of the sublime takes its outset in post-Lacanian reconstructions of psychoanalysis and makes explicit a sublime desire to merge with the mother and the land, rather than mask this oral, primordial desire. The Oedipal sublime represses the desire for pre-Oedipal bonding with the mother's body, while in the pre-Oedipal sublime these energies, geothermal in nature, are allowed for, Yaeger argues. Sara Mills shows that Yaeger here opens for a new self-other relationship where otherness is not repressed (Mills 2000). These ideas are further close to Luce Irigaray's ethics of sexual difference that I have translated as the logic of the umbilical cord (Birkeland 2000, see chapter thirteen).

A feminine sublime will therefore allow for geothermal and bodily energies that take other routes to aesthetics and the beautiful. It will allow for many things, also for the revenge that wells up in women who refuse to adapt to the codes of a dominant culture that demands female propriety or silence, Yaeger argues. I suggest that this feminine sublime sheds light on both Mary Wollstonecraft's Scandinavian letters and Lavinia's story. In addition, I would suggest that there is a connection between Wollstonecraft's understanding of the relationship between body and mind and the sensible transcendental, which according to Luce Irigaray refers to an experience of the simultaneously transcendent and immanent functions of being (Whitford 1991, Irigaray 1993b).

Chapter 12

The Dawning of the Midnight Sun

A place in the world

Lars is in his seventies and is travelling with his wife to the north. He has lived in a coastal area in the north of Europe all his life, working as a fisherman, sailor and farmer. Lars grew up in a fjord by the North Sea. The farms in the area usually combined fishing and farming, and it was a very common way of life along the coast. When they reached school age, they had the opportunity to go to school but not for the whole school year. The children had to walk a long way to the school building, Lars remembers, six days a week. The war (World War II) broke out soon after he had finished his schooling, and he decided to stay home with his parents to help on the farm or do a little fishing along the coast. When the war was over, Lars continued being a fisherman and sailor on fishing vessels and smaller ships along the coast as crew. He joined larger fishing vessels for many years. He never had his own boat. He has also worked on cruise ships with tourists. He has seen the coasts of Norway, the Mediterranean, England, Northern France, Denmark and Sweden. When he was young, his greatest dream was to see the North Cape. In the 1950s, he actually had the opportunity to see the place. This happened before the road came to the North Cape, and there was actually nothing there, not much of a building, Lars says. He remembers standing at the edge of the cliff watching the cruise ships coming and going, anchoring up in Horn Bay and letting the passengers off to climb the steep trail up to the summit. The greatest experience at North Cape was seeing the midnight sun, Lars says. It was a bit emotional, he recalls laughing, and it is something that he treasures very much. A dream come true.

When Lars married, he settled on the farm and raised a family. He and his wife have four children. They produced milk and some beef. Lars and his wife worked on the farm until a few years ago, when his wife fell ill and could not work anymore. Since then she has depended on her husband's care. When he had told his wife that he had bought these tickets, she got very worried and upset, since she did not think they could go anywhere with her wheelchair. Travelling on the *Hurtigruta* along the Norwegian coast has been a dream for them both, and now their wishes are fulfilled. He does not think for a second that his wife regrets it, and everything works out fine.

To Lars the special experience of being at the North Cape is seeing the midnight sun. On the other hand, there is nothing special about the midnight sun at the North Cape, Lars continues, since she is probably not any different at the North

Cape than she is where he lives. She goes down in the sea at the North Cape as she does at home and that is very beautiful. There is one major difference, though. Lars explains that he can see the sun go down and then rise again in the sky in the north, without it disappearing below the horizon. This is the most delightful thing about the midnight sun to Lars; He can see the sun descend and then ascend. He describes the sun as feminine, and talks quietly about the nothingness that reveals itself for him as meaningful when he sees the midnight sun rise, which means that nothing stops him seeing the sea and the sky merge in the horizon. He explains that he has done a lot of thinking about the midnight sun. There are some places in his homeland, and elsewhere in the world, where he can experience nothingness, he explains.

He was familiar with what he would see at the North Cape. He had seen pictures of it lately, so it was no big surprise to him to see the big building and the changes in the man-made environment constructed there. What surprised him, though, was how vast an area it was. Even though he has been there before, he could not remember it being such a large area. He was also surprised by the large number of campers. The finest thing about North Cape at this time, he says, was finding the view from the site, which is the same as it has always been. He did not do a lot of thinking there, but found it magnificent to have come to such a place and have such a view. And he thought it would have been nice to be there at midnight, which they did not do this time, to see the midnight sun.

Lars says that nature is important to him. Even though he takes care of his wife 24 hours of the day both at home and on this trip, he still has the opportunity to spend time watching the changing scenery and the coastline. He is very fascinated by the sea and the experience of nature from sea. He has always enjoyed outdoor walking in the mountains near the farm. The finest thing about nature is that he can watch nature and experience beautiful overviews, and share his time in nature together with a flock of young birds flying in front of him while walking. Lars tells me about one of his best experiences, which refers to seeing the small skerries named Roqual west of the Hebrides from the viewpoint of the sea. This memory is from a long time ago when he was working as a fisherman. Lars says there is fish in the sea there. When you get away westwards at sea in a ship, he explains, you see how the land disappears little by little, and finally you only see the sea. After a while, you start to see Roqual, and it is very exciting. The skerries are more like cliffs standing upright in the sea. These cliffs resemble the cliffs at North Cape, which stand upright from the sea vertically.

There is much wonder in Lars' experiences of the world. He has always been very curious about seeing the outside world, he explains, but he has also felt very much a farmer, taking care of what his forebears built and created. Lars has learned from his years at sea that the local world is a small world. He acknowledges how important travelling and meeting the larger world is. There are many good and fascinating things to see and experience outside the local world. Lars mentions that Algeria is a very fascinating country to visit, with its very different culture, and with very different conditions of living compared to Northern Europe.

Lars has many memories from his long life, and even though there has been little leisure for a farmer like Lars, he keeps his memories alive by remembering and retelling them to himself and the family. He recalls in particular a life full of work, from morning to night. He used to wake up at six and go to bed around eight in the evening, he explains. In the summers, there was even less spare time. After the children had grown up, Lars and his wife had the opportunity to go on vacation. They usually left the farm for one or two weeks. It was impossible to have a vacation while staying at the farm, because there were so many things to do. It was good to get away and relax. He and his wife have travelled within their home country, and they have mostly visited meetings and rallies organized by the Mission of Seamen during the summers. They have never visited foreign countries together. He tells me that he dreams of visiting the Middle East, but he fears the trip would be too hard on his wife. She cannot walk naturally. Lars has decided that as long as he can, he will stay with his wife at home and help her. It benefits her to stay at home, he says. He thinks this is much better for her than staying at a nursing home. Since she became ill, they have not travelled very much, only short trips to visit family and relatives and some meetings at the weekends. The trip to the north on the *Hurtigruta* is an exception and the realization of a dream, and both Lars and his wife feel content after having seen the North Cape.

Dwelling, place and "the feminine"

Lars' story is a story full of wonder. It is a story about the wonders of dwelling and creation of place. His story shows that making place is relative to the experience and practice of dwelling. Below I will develop some thoughts about dwelling and lived place in a northern world. The term dwelling was developed in philosopher Martin Heidegger's later works, where he spoke about place as a condition for being, or place as an existential (Heidegger 1971). According to the philosopher Carol Bigwood, Heidegger understands place as a fundamental characteristic of the human being, as letting-be, and release of thinking and creativity (Bigwood 1993). The geographer John Pickles reads Heidegger's construct of dwelling simply as a creation of place and dwelling place (Pickles 1985).

Heidegger writes that building makes dwelling possible, but buildings are not dwellings. Dwelling is a human way of being on earth. It is to spare or preserve the fourfold of Earth and Sky, Mortals and Divinities. Dwelling happens on earth, and exists under the sky, and means looking after or taking care of the earth and the sky. Human beings save the earth, receive the sky, awake the divinities and initiate their own nature, according to Heidegger. Caring is not to stay on the earth or under the sky. Caring is to stay with the things and locations that provide the places for daily dwelling. The human state of being is to stay with things. The relationship between human beings and place is simply dwelling. Dwelling, as Heidegger understood it, is a process where the lived place of human beings becomes a personal place: a home.

Dwelling is not a closed term. Rather, it is an open term that includes the possibility of including that which may exist beyond the immediate horizon of home. This turns dwelling into a project, since dwelling has a direction and a path. Human placiality is further characterized by being directional and intentional because it has a direction towards the world and things already. Directions of left and right are examples of the directionality of human spatiality. Human placiality is different from geometric spatiality. Human beings cannot move in geometric space, Heidegger writes, they can only change their 'here'. Distances cannot be crossed, but are projections from the place one is involved in, which is a constant (and changing) here and now. It also means that 'place' comes before 'space' (Casey 1997, Malpas 1998, Olwig 2001 and 2002). Space exists, but is neither external object nor an inner experience, according to Heidegger (Heidegger 1971).

Carol Bigwood shows that Heidegger's understanding of dwelling and place romanticizes place and affirms an often ethnocentrically German earth, a nostalgic construction of a native land, thus reifying and fixing the meaning of both being and dwelling. Feminist philosophers have pointed to Heidegger's taken-for-granted masculine constructions of being (Bigwood 1993, Irigaray 1993, Mortensen 1994). They show how the human being is represented as a neutral being, a non-sexed being, and how sexual difference has remained hidden in the discourse on dwelling. The central question for feminists is whether being comes before sexual difference, or whether one thinks sexual difference is more primordial than being. Irigaray uses Heidegger's own words against himself. She shows that Heidegger's view that human beings have forgotten the question of the meaning of being is also a forgetting of the question of the meaning of sexual difference (Irigaray 1993). What does it mean to be a woman, and what does it mean to be a man? Sexual difference comes before being, Irigaray insists, while stressing the wonder that is present when discovering being. The wonder in Irigaray's and Heidegger's thinking sheds light on Lars' wonder when seeing the midnight sun with a feminine figuration. The affirmation of life and earth that is so present in Lars' story shows that wonder is an important aspect of both place and dwelling, and as we will see, this affirmation is an affirmation of sexual difference.

Two impressions from Lars' story have amazed me. The first is that Lars described the midnight sun as a 'she', and the second is that there is a proper way of seeing 'her'. Seeing the midnight sun is central to Lars' experience of North Cape. The midnight sun is important for other visitors to the North Cape, but it has been difficult for many to explain why the midnight sun is so impressive. Lars' story reminds us about the symbolic meaning of the midnight sun, which is seeing the sun turn the night to a new day. In this sense, Lars' story is about the meaning of the midnight sun, and about ways of seeing the sun. One must see the sun turn, and this can be done at particular locations on the earth above the Arctic Circle. In Lars' view, the proper way of seeing the midnight sun makes the observer a participant in the event. Seeing the midnight sun is not a passive act, it is active participation, where one takes part in the change from night to day, and which transcends the dualism between observing subject and observed object. The sun is recognized as an active force, as is the rotating and living earth, and the reflexive and intentional watching of the sun from the surface of the earth by human beings like Lars.

Carl Gustav Jung and others have described such states through the construct *participation mystique*, or a mystical union (Brooke 1991). Such participation creates a bridge between the external and the internal world, the being of the world and the human being. It is an intentional connection, which expresses consciousness-of-the-world. In Jung's view, human beings' access to the world goes through psychological life, and Jung's own experiences of such access shed light on Lars' story. The sun had a particular meaning for Jung because of an event during a foot walk to Mt Elgon in East Africa (Brooke 1991, Jung 1995). At the summit he found a dawning significance in things while seeing the sun shooting up over the horizon. The light seemed to penetrate the structure of things and objects, according to Jung, which eventually made him feel as if he were inside a temple. It was the place for timeless ecstasy. According to Brooke, metaphors of darkness and light are the primordial metaphors for the understanding of human life to Jung. This experience expresses Jung's personal myth according to Brooke. The world became a temple in a time-less monumental space, but the event nevertheless took place at a particular location. From this experience, Jung learned that human beings do not invent consciousness, but that consciousness evolves and reveals itself through the moment and image of the dawn.

The sun in the north is the same sun that one sees in Africa, and they are the same source of light, but the northern sun as temple is different. We might describe the southern sun and the northern sun as two poles in the experiences of darkness and light. The northern sun remains above the horizon during summer time. I suggest that life, death and renewal (the rhythm of nature) are in the centre of the meaning of seeing the midnight sun at the North Cape. In central Europe, the sun rises in the east, but it is different above the Arctic Circle. During winter, the sun does not appear at all, while during summer, the sun descends and ascends in the north. In the north, nature represents austerity, indifference and barrenness, qualities that are more or less death-like. Travellers I spoke to felt that they were indifferent and small compared to northern nature. Many associated the northern climate with being cold, harsh and barren in the summer and the winter. Habitation of the north is risky, because of the struggle against darkness, the cold and winter. In this death-like image of nature, the sun is an even larger image of life, birth or renewal. Seeing the midnight sun is possible at this latitude for a few weeks during the summer, because of the earth's changing position in relation to the sun over the year. When the sun ascends in the horizon in the north in the middle of the night, silence and astonishment seem to be the first reaction. Therefore, it is not unexpected that many travellers also identified northern nature with the sun, the midnight sun, which represents the life-giving quality of northern nature. The sun is then associated with creation of new life, survival and the upholding and recreation of life. When the summer comes, the north has transformed itself into a heavenly place of eternal light, embracing both day and night in a continuous day.

People living in the more temperate regions do not experience these rhythms between light and darkness in the same polarized way. The seasonal changes become extreme opposites, and provide a dimension to life not experienced in Africa or in central Europe.

The geographer Yi-Fu Tuan writes that life on earth in cosmographic belief depends on events in the sky (Tuan 1977). What the sun, moon and stars do affect life on earth. When the sun, moon and stars sink below the horizon, it is as if they were taking a journey to the underworld, or a counter-heaven, Tuan writes. If one lives above the Arctic Circle, which marks the border for the appearance of the midnight sun in the horizon, one has to relate to the particular rhythm of the seasonal changes over the year. In these areas, the rhythm of day and night extends and blends with the cycle of the year. This temporal change seems like a movement between one long day lasting all summer and one long night lasting all winter. Everything that makes a difference becomes polarized in terms of day and night, summer and winter, warmth and cold, light and darkness. The fight for life is a real fight against the colonization of life by the long, cold and dark winter. Compared to the southern sun, there is a much stronger polarization of light and darkness in the north.

I would suggest that we look upon the north point and the meaning of the North Cape as an encounter with a particular and forgotten creation myth in the secularized regions of modernity (Birkeland 1999). The northern sun and the midnight sun play a particular role in this myth. Human beings have always created myths of a first place as a mysterious origin of nature and culture, and therefore creation myths are central in religious belief. Estella Lauter argues that myths are just like dreams constituted as another reality, through images, art, literature or in other ways (Lauter 1984). A myth is a story or a symbol that is repeated many times until it is accepted as truth. It is a shared or collective agreement that explains some aspects of the unknown that differs from scientific knowledge because it is accepted as true even if it is proven untrue. Myths have a mediating power between the known and the unknown, and contribute to explaining what is not possible to explain in ordinary ways. Different myths are realized in different situations, in initiation, marriage, birth, in the change of the four seasons of the year, and in the change between night and day. The yearly rhythm between work and holiday is one situation that may call for the projection of mythical images.

Parallel creation myths have existed in different religious beliefs. Creation myths concern the fundamental questions: who created the world? Where do I come from? Jungian psychoanalyst Marie Louise Von Franz argues that whenever human beings arrive in a new and strange place, they have tended to project images that express the basic myths of creation in their culture (Von Franz 1995). Creation myths have arisen in particular from projected images of the familiar in an unfamiliar place, and are performed and repeated under certain conditions, Von Franz writes. When medieval peoples, for example, set foot in a new land they repeated creation myths as a manifestation that the land had not formerly existed. After arriving in the new land, it entered their consciousness and they could create the new land and settle. Thus, creation is about consciousness that is awakening, where consciousness is consciousness-of-the-world.

I will show that holiday travel to North Cape calls for the projection of particular images connected to creation myths, and that the dawning of the midnight sun may stand in the centre for a creation myth that honours the becoming and flow of life, or life process, what I previously have associated with the feminine principle. This rewriting and recreation of the mythic meaning of the sun is therefore about feminine creation, female imagination and a search for a symbolic language adequate for women. This work is symbolic, because being human is to have and use language, amongst other things, but it is particularly important for women. Women especially must create symbols and images that confirm and express the female difference. Luce Irigaray argues that women must become divine women, because this is necessary for a woman to become a true female subject and achieve a place in the world for herself, and not only for others (Irigaray 1993b). For Irigaray, it is clear that the imagination and the use of language are important in divine creation, which includes a positive connection between women and religion. She points to the lack of a female God, a female trinity consisting of mother, daughter and spirit. The final element of women's place making would thus be to create an understanding of the divine with a feminine or female figuration or personification.

The sun, and in particular the midnight sun, can play an important role here. Luce Irigaray discusses the relation between women and the divine by mentioning women's connection to heavenly bodies like the moon and the sun. It has become an unquestioned truth in western culture that the moon is associated with femininity, while the sun is associated with masculinity. The rising sun is a symbol for understanding, consciousness, thinking and knowledge. In classical mythology, the meaning of the sun is closely associated with hero myths, where the sun in the figure of the hero fights and wins over darkness. According to Miranda Green, European mythology outside of the Greek pantheon provides many myths of the sun and moon that question the Greek monopoly on sun and moon myths (Green 1991). On the one hand, the sun is associated with life, creation and healing, fertility and light, heroic journeys and the conquering of death. On the other hand, the sun is also associated with destruction and death, power and control and the eye of the universe. The sun reveals a conflict between good and evil, light and darkness, life and death, summer and winter and positive and negative, according to Green, but she does not discuss how this conflicting meaning is related to sexual difference.

The historian of religion, Mircea Eliade, argues that the sun in classical mythology is opposite in meaning to the moon, which is related to masculine and feminine qualities (Eliade 1987). The sun is associated with intelligence, consciousness, power, autonomy, authority, creativity and knowledge, in classical terms very masculine characteristics. On the other hand, the moon is associated with feminine qualities: birth, death, becoming, cosmic darkness, water, madness and the unconscious. Irigaray and Eliade show that at some time in ancient history the sun goddesses were replaced with male sun gods, in particular Zeus and Apollo, in Greek mythology. Irigaray writes that certain problems arose when the goddesses of fertility and natural season were replaced and suppressed (Irigaray 1993b). The earth and fertility were no longer honoured as before. Mircea Eliade has also identified this change of meaning in sun myths in Greek mythology. He shows that over time the heroic struggle between light and darkness was transformed (Eliade 1987). The sun became associated with intelligence and consciousness without its other, the meaning of darkness. Eliade suggests that this produced rationalization and a cultivation of consciousness to such a degree that the place of darkness in the mythic order was lost. The sun as deity was replaced with pure ideas, he writes. Irigaray shows however that this interpretation is not at all clear and uncontested even in western culture, and explains that certain cultures link the sun with women and the moon with men (Irigaray 1993b). Even in Greek culture, one can find this in the myth of Demeter, who is associated with the solar seasons. Demeter's daughter, Persephone or Kore, embodies the sun while she stays with her mother on earth for half the year. The sunny season is the season of Persephone.

Re-telling the myth of Demeter and Persephone to invent the feminine divine provides other directions as well for a revival of the honouring of earth and fertility. Miranda Green points out that the sun does not have identical meaning in the mythologies around the world (Green 1991). For example, worship of the sun has been absent in the hotter regions of the world, she says, because the sun in these areas was associated with destruction of life rather than creation of life. Worship of the sun as a provider of life has been particularly important in the northern regions of the world, according to Green. An association between the sun and fertility, creation, and conqueror of death can be traced in the northern areas of Europe.

Goddess worship was important in ancient Greece, as it is in all maternal or fertility-oriented religions. It is interesting here to look at the mythologies of the indigenous Sami who inhabit the northern parts of Scandinavia, Finland and Russia and the mythologies of the northern people. We know that people in the northern parts of Europe in ancient times worshipped both paternal and maternal divinities. According to Gro Steinsland, historian of religion and expert on Norse religion, the world of gods contained a heterogeneous and nuanced idea of the divine in Norse culture (Steinsland 1997). Steinsland argues that this represented a much more sophisticated view of the pantheon than is found in Judean-Christian religion. Writing on Sami religion, historian of religion May-Lisbeth Myrhaug argues that Sami religion has an even more developed goddess worship than Norse religion (Myrhaug 1997). The Sami worldview holds that the universe is filled with deities both above the heaven, in the heaven, on the earth and underneath the surface of the earth. This is a complex worldview where gods and goddesses create a unity or balance between the feminine and the masculine principle. An important creation myth is about the sun. In Sami religion, the sun has a feminine figuration. The sun (*Beive*) is called queen in heaven, she has power and influence over life on earth, and is expressed by an image where four rays spread out from a centre. These rays symbolize the earth's Four Corners, and illustrate the placement of all living things in relation to the sun. In the moment of creation, the soul was carried to each corner until it was given a body by the mother goddess (*Máttaráhkká*) or the Earth Mother in the final fourth corner.

Chapter 13

Making Place, Making Self: Choragraphy

The arrival at the North Cape

In this final chapter, I would like to bring the discussions in the previous chapters together via a critical reconstruction of place in "the feminine". I will discuss the implications of the journey towards the north and the North Cape for the conceptualisation of place. I will start by coming back to the story of Sofia, whom we met in the introductory chapter, and who is a figuration of the change in the conceptualization of place through the encounter with the north. In this concluding chapter, I will write Sofia as place – she is place in "the feminine" – from the perspective of being a female self, a feminine place. This is made possible by the actual arrival at the North Cape.

Sofia knew little about the north of Norway, but she had an understanding of the north as a necessary reference point in an internal geography. When Sofia started walking, the North Cape was only a point on the map, she said. She only knew it was the end of Europe, the north point. She did not know very much about Norway in the first place. She knew of the fjords in the western part of the country, and she had read about snow in the winter. The North Cape symbolizes one of the four cardinal points in western cosmology. These points have been important for human being's orientation throughout history. This is obvious to geographers, who learn about the long history of mapping the *terra incognita* and the practice of cartography. Human beings still use these points for orientation in modernity, as they are part of the way the world is understood. However, the meaning of the cardinal points is mostly taken for granted today. They are found in maps as a part of modern world-views. The maps are there, as given, while the mapmakers have disappeared from the scene (De Certeau 1984). Sofia's story shows that we should not take the maps for granted. Instead, Sofia's story shows that human beings to a greater extent should make their own maps and create their own cardinal points. This is particularly important for women, who have had to use *man-made* maps of the world and of the self.

As Sofia's story shows, the north is the most important of the cardinal points. The north was so important for her orientation in the world that she had made it a point in a subjective map of her self. When the cardinal north is unknown, how does a woman learn about it and make it her own? Sofia travelled to make her own north through first-hand experience. As Sofia walked farther and farther north, she learned more and more. She learned little by little, she said, because walking takes time and she can only move step by step. She learned about life in the north, its people and nature, and in particular about strength. She learned to become strong during her walk. At first she was very fragile, but she got more energy over time. She learned that she had to look for strength – as light – inside, because the north is the kingdom of darkness, she said. One has to find meaning inside, not survival in itself, but life and light and warmth that animate her self. Today people do not believe so much in themselves, Sofia said. People are more concerned about finding warmth and light in the external world, in things, other people and material wealth. In the north this is impossible. Meaning, strength and power must come from within and from experience. When she arrived at the North Cape, she felt she had come to a special place, but she could not see this place in the external world. There was nothing to see. She had walked as far as she could go on mainland Europe, and the North Cape meant no more ground to walk. This was the arrival in the north. The North Cape was special, not because she found something particular there, but because she made the arrival meaningful in the context of the long walk.

Sofia met many people who said they were going to the North Cape because it was something they had to see. They had been to Machu Picchu and they had seen Fujiama, so now they were going to see the North Cape. To them, it was just another famous point to see. The people Sofia met could not express the experience of the attraction of the North Cape. They always talked about the others' experiences, not their own. They did not have a language that expressed the attraction. Is it because they had not walked the distance? Or is it because they could not see the north in the external world? What is the North?

In the Western hemisphere, the North is viewed as the most important cardinal point. There are differences between the cardinal points. The North and South are located at precise points on the globe (a globe as an abstract co-ordinate space consisting of lines of longitude and latitude). In fact, the lines of longitude converge at the North Pole and the South Pole. In addition, the North and South are magnetic poles. This is not possible with the East and the West. There are no poles in the East and the West, and there is no magnetic energy connecting them. This is easy to see when you look at the globe from the outside, but it does not help much when you actually get to the North Pole (or South Pole) because you do not arrive at any specific place that is visibly distinct. There is actually nothing to see. A similar point can be made with regard to the North Cape. What seems to make the North Cape remarkable is the vertical line of the cliff that forms a *marquer* for something that cannot be seen (which is the North). The North Cape is not a sight to be seen but something from which to see a sight, which cannot otherwise be seen. It is not a sight, but a site. Travelling to the North Cape is thus a search for the meaning of that site, which cannot be seen as reaching a visible and fixed truth. To see anything, the traveller has to turn within, thus demonstrating that the truth of the North Cape is not to reach or see something visible in the external world. It is to arrive at a place in one's internal world where one's experiences of place and self are fundamentally transformed because they converge and unite. Sofia's topophilia, the intimate and affectionate ties that were created between her self and the North Cape, confirms that place is more like a field of care, described by Gaston Bachelard (1994) and Yi-Fu Tuan (1974).

Sofia was told she had lost her north. I think this is incorrect. The north was not something she had lost, because she had never had or known her north. The cardinal North has never existed in "the feminine" sense for Sofia. Sofia's story shows that the change – the transformation of the north from unknown to known – is concrete as experiences unfolding in the life-world. To Sofia, the journey was an experience of a personal transformation that took place in her life-world, as a continuously moving place-world. From this transformation the understanding grows that the north does not exist outside of the life-world. The north is not a fixed point or a universal or absolute point of meaning on a map. The north is that immanent realization that the self is a place, and that place is a vaster, deeper and larger self that one cannot know without some kind of journeying or work. Sofia's journey to the north made the cardinal north, the North Cape, a feminine place in the life-world. As she now knows her personal north, she will also know her personal east, south and west.

What can we learn from Sofia in this sense? What can we learn about place? Sofia's topophilia represents a critique and a renewal of humanist philosophers and geographers' constructions of place. I suggest that we see Sofia's journey as a personification of the transformation of place from object to subject, and ask with the words of Luce Irigaray: but what happens when the object starts to speak? (Irigaray 1985).

Chora and the metaphysics of place

What is place? As we have seen in the previous chapters, place has been represented in terms of woman and the feminine to such a degree that the discourse on place is a gendered and sexed discourse. Place has been an object in a discourse. The subject in geography is a male self set apart from his object of study, places, landscapes, natures, the world endowed with social meaning and status. Geography has become place-less, where places do not exist in and for themselves, only as objects in discourse and resources for living. Places do not do anything, they are being done to. As we have seen in the previous chapters, place has be given essential, fixed and stable qualities, represented as the ground upon which everything rests. Place as ground is named Woman, a ground that has not been given positive self-definition and has not defined *herself*.

Gillian Rose uncovered the feminisation of place in geography, but this is not only a challenge for geographical discourse. The sciences draw on a long and silent tradition in philosophy where place has been feminized since the beginning of philosophy. *Chora* was a concept connected to geographical discourse in ancient Greek philosophy generally, and it was clearly feminized. Plato, for example, discussed *chora* in *Timaeus*. The etymological meaning of *chora* is the Greek word *choros* which means place (Olwig 2001). In Greek discourse, *chora* is related to place, but not to space (which is *topos*). The meaning of both space and place in early geographical discourse is indebted to Claudius Ptolemy whose ideas have influenced geographical thinking ever since, and indeed still do. For Ptolemy, geographical knowledge was divided into chorography, topography and geography. It is only chorography which dealt with form or the shape of actual land or country as it is seen from within the land. Topography (*topos* as space) refers to knowledge of the world by way of geometrical principles, while geography is the representation of the general features of the earth, according to Olwig (ibid). When Ptolemy's ideas were rediscovered during the fifteenth century, they brought forward ideas of place that transformed and reduced its chorological aspects to topography, or space. The rediscovery of Ptolemy's geography was important for the rethinking space, as Descartes did, but something went wrong in this rediscovery. The Greek distinction between place and space was erased. Descartes did much to confuse the meaning of place and space, and over time the meaning of place was subsumed under the concept of space. Many have argued that this may be the key cause why space and place get so confused in current geographical debate (Olwig 2002; Casey 1997; Malpas 1998). There is a tendency today to talk about place in ways in which place refers to a topological space, or a geometrical space, and there is a tendency to confuse the ontological status of place as the lived world, or land as it is lived from within, with space which has nothing to do with place at all (see chapter seven).

Ptolemy's chorography drew on Plato's understanding of *chora*. Though *chora* means place, what determines place? Did Plato do anything to provide *chora* with a positive self-identity? Or is *chora* objectified and defined as outside of discourse from the very beginning? Plato feminized *chora* and described her as a receptacle with a decidedly feminine gender. According to the philosopher Elizabeth Grosz, *Timeaus* is a cosmology. It is an attempt by Plato to explain the universe, the divine creation of the cosmos and earth (Grosz 1995). Grosz shows how Plato takes his outset in a series of binary oppositions that characterize Western thinking (being – becoming, the intelligible – the sensible, ideal – material, divine – mortal) that are related to the relationship between reason (mind) and the material world. Grosz shows that the opposition between being (that which is unchanging, the world of Forms and Ideas, the perfect), and becoming (that which is sensible, subject to change and so forth, the imperfect), may look simple, but that it is hard to use this opposition as an explanatory model because it presumes a mediation or mode of transition.

Grosz argues that Plato introduces *chora* as a mediating bridge and that it represents a third or intermediate category (Grosz 1995). However, Plato is not consistent, Grosz argues. He suggests that *chora* shares properties of both Forms and Ideas, but at times he argues that *chora* does not have anything in common with either Forms or Ideas. *Chora* seems to be enigmatic and with no attributes of her own but still she is not without attributes. Grosz argues that Plato cannot specify any particular qualities or properties of *chora*, because he writes as though *chora* were the mother of all qualities without having any qualities herself except the capacity to 'take on, to nurture, to bring into existence any other kind of being' (ibid:114). *Chora* thus becomes a condition for the material world. She is like a screen for the projection of images of changeless forms since she receives, takes in and possesses without leaving an impression. *Chora* does not have any self-identity. She maintains but nothing supports her. *Chora* brings being into becoming but has neither being or becoming herself, as Grosz reads Plato. The philosopher Edward Casey (1993, 1997) has suggested a similar understanding of *chora* within which he sees *chora* as a necessity, as the seat of the emerging cosmos, as matrix, as pregeometric and elemental.

The philosopher Jeff Malpas interprets Plato similarly, but focuses more on *chora*'s relationship to becoming (Malpas 1998). *Chora* is like a receiving principle and a mother to Plato, and Malpas argues that *chora* is about 'the manner in which things come into being and in which one thing can change into something else' (Malpas 1998: 26). *Chora* is about becoming, and Plato uses the images of mother, father and child to describe becoming, Malpas writes:

> That which becomes Plato compares with a child; that which is the model for that which becomes he likens to a father; and that in which becoming takes place – into which it is received – he compares to a mother. This 'mother' of becoming, which Plato also refers to as the receptacle or nurse of becoming, is the place in which the qualities of the thing that comes into being appear (Malpas 1998: 27).

Aristotle understood place in other terms. Malpas shows that Plato and Aristotle are both concerned with place rather than space and that there are important differences between these two philosophers. Plato's concept of place refers to containment, while in Aristotle's thinking place refers to containing bodies, to interval or magnitude. Both understand place as particular. It is important to bear in mind that Aristotle's understanding of place has been changed or misinterpreted and later has given rise to place as extension. Place as extension (or as space, which was the superior concept for Descartes) is something that is infinite and blank like an empty box where all things can be located.

In the history of philosophy over the centuries, the Cartesian grammar has thus led to an eradication of place. Space became the term. The Cartesian grammar regarded space as an abstract three-dimensional grid (geometrical space, or topology) dissociated from nature, place and the body. As with the concept of place, space was not gender-neutral or free of sexed meanings and connotations, as we have seen in the previous chapters. In the modern era, space has been given feminine meaning, and the philosopher Luce Irigaray shows that this is not coincidental. There is a dissociation between time and space related to other pairs of concepts, those of body and soul, sexuality and spirituality, the inside and the outside (Irigaray 1993). Space is a disembodied and fleshless concept. Irigaray shows that time became the interiority of the male human being, while space has become its exteriority (1993a:7). Space has been coded as absolute, as apolitical and of little interest compared to time. Time is coded as dynamic, transitory or changing. Space and place are placed outside of history, progress, civilisation, science, politics and reason (Rose 1993, Massey 1994, Grosz 1989). This pairing of opposites is, it is argued, related to sexual difference in problematic ways since it reveals a paradoxical discourse that presumes identity between space (and place) and woman but does not accept that this identity should have anything to do with what matters (like history, science, politics, being). Space and place (and woman) is a ground with no ontological value. It is matter, but does not matter. This does not make sense.

This paradoxical presupposition is also widespread among feminist thinkers and researchers. A feminist and (Lacanian) psychoanalytical example relevant to the present discussion is Julia Kristeva's writings on the semiotic *chora*. Kristeva drew attention to *chora* in *Revolution in Poetic Language* (Kristeva 1984, see also chapter eight). Kristeva theorized the structured and structuring subject in dynamic terms as *a subject in process/on trial*. She described signifying practices as the result of heterogeneous forces that include both conscious and unconscious processes. *Chora* forms a part of the unconscious processes related to the structuring forces of early mother-child interaction. These forces exist pre-discursively or pre-symbolicly and work like a rhythmic space, like an origin of meaning. They are associated with what she terms semiotic dispositions or language. *Chora* is characterized by bodily rhythm, repetitions, and fluctuations and signifies everything from distinct mark, trace, index, sign, proof, marks and figurations which originate through the early relations between mother and child (Kristeva 1984: 25). *Chora* is more like a process than a language, it is both destructive (fixed) and creative (fluid), and the place where the human being is generated and negated in both discontinuity and flow. *Chora* is both fixed and in flux.

Central to Kristeva is that *chora* is not possible to represent since the semiotic may not be directly or immediately accessible. *Chora* comes before symbolic language and refers to the mother's time and space instead of the father's time and place. *Chora* comes before topography, before linear time and abstract space, since it articulates the time and space of the mother. Every description of *chora* moves in-between both semiotic language and symbolic language, but Kristeva does not understand *chora* as an origin for a female imagery since she makes her dependent on symbolic language for her to exist. *Chora* exists only as a possibility.

It is clear that Kristeva engenders *chora* feminine since it is associated with the early mother-child interactions. Kristeva understands *chora* as feminine place but uses the term without much discussion. This is problematic because *chora* thus stands in an ambiguous relation to language and representation. One reason for this is Kristeva's use of Lacanian psychoanalysis. *Chora* cannot be determined and she is still determined only in relation to paternal language. There is no positive self-identity in relation to maternal language in Kristeva's view. I will argue that this shows that the paternal and maternal principles are asymmetric in relation to representation and language. I argue that this forms part of an ongoing masculinization of the reduction of chorology into topology.

I would like to elaborate this argument by exemplifying the difference between thinking space as extension from place as interval. The example is from Jacques Derrida (Derrida 1995; Grosz 1995). Derrida sees *chora* as playing a role in cosmology, but he sees her as a product of discourse and therefore inadequate and non-true. Nobody can speak directly of *chora* since *chora* is like a dream. She is located between the two, neither one nor the other (Derrida 1995: 126). In addition, he sees it as impossible to describe *chora*, to give it a meaning, because only that of the father and son can be given meaning. Derrida thinks that Kristeva's *chora* is nothing but metaphysics. By stating the existence of *chora,* Derrida thinks that Kristeva presupposes a belief in *chora* independent of experience. According to Derrida, it is not possible to grasp the meaning of an object, a concept or a person in an immediate way, innocently or directly, through language (Fürst 1998). This is what Derrida refers to with his understanding of the metaphysics of presence, which suggests an identity between speech and presence (or essence). A metaphysics of place would imply that it is possible to grasp place in an immediate way, without mediation. Kristeva and Derrida are opponents of a metaphysics of place, the trap of essentialism.

I would argue, however, that both Derrida and Kristeva reduce all meaning of *chora* and of place to a determination via symbolic language. This is the trap of constructivism. I would like to criticize essentialism and constructivism in the light of the phallogocentric determination of this pair of opposites. Derrida and Kristeva both treat *chora* in terms of extension or space, a non-material yet material entity that is not meaningful without inscription from the outside. Derrida has a problem with presence, according to Elisabeth Fürst (1995) and argues that this is an escape away from essence, leaving perception, the body and being. There are no living human beings in Derrida's philosophy, and this is understandable given that he is a philosopher-linguist and not a social scientist. A theory of meaning making for the social sciences will, however, need to relate to the level of agency and real flesh and blood humans. The question of language use has been in focus among the French feminists, and they – in different ways – take up Derrida's ideas with a much closer reading of the production of meaning from the perspective of the body and the female body. Julia Kristeva does not have the same problem with presence as Derrida. In her theory of meaning production, *heterogeneity* represents the exit from dualist thinking. Heterogeneity is material, associated with the pulsating drives of the body, which create not only symbolic or linguistic movement, but movement in the body and psychic space (see chapter eight). In Kristeva's view of meaning making, tension between the feminine and the masculine is allowed but is not solved or transcended.

Both Kristeva and Derrida see language as masculine and phallocentric. When Kristeva argues that symbolic language is necessary to represent *chora,* this means that she understands *chora* in terms of a topological rather than a chorological way of thinking. This does little more than to restore both place and woman as unconscious, repressed or unspoken foundations for philosophy and western thinking. Derrida nevertheless likens *chora* to a dream. This implies that the language of *chora* is the language of dreams, myths and the mythical world. *Chora* is different, and close to an understanding of woman as border/that which exceeds all borders. This would imply that *chora* is close to pure difference, since pure difference cannot be written, cannot be fixed and refuses all categories. This has been interpreted as the power to hold open the question of truth; Woman refuses to fix truth, while man wants to close truth, according to J. Peter Burgess (Burgess 2000). This reveals that *chora* exists, but not in a way that can be expressed via language, as these writers understand language.

The philosopher Elizabeth Grosz reads Derrida as primarily interested in disturbing the logic that tries to describe *chora* positively, but this is not enough for Grosz (Grosz 1995). *Chora* has been given a mediation function by Plato, and Grosz argues that *chora* may create a founding concept of a philosophy of femininity that does not severe the connection to female corporeality (Grosz 1995:113). She rewrites *chora* without making it a theory of place as feminine. *Chora* has undoubtedly many of the attributes of pregnancy and maternity, but still lacks the one thing that makes her alive. The material *chora* cannot exist without ideas impressed upon her.

The question is what is lacking in order for *chora* to write herself. I would maintain that the distinction between place and space is important for an understanding of embodied, pure difference, and for rewriting place in "the feminine". In other words, we need a new chorography to write place in "the feminine". Perhaps a *choragraphical* way of thinking would be more proper for writing place in "the feminine"? As I will argue, Luce Irigaray's ideas on the ethics of sexual difference may contribute to that revelation. By drawing on Irigaray's ideas, who rewrites Aristotle's idea of place as interval, I will be able to provide a language for *chora* so that she writes herself, as *choragraphy*. Central to this work is the understanding of the relationship between language, gender and sexual difference.

Language, gender and sexual difference

Luce Irigaray focuses on the living and sexed body as the source of creation of meaning (Birkeland 2000). Irigaray's project is in some senses similar to Kristeva's, since both focus on the early experiences of the child for development of language and meaning. Where Kristeva is interested in the child's relationship to the father and the paternal (masculine) principle, Irigaray is interested in the child's relationship to the mother and the maternal (feminine) principle. In many of Irigaray's works, she argues that language is both sexed and gendered (see for example Irigaray 1993b). Language is neither indifferent to gender nor sexual difference. In the English language, gender and sexual difference refers to different things. How is gender different from sexual difference with reference to language, and thus to the creation of meaning and experience? Following Christine Battersby,

I argue that we must focus on the 'female' rather than the 'feminine' (Battersby 1998). 'Femininity' refers to gender, connected to behavioural and affective differences. 'Female' refers to sex, connected to bodily and extensive differences, or the bodily, biological or physiological differences between men and women. Assigning someone to the category 'female' is not the same as assigning someone to the category of the 'feminine' (ibid: 21). To speak of sexual difference means to refer to bodily and extensive differences, how these influence human practices, of which linguistic practices are only one outcome.

Irigaray's view is that sexual difference is essential for language (Irigaray 1993b). This does not exclude gender differences in language, but in the western world, gender differences become increasingly dissociated from sexual difference, Irigaray argues. The new reproductive technologies introduced in the western world have widened this gap between gender and sexual difference and created equal opportunities for women in many areas of society. This development is good but it does not mean that language necessarily incorporates sexual difference. Language may still be sexed (Irigaray 1993b: 201). Western philosophy has produced a connection between language and the morphology of the male human being, centred on the symbolic meaning of the phallus, which defines sexual difference in terms of presence or absence. You either have it or you do not. There is only one difference, which is the male difference based on male bodily morphology (Birkeland 2000). This has created phallocentric language, which refers to the centrality of male symbolism and imagery in the construction of meaning. There is a conflict at the cultural and symbolic level, a so-called war between the sexes on a symbolic or imaginary level, where the vocabulary of fertility/sterility, creation/destruction, mother/father, health/sickness understood in a dualist and hierarchical way expresses a non-harmonious relation between male and female imagery (Irigaray 1993b: 58). Irigaray argues that the western world has operated only within the system of male imagery, which becomes destructive without a harmonious relation to female imagery. Irigaray argues that it is necessary to try to create balance on the symbolic level and argues for both masculine and female symbolism and imagery, so that rationality, concepts and language use could be fertile according to two symbolic systems. From this, we may conclude that conscious work towards restoration, forming and recreating feminine imagery may strengthen not only women's language and place in the world but also contribute to healing the relationship between the sexes on a symbolic level. This presupposes that feminine imagery represents a qualitative difference with regard to how difference is dealt with. Feminine imagery should therefore not apply a dualist-hierarchical organization of differences or represent the only solution for viable place making. Such responses only revert back to the problem of dualist thinking, and therefore represent no real transcendence. There should be real face-to-face communication between male and female imagery to create viable symbolic exchange. In Irigaray's later works, we see a turn towards such symbolic exchange with her new interest in the expression and ways of love (Irigaray 1996, 2002).

Irigaray envisions a language where everyday experiences of the world, of places, bodies and nature, can be expressed in a language that distinguishes between yet respects male and female symbolism. The words male and female here refer to a basic and fundamental symbolism that consists of two sets of imagery. This different language refers to the linguistic practices by persons or groups of persons (*langage*) and not the structure of language (*langue*) (Whitford 1991: 42).

Therefore, to have an understanding of gendered language is not the same as having an understanding of language as related to sexual difference. Even though socially constructed gender relations shape language, we must in addition ask in what ways language use reflects male or female imagery connected to male and female bodily morphology. Actively adopting a perspective of sexual difference implies more than accepting language as gendered. I would argue that an understanding of place in "the feminine" depends on making a distinction between gender and sexual difference. Gender difference does not sufficiently describe the way language is connected to sexed bodies and experiences. Having an understanding of place in a gender perspective is not the same as having a concept of place from the perspective of sexual difference. To talk about gendered place, we also need to ask in what ways men and women need a sexed language to create different understandings of place, and in what ways such discourses represent an affirmation of alternatives to masculinist discourse. This also means that male imagery is not implicitly masculinist.

The first place

How can geography draw on female imagery, female symbolic systems and create discourses on place in "the feminine"? The focus should be on the way existing language structures meaning, and how we can create a language suitable for writing the feminine difference. A woman-centred focus on feminine difference, as I understand it, means working for a strategic reorganization of the existing social and symbolic order in a way where "the feminine" may be thought as different without defining it as the opposite of the masculine. With reference to the difference between men and women, it means understanding the specificity of the female body as positive but different from the male body. And, with regard to the differences between women (and men), it means understanding the differences between women (and men), as well as the differences within each woman (and man), as positive (Harding 1986; Flax 1987; Scott 1988; Fraser and Nicholson 1988). The following discussion will be based on the ideas of Luce Irigaray, who from a post-Lacanian feminist psychoanalytic perspective has argued that western philosophy has depended on a dualistic and hierarchical understanding of the meaning of the difference between the feminine and the masculine (Irigaray 1985, 1993). This way of thinking has consequences for the understanding of place (Rose 1993; Birkeland 1999, 2000).

Although Irigaray does not discuss *chora* herself (though she has discussed it indirectly in *Speculum* (Irigaray 1985), she takes the understanding of place much closer to the living body. In *Ethics of Sexual Difference* she writes that our age is the age of sexual difference (Irigaray 1993). Sexual difference could in fact represent our salvation if we thought it through, she argues. Irigaray writes from a symbolical order based on female genealogies and a feminine symbolic appropriate for women. Irigaray shows that the human being has always been written in the masculine form while woman as subject has been non-existing. The reason is that human beings have forgotten the meaning of sexual difference. To Irigaray, sexual difference should be viewed as a question connected not only to principles of justice specific to the two sexes but an inclusion of the female principle in spiritual and symbolic life. Irigaray's ideas in *Ethics* take us from the immanent ground of being to the transcendent realms, and show that these are not separated and divided according to a sexual division of labour. She shows, rather, that these are connected. She inscribes the connection between the immanent and the transcendent with the introduction of the sensible-transcendental aesthetic subject.

Irigaray argues that it is necessary to rethink the concept of place on ethical grounds in terms of sexual difference. The sensible, the earth, the ground and place must be connected with the transcendental. The construct of place must be reconceptualized, and its place in philosophy in terms of its double relationship to the immanent and the transcendental must be restored. Irigaray shows that rethinking place is crucial for an understanding of sexual difference:

> The transition to a new age requires a change in our perception and conception of space-time, the inhabiting of places, and of containers, or envelopes of identity (Irigaray 1993a: 7).

and:

> We must, therefore, reconsider the whole question of our conception of place, both in order to move on to another age of difference (each age of thought corresponds to a particular time of meditation on difference), and in order to construct an ethics of the passions (ibid: 11-12).

The starting point for rethinking place is the body. The body is the most concrete place that exists and it is the very first place a human being senses. Every child senses the world as a female and feminine world through the mother. The mother is the world, she is the first place. Irigaray stresses the need to give the relationship between place and woman a positive value, and argues that we cannot ignore thinking of place as feminine. The consequence is that it is not possible to think space and place without thinking sexual difference. Any discourse on place is simultaneously a discourse on sexual difference.

There are huge consequences if one forgets the mother's body as the first place, according to Irigaray (1993a: 10). One is evident in the so-called Oedipus complex (Irigaray 1985). The development of sexual difference, according to Freud, is marked by the entry of this complex in a child's psychic life. The pre-Oedipal is thus a particular place connected to the mother, from whom it is necessary to separate, according to Freud. A child thus has to create distance to the mother, and identify with the father to establish sexual identity. The Oedipal exists through the creation of a border to the pre-Oedipal. Irigaray says that the meaning of place in western thought has been Oedipalized, whereby the meaning of place is associated with the pre-Oedipal connecting place with early mother-child relations and mothering in general. Thus we may say that any border in society resembles this first border. Irigaray would go as far as saying that an isomorphic similarity exists between the materiality of the body in the relation between mother and child and the form and shape of the materiality of social space, of places in the world. Border-making in the real world can therefore be seen as an extension of the work to establish identity as different from the first place.

In relation to this, the western way of distinguishing between time and space can be seen as a particular version of the Oedipal fixation on borders. Irigaray shows that the dissociation between time and space is related to other pairs of concepts, like woman and man, body and soul, sexuality and spirituality, inside and outside (Irigaray 1993a). Indeed, space regarded as extension or geometrical space is the perfect example of a disembodied and fleshless concept of place. This space is not lived, Irigaray argues, it is a construct of the mind that is created as a solution to the threat of the maternal first place. It is an explanation of why there is such a thing as a world, materiality and real stuff like flesh and blood, sweat and tears, suffering, joy and happiness. Irigaray criticizes the consequences of such border-makings; time has become interior to the human being, while space has been exteriorized.

A second example of the lethal consequences can be found in western culture's creation myths. Irigaray rewrites the Judeo-Christian creation myth in a fascinating but disturbing switch (Birkeland 1999). In Irigaray's version of the myth, the mother and womb, that body-place of first beginnings, is the origin of an ancient creation myth that has been forgotten for a very long time but which may become the new creation myth of our time. In this creation myth, place takes an important meaning. Irigaray draws on an Aristotelian understanding of place as interval. In the beginning bodies and places existed, according to Irigaray (Irigaray 1993a). Place was actually body-as-place. The mother was the place for the child-to-be, and woman was the place for the encounter with another human being. This place was a maternal-feminine embodied place. This place was a double, because she was both mother and woman. She was both enveloped in a body and enveloping with the womb. She was open both to herself and to the other outside herself. This made woman-as-place into a place-in-motion. Woman-as-place was an envelope and an opening. And as envelope and opening she was never complete envelope or open, but porous or half-open/half-closed.

In the western world, this maternal-feminine place has become threatening because of the unconscious power it holds over human beings, Irigaray argues. It is the abyss, the ground. This is why discourses on place are concerned with border-makings. The philosopher Christine Battersby reads Irigaray's ideas as a discourse on boundaries (Battersby 1998). She shows that concepts of identity in western philosophy have focused on the boundaries of the self, and the difference between self and non-self. Battersby writes about personal identity but this can very well be extended to place identity. She argues for a way of thinking where identity can be based on fluidity or flow, rather than on spatial containment and its logic of either-or. As Battersby suggests, we can think of identity in terms of mother-child relationships. This means that identity is permeated with difference. The border between self and non-self is not characterized by antagonism or containment, but in terms of patterns of flow, according to Battersby. Identities of place may no longer be thought of in terms of a there or a here, but as identification with-in place, in flow or process.

I have translated this fluid metaphysics as the logic of the umbilical cord (Birkeland 2000b). It is Irigaray herself who has suggested the umbilical cord as an image for the power of motherhood and the maternal principle. She views the umbilical cord as a parallel to the phallus as a symbolic expression for the paternal principle. Instead of seeing the paternal principle as an expression of the social and symbolic order, she views order and power from the maternal principle, where phallic power is far from all-powerful. Phallic power is a masculine version of the power of the first place and the logic of the umbilical cord (Irigaray 1993, Birkeland 2000b). The word for power that would be equivalent for this logic is power as creation. This power is not to have power over someone or something. It is rather power as flow, as empowerment, as that which exists between, as that exchange of flow between the mother and the child, via the image and reality of the umbilical cord, symbolized by the fluid flowing from mother to child and the growing life flowing from the child.

This concrete manifestation of power is a time-place not yet separated in a here and a there, a before and an after, you and me. The interesting point is to recognize it as a concrete place that refuses the logic of either-or. This represents a possibility to view the body of the mother as a source of female imagery and identification in language for both men and women. It does not represent a fixation of identity as if it were a closed space, but identification as process and change, as a fluid and moving event, pulsating life.

There is yet another aspect to the revitalization of female imagery to discuss with regard to place. When discussing body-as-place, as Irigaray does, we encounter the conflict between valorization of the mother's body in feminist discourse and the devalorization of the same mother's body as a sexual body in masculinist discourse. The woman's body – and the first place – exist in a conflict, as mother and lover, in both ways treated as object not subject. The rewriting of place in terms of woman must also address this second aspect of female imagery, and below I will extend this discussion with regard to the dawning of the midnight sun at the North Cape.

Female speculation: The sun at midnight

At the outset of this chapter I argued that the life-world must be understood from the perspective of sexual difference. In this section I will turn again to embodied, female self (as place, *chora*) and evoke the second aspect of body-as-place through female speculation and the image of seeing the sun at midnight. Luce Irigaray has clearly challenged phenomenology's forgetting of sexual difference. She shows that there is a connection between the idea of the ego, self and visibility in the western world that can be traced to Freudian ideas and the tendency to view the phallus as the visible symbol of the masculine self. Such a discourse on boundary-making divides the inside from the outside, the invisible from the visible, the feminine from the masculine and the female from the male. The inside is invisible, as is shown in Freud's understanding of sexual difference. This means that woman appears as a castrated man because she lacks the visible thing. There is nothing to see, woman is a dark continent. Woman is a mirror, a sort of foundation that gives man his image, thus repeating it as the same (Irigaray 1985: 54). The feminine is connected to interiority and the invisible, while the masculine is connected to exteriority and the visible. Literary theorist Philippa Berry argues, however, that Irigaray figures the feminine in terms of interiority and as a 'feminine, genital eye, which looks inward rather than outward' (Berry 1994: 233). This explains the visual bias in western knowledge production, where woman is not only ground but also mirror, in Irigaray's view. Being, however, does not have to be visible. Being does not have to appear as visible for it to *be,* and being is not equal to that which appears (Irigaray 1985 and 1999; Whitford 1994; Berry 1994; Mortensen 1994; Thrift 1999).

Philippa Berry has argued that the central *motif* in Irigaray's book *Speculum* is the mirroring of phallocentric thought (and its phenomenology) through a burning mirror, the speculum, that sets things *on fire* (Berry 1994: 230). It is yet another of western philosophy's dualisms that is deconstructed here: the opposition between spirit and matter, the divine and the earthly. Irigaray creates a connection between woman and spirit. Berry sees Heidegger's interest in spirit in terms of a connection between the visual, truth and understanding (*aletheia*) as important for Irigaray's feminist interpretation of truth, light or enlightenment and understanding. Both Heidegger and Irigaray want to set speculation *on fire* in order to gain understanding. The image of fire is central for Irigaray for other reasons, as well. As sexual and spiritual in a female sense, the female fire is akin to the meaning of the untranslatable word *jouissance* which can mean something like eye-opening ecstasy, bliss and delight, play, pleasure, plurality, fluidity and tactility; it is excess and also excessive, it makes it possible to see through and also beyond. It is seen as *gynesis,* as that process which sets woman into the becoming of discourse and writing, as Alice Jardine argues (Jardine 1985). Hélène Cixous refers to this process as that which is necessary for women to write as women, writing with white ink (Cixous 1981). It is the 'indefinite flood in which all manner of developments can be inscribed' (Irigaray 1985:229).

Irigaray stresses the darkness that precedes or is the result of oculucentric vision (Irigaray 1985). There is a blind spot that eludes the lens of oculucentrism and this dark continent is figured feminine. Irigaray wants to reveal the blind spot in this phallocentric speculation, to see through it darkly. She does so by comparing it to the 'virgin of the eye' or the pupil in the eye, which is designated as *kore* in Greek, and which further provides association to the myth of the Greek goddess Kore or Persephone (Berry 1994: 232). The Kore thus focuses on interiority instead of exteriority, on the inward, genital eye in a movement that points back towards the maternal and the origin, according to Berry. The feminine eye as *kore* is a point of darkness that refers to the crisis of vision in the labour to reach understanding or truth (*aletheia*). The crisis of *kore* is that it is a field in itself, non-representable and enigmatic, that undermines consciousness since it invites us to look behind the eye/I.

How could it be possible to look behind this eye/I phenomenologically speaking? According to Philippa Berry, Luce Irigaray brings a feminine materiality to *aletheia*, or truth, by associating it with the pre-Oedipal stages of psychic development (Berry 1994, Mortensen 1994). Irigaray has discussed this with reference to Plato's parable of the cave, which is an image of the womblike place which the philosopher must work himself out of in order to gain enlightenment or *aletheia* (Irigaray 1985). This parable of the cave shows that enlightenment, or walking out of the cave towards the light, also leaves a big shadow behind. This same turning towards the light is also found in Heidegger's understanding (Berry 1994). It thus seems that Heidegger's conception of truth is only partial, since behind the light and enlightenment of the clearing there lies a shadow that is not yet discovered. What I draw from this discussion is that there is an in-turning and an entry into a particular invisible realm in the path towards a female or feminist clearing, a feminine place as *chora*, which would imply a change in the meaning of the self. When one looks behind the I/eye, the self will never be the same.

By employing the metaphor of the speculum Luce Irigaray has developed a feminine form of understanding as an inner fire that concerns embodied language and vision. The speculum is an instrument that Irigaray applies in an investigative – speculative – way. Used in this way it becomes a burning glass, a concave textual, which is used to magnify an inner fire or an inner female spirit that comes into being (Berry 1994). The speculum becomes similar to a burning glass that works to reveal and unveil truth in an explosive, flaming way. The unveiling will direct its burning eye of the feminist speculum towards revealing the feminine multiple being as a geographical self. It is done from the state of becoming as a continuing transformation, in order to recover and reinterpret a 'buried feminine darkness, in those shadows upon which representation depends' (ibid: 238-239). Berry concludes that through the image of the burning glass the division between seer and seen, masculine and feminine, spirit and matter, the divine and the earthly, same and other and day and night is undone. But not only undone, I would argue, since a link and a union between opposites takes place from which place in 'the feminine' is born.

When one looks behind the I/eye, the self will never be the same. And so will it be when one looks behind the North Cape. Arriving at North Cape is both a discovery and a transformation of the understanding of place. When one encounters the land of the north, there is nothing to see, if one's search takes its outset in a connection between *aletheia* and visibility. There is only sea and sky left, no more ground. There is only water, air, no more earth. If you stand at the North Cape and see beyond the water, earth and air, you discover fire, illuminated by the movement of the sun. Seeing the sun descend and ascend at midnight is a revelation of fire, the fire aspect of a feminine elemental geography. It is fire that was missing from Sofia's elemental geography. Fire is immanent in the flow of love, in creativity, in will and in life force, or Eros. This discovery is possible when one experiences the sun turn the night into a new day. Seeing the sun at night is paradoxical. It is done at a time of the day when the moon is the only light in the sky. The night is the time when the I/the eye is asleep. The night represents night-consciousness. The midnight sun is thus an image of darkness as a source of light, warmth and fire, and it is utter creativity because it comes into being from nothing. Looking at the midnight sun at North Cape represents a sudden and fiery revelation of the meaning of becoming. The midnight sun represents the becoming of the feminine sensible-transcendental, the loss of a border between self and non-self, and symbolizes the connection between place and non-place, which is other and larger than the self and place, the geographical self.

This mediation between matter and spirit appearing at the North Cape as that (umbilical) cord connecting earth, water and air with sun-fire is possible for the sensible transcendental subject. The sensible transcendental is a figuration used by Irigaray to link the pairs of opposites in dualist thinking, that between spirit/mind and matter/body, imagination and ethics (Whitford 1991: 150). This figure relates directly to ground, body and place. The sensible transcendental is a subject which is not cut off from his or her own becoming. She and he integrate two kinds of fertility: the fertility of women and the fertility of men connected to bodies and to the spiritual and intellectual realms. The word transcendental (which is a concept with differing meanings) in this context refers to the sphere of interest of the subject/thinker/philosopher. In conventional philosophy, the transcendental is cut off from the ground and incorporates a symbolic division between a higher and a lower form of thinking that is in addition related to the division between men and women. I argue against this view aided by Irigaray, who suggests that both sexes need to be 'fertile according to the spirit' (Irigaray in Whitford 1991: 156). And it also means that both sexes need to be seen as fertile according to body, and thus to ground and place, I would add. There is a symbolic division between the sexes regarding the divine and cosmology, which has powerful consequences if the sensible is cut off from the transcendental. We might say that Irigaray refuses to separate the aesthetic from the political, the spiritual from the material. The symbolic marriage between the material and the spiritual, feminine and masculine, creates life, mobility, and fertility for both sexes.

Choragraphy

In this book I have turned the attention to geographies of the self and place by addressing the relationship between tourism, subjectivity and self. Sofia's journey has been a guide to the north, and her story has shown that the North Cape is not a sight, but a site. The north is not visible truth. There is nothing to see. To see anything, the traveller has to turn within his or her own self, thus demonstrating that the truth of seeing North Cape is fundamentally embodied and revealed through the place-image of the midnight sun which magnifies an inner fire. As Sofia's extraordinary journey took place outside organized tourism, this geographical journey has taken place outside of mainstream masculinist geography. It is still geography, for what can geography be if it does not also account for real women's geographies?

Sofia's journey to the north was initiated as a search for her personal north point. Her story has structured the narrative logic of this book's discussions by presenting a woman-centred point of view. I have argued that sexual difference is central to the making of self and place. By journeying to the North Cape the female self is created as a movement between the feminine and the masculine, between the maternal and the paternal, in complex interactive processes. It is not a journey from A to B in terms of fixed points but an open process characterized by openness in both internal and external worlds. Sofia's journey has shown that sexual difference is a complex process that produces a change in the meaning of self as something that exists within and place as something that exist without. Instead, the journey suggests an end to constructions of self and place as a subject-object relation and a beginning of seeing self and place in terms of a subject-subject relation. The theoretical journey has implied work on phenomenology and post-Lacanian psychoanalytic feminism in a way where these traditions are able to communicate with each other. I went back and forth between these two traditions until I reached the North Cape, that point in my argument where opposites converge, and where I conclude that the self is a geographical place and where place is a geographical self.

Writing place in "the feminine", as was introduced in chapter one, has needed female imagery based on female genealogies. It has also needed harmonious relations between female and male imagery in the symbolic order. Place-making, as I see it, is thus a continuous process of difference where place is both within and without, both interior and exterior. Places are patterns of flow. Place is not unitary or contained, and the boundaries between places are not closed, autonomous or impermeable. Place is potential place, she and he is flow, revealing what it means to dwell. This is a non-Oedipal understanding of place. This way of understanding place should not be regarded as the only solution to discourses on place. It is not a question of fixing the meaning of place. What is at stake is how this experience, phenomenon, image and reality of place comes into being, how it transforms masculinist imagery into heterosexual imagery useful for the becoming of the differences of two sexes. The central concern is not to have place identity, but to be place and to make place. Place is not woman, but place-making is also a bringing forth of female imagery. It is a fluid way of dwelling. There is sensitivity to the possibilities for another way of planning, building and living with and within place.

In this conclusion, I want to use these ideas to rewrite sustainable concepts of place and self (see Braidotti 1999). When I use the word sustainable, I treat it in a very loose sense. I am not using it in an instrumental sense of the word but to evoke the logics of the umbilical cord and the flow of feminine imagery – thinking about things and people in a way where everything is related to everything and where everything affects everything. It is thinking the immanent and the transcendent simultaneously. The interconnectedness of self and place shows that we, humans, need to reconnect with our material basis, to our own bodies, other bodies, our non-human others, and to the first place. I would therefore suggest a politics of difference in a sustainable sense.

Geographers are, and should be, concerned with the production of space and place. I argue that the concept of place does and should play a very important role for a sustainable future. The western world is obviously not a good dwelling place. What we have are placeless places and lack of dwelling. Humans have not been able to create good dwelling places for themselves (or for their non-human others). I think we have to see this placeless-ness as a social and cultural disease caused by a lack of relationship to the first place. Place can potentially be a feeling of being at home in our body-place in a way where difference is allowed for. I think this would be a sense of home where difference is met with wonder. It would lead to the possibility of belonging in a new way where place is humane and where humans *are* place.

Irigaray teaches us to think of the body as a place. Not only our own body is a place, but our bodily memory bears the traces of our mother's body as the first place, consciously or unconsciously. The consequence is that it is not possible to think of place without co-thinking our history as our mother's children, seated in the particular place of mother-child interaction. And our civilization also bears the traces of dependency to place. As a forgotten place of culture's memory it provokes both a strong fascination and great fear when dealing with place as the ground for culture's being. By remembering our mother's body as the first place for all of us, men and women, we are also reminded of the non-human world as the first place for culture. This means, quite literally and in other ways, that any discourse on place is also a discourse on Woman (Mother).

This could be seen as a starting point for a new emergence of a power of place, coming from the body, from place, and the more-than-human. This power of place cannot appear without translation. Re-inscribing place with a new meaning needs place-writing. According to the philosopher Val Plumwood (2002), it is important to engage with some sort of translation, narration of intentionality and communicativity to understand the power of place. Place and self exist, but must be given social relevance through interpretation and contextualization. The language of place does need the forming of relationship to place to relate dialogically to place. While Plumwood argues for place-writing to be seated in the creation of multi-layered relations to place, it is also obvious that this is highly problematic for western culture. This interpretation, this narration, is exactly what I suggest in this conclusion by writing place in "the feminine", or *choragraphy*.

As first year students of geography, we learn about chorography. Another name for geography has for a long time been chorography. I consciously invoke the term *choragraphy* as a metaphor for writing place in "the feminine". In ordinary language, chorography is the geographical description of place or region, or the study of geographical distribution. When I use the word *choragraphy* it means writing place as that power from within. I suggest that geographers focus on place in "the feminine" by writing place as subject. I suggest we should not only write but relate to place as subject, treating place as a she, as fore-mother, and affirm the dependency on her as the seat for our becoming. I look forward to geographical genealogies of place, both female and male, emergent places and plural place-worlds. Places made habitable, and habitable because of the power of place.

Bibliography

Abram, D. (1996), *The Spell of the Sensuous: Perception and Language in a More-than-Human World*, Pantheon, New York.

Adam, B. (1990), *Time and Social Theory*, Cambridge, Polity Press.

Adler, J. (1989), 'Origins of Sightseeing', *Annals of Tourism Research*, Vol. 16, pp. 7-29.

Alvesson, M. and Sköldberg, K. (1996), *Tolkning och reflektion*, Studentlitteratur, Lund.

Anderson, K. and Gale, F. (1992), *Inventing Places*, Longman Cheshire, Melbourne.

Åquist, A.-C. (1994), 'Idehistorisk översikt', in J. Öhman (ed), *Traditioner i Nordisk kulturgeografi*, Nordisk Samhällsgeografisk Tidskrift.

Aronsson, L. (2000), *The Development of Sustainable Tourism*, Continuum, London.

Atkinsson, P. and Hammersley, E. (1996), *Feltmetodikk*, Ad Notam, Oslo.

Auge, M. (1995), *Non-places: Introduction to an Anthropology of Supermodernity*. Verso, London.

Bachelard, G. (1994), *The Poetics of Space*, Beacon Press, Boston.

Bærenholdt, J.O. and Simonsen, K. (2004), *Space Odysseys, Spatiality and Social Relations in the 21st Century*, Ashgate, Aldershot.

Bærenholdt, J.O. et al (2004), *Performing Tourist Places*, Ashgate, Aldershot.

Battersby, C. (1998), *The Phenomenal Woman. Feminist Metaphysics and the Patterns of Identity*, Polity Press, Oxford.

Barth, F. (1961) Nomads of South Persia, Oslo University Press, Oslo.

Basso, K.H. (1996) *Wisdom sits in Places. Landscape and Language among the Western Apache*, University of New Mexico Press, Albuquerque.

Bauman, Z. (1996), 'From Pilgrim to Tourist – or a Short History of Identity', in S. Hall and P. Du Gay (eds), *Questions of Identity*, Sage, London.

Becker, U. (2000), *The Continuum Encyclopedia of Symbols*, Continuum, New York.

Bell, D. and Valentine, G. (1995), *Mapping Desire. Geographies of Sexualities*, Routledge, London.

Bender, B. (1993), *Landscape: Politics and Perspectives*, Berg Publishers, Oxford.

Berg, N. and Forsberg, G. (2003), 'Rural Geography and Feminist Geography', in J. Öhman and K. Simonsen (eds) *Voices from the North. New Trends in Nordic Human Geography*, Ashgate, Aldershot.

Berger, T. and P. Luckmann (2000), *Den samfunnsskapte virkelighet*. Fagbokforlaget, Bergen.

Berman, M. (1981), *The Re-enchantment of the World*, Cornell University Press, Ithaca, N.Y.

Berry, P. (1993), 'Woman and space according to Kristeva and Irigaray', in P. Berry and A. Wernick (eds), *Shadow of Spirit: Postmodernism and Religion*, Routledge, London.

Berry, P. (1994), 'The Burning Glass: Paradoxes of Feminism Revelations in Speculum', in C. Burke, N. Schor and M. Whitford (eds) *Engaging with Irigaray*, Columbia University Press, New York.

Bertaux, D. (1981), *Biography and Society. The Life History Approach in the Social Sciences*, Sage, Beverly Hills.

Bigwood, C. (1993), *Earth Muse. Feminism, Nature, and Art*, Temple University Press, Philadelphia.

Birkeland, I. (1995), 'Om å skrive feministisk geografi', *Nordisk Samhällsgeografisk Tidskrift*, Nr 21, pp. 32-40.

Birkeland, I. (1997), 'Visuell erfaring som situert kunnskap', *Sosiologi i Dag*, Vol. 27, pp. 73-89.

Birkeland, I. (1998), 'Nature and the "Cultural Turn" in Human Geography', *Norsk geografisk tidskrift*, Vol. 52, pp. 229-240.

Birkeland, I. (1999), 'The Mytho-Poetic in Northern Travel', in D. Crouch (ed.), *Leisure/Tourism Geographies*, Routledge, London.

Birkeland, I. (2000a), 'Luce Irigaray: mors makt', in I. B. Neumann (ed.), *Maktens strateger*, Pax, Oslo.

Birkeland, I. (2000b), 'Representasjoner av Nordkapp og norsk natur 1860-1900', in I. Birkeland and B.L. Hanssen (eds), *Menneskers rom*, Unipub, Oslo.

Birkeland, I. (2002), 'Sted som metafor for kvinnelig subjektivitet: Reisen mot nord', *Kvinneforskning* vol. 26, pp. 83-97.

Blom, G.A. (1992), *Nidaros som pilegrimsby*, Småskriftserien, nr 6, Nidaros Domkirkes Restaureringsarbeiders Forlag, Trondheim.

Blunt, A. (1994), *Travel, Gender, and Imperialism*, Guildford, London.

Blunt, A. and Rose, G. (1994), *Writing Women and Space: Colonial and Postcolonial Geographies*, Guildford, New York.

Bohls, E. (1995), *Women Travel Writers and the Language of Aesthetics*, Cambridge University Press, Cambridge.

Bondi, L. (1991), 'Feminism, Postmodernism, and Geography', *Antipode*, vol. 22, pp. 156-167.

Bondi, L. (1997), 'In whose words? On Gender Identities, Knowledge and Writing Practices', *Transaction of the Institute of British Geographers*, vol 22, pp. 245-258.

Bondi, L. et al (2002) *Subjectivties, Knowledges, and Feminist Geographies*, Rowman and Littlefield, Lanham.

Bourdieu, P. and Waquant, L. (1992), *An Invitation to Reflexive Sociology*, Polity Press, London.

Braidotti, R. (1991), *Patterns of Dissonance*, Polity Press, Cambridge.

Braidotti, R. (1994), *Nomadic Subjects*, Columbia University Press, New York.

Braidotti, R. et al (1994) *Women, the Environment and Sustainable Development*. Towards a Theoretical Synthesis, Zed Books, London.

Braidotti, R. (1999), 'Towards Sustainable Subjectivity: A View from Feminist Philosophy', in E. Becker and T. Jahn (eds), *Sustainability and the Social Sciences*, ZED Books, London.

Brooke, R. (1991), *Jung and Phenomenology*, Routledge, London.

Bruner, E. (1991), 'The Transformation of Self in Tourism', *Annals of Tourism Research*, Vol. 18, pp. 238-50.

Bruner, E. (1994), 'The Ethnographer/Tourist in Indonesia', in M.-Fr.Lanfant et al (eds) *International Tourism. Identity and Change*, Routledge, London.

Burgess, J.P. (2000), 'Jacques Derrida: Maktens begrep, begrepets makt', in I.B. Neumann (ed.), *Maktens strateger*, Pax, Oslo.

Burke, E. (1958), *A Philosophical Enquiry into the Origin of our Ideas of the Sublime and Beautiful*, Routledge and Kegan Paul, London.

Buttimer, A. (1976), 'Grasping the dynamism of lifeworld', *Annals of the Association of American Geographers*, Vol. 66, pp. 277-92.

Buttimer, A. (1980), 'Home, Reach and the Sense of Place', in A. Buttimer and D. Seamon (eds), *The Human Experience of Space and Place,* Croom Helm, London.

Buttimer, A. (1985), 'Nature, water symbols and the human quest for wholeness, in D. Seamon and R. Mugerauer (eds), *Dwelling, Place and Environment*, Columbia University Press, New York.

Buttimer, A. (1993), *Geography and the Human Spirit*, Johns Hopkins University, Baltimore.

Buzard, J. (1993), *The Beaten Track. European Tourism, Literature, and the Ways to 'Culture'*, Clarendon Press, Oxford.

Casey, E. (1993), *Getting Back into Place. Toward a Renewed Understanding of the Place-World*, Indiana University Press, Bloomington.

Casey, E. (1997), *The Fate of Place*, University of California Press, Berkeley.

Catz, C. (1996), 'The expeditions of conures', in D L. Wolf (ed), *Feminist Dilemmas in Fieldwork*, Westview Press, Boulder.

Chambers, I. (1994), *Migrancy, Culture, Identity*, Routledge, London.

Chanter, T. (1995) *Ethics of Eros. Irigaray's Rewriting of the Philosophers*. Routledge, New York.

Christoperson, S. (1989), 'On being outside "The Project"', *Antipode*, Vol. 21, pp. 83-89.

Cixous, H. (1981), 'Sorties', in E. Marks and I. de Courtivron (eds), *New French Feminisms*, Harvester, New York.

Cixous, H. (1981), 'The Laugh of the Medusa', in E. Marks and I. de Courtivron (eds), *NewFrench Feminisms*, Harvester, New York.

Clifford, J. (1986), 'Introduction: Partial Truths', in J. Clifford and G. E. Marcus (eds), *Writing Culture*, University of California Press, Berkeley.

Clifford, J. (1992), 'Travelling Culture', in L. Grossberg, C. Nelson and P. Treichler (eds), *Cultural Studies*, University of California Press, Berkeley.

Clifford, J. (1997), *Routes. Travel and Translation in the late Twentieth Century*, Harvard University Press, Cambridge.

Cohen, E. (1979), 'The phenomenology of tourist experiences', *Sociology*, Vol. 13. pp. 179-201.

Cohen, E. (1988), 'Authenticity and Commodification in Tourism', *Annals of Tourism Research*, Vol. 15, pp. 371-386.

Cohen, S. and Taylor, L. (1976), *Escape Attempts,* Routledge, London.

Coleman, S. and Crang, M. (2002), *Tourism: Between Place and Performance*, Berghahn

Books, Oxford.

Crang, M. (1999), 'Knowing, tourism and practices of vision', in D. Crouch (ed), *Leisure/Tourism Geographies*, Routledge, London.

Cronon, W. (1996), 'The Trouble with Wilderness; or Getting Back to the Wrong Nature', in W. Cronon (ed), *Uncommon Ground. Rethinking the Human Place in Nature*, W.W. Norton, New York.

Crouch, D. (1999), *Leisure/Tourism Geographies. Practices and Geographical Knowledge*, Routledge, London.

Culler, J. (1981), 'Semiotics of Tourism', in *American Journal of Semiotics*, Vol. 1, pp. 127-140.

Curtis, B. and Pajaczkowska, C. (1994), 'Getting there': Travel, time and narrative', in G. Robertson et al, *Traveller's tales*, Routledge, London.

De Certeau, M. (1984), *The Practice of Everyday Life*, University of California Press, Berkeley.

Denzin, N. (1989), *Interpretative Biography*, Sage, London.

Derrida, J. (1995), *On the Name*, Stanford University Press, Stanford.

Dinnerstein, D, (1977), *The Mermaid and The Minotaur*, Harper & Row, New York.

Douglas, M. (1966), *Purity and Danger*, Routledge, London.

Døving, R. (1993), *Syden – Fritidens land og dets folk*, Hovedoppgave, Institutt og museum for antropologi, Universitetet i Oslo, Oslo.

Edensor, T. and Kothari, U. (1994), 'The masculinization of Stirling's heritage', in V. Kinnaird and D. Hall (eds), *Tourism: A Gender Analysis*, John Wiley and Sons, Chichester.

Eliade, M. (1987), *The Sacred and the Profane*, Harcourt Brace, Orlando.

Entrikin, N. (1991), *The Betweenness of Place*, The Johns Hopkins University Press, Baltimore.

Evernden, N. (1985), *The Natural Alien*, Toronto University Press, Toronto.

Feld, S. and Basso, K. (1996), *Senses of Place*, School of American Research Press, Santa Fe.

Fisher, A. (2001), *Radical ecopsychology. Psychology in the service of life*, SUNY Press, New York.

Flax, J. (1987), 'Postmodernism and gender relations in feminist theory', Signs, Vol. 12, pp. 621-643.

Flax, J. (1990), *Thinking Fragments. Psychoanalysis, Feminism, and Postmodernism in the Contemporary West*, University of California Press, Berkeley.

Fog, J. (1994), *Med samtalen som udgangspunkt*, Akademisk Forlag, København.

Fraser, N. and Nicholson, L. (1988), 'Social Criticism without Philosophy – An Encounter between Feminism and Postmodernism', *Theory, Culture and Society*, Vol. 5, pp. 373-394.

Frawley, M. H. (1994), *A Wider Range: travel writing by women in Victorian England*, Fairleigh Dichinson University Press, Rutherford NJ.

Freeman, M. (1993), *Rewriting the Self*, Routledge, London.

Fürst, E. L. (1995), *Mat – et annet språk*, Pax, Oslo.

Fürst, E. L. (1997), 'Poststrukturalisme og fransk feminisme', in E.L. Fürst and Ø. Nilsen (eds), *Modernitet. Refleksjoner og idébrytninger*, Cappelen Akademisk, Oslo.

Gadamer, H.-G. (1989), *Truth and Method*, Sheed and Ward, London.

Gottschalk, S. (1998), 'Postmodern Sensibilities and Ethnographic Possibilities', in A. Banks and S. P. Banks (eds), *Fiction & Social Research*, AltaMira Press, Walnut Creek.

Graburn, N. (1977), 'Tourism: The Sacred Journey', in V. Smith (ed), *Hosts and Guests. The Anthropology of Tourism*, University of Philadelphia Press, Philadelphia.

Gray, J. (1999), 'Open Spaces and Dwelling Places: Being at Home on Hill Farms in the Scottish Borders', *American Ethnologist*, Vol. 26, pp. 440-460.

Green, M. J. (1991), *The Sun-Gods of Ancient Europe*, B.T. Batsford, London.

Gregory, D. (1994), *Geographical Imaginations*, Blackwell, Cambridge.

Gregory, D. (1995), 'Lefebvre, Lacan, and the production of space', in G. Benko and U. Strohmayer (eds), *Geography, History and Social Sciences*, Kluver, Dordrecht.

Gren, M. (1994), *Earth Writing*, Department of Geography, University of Gothenburg, Gothenburg.

Gren, M. (1996), 'Visible/invisible boundaries', *Nordisk samhällsgeografisk tidskrift*, Nr 22.

Grosz, E. (1989), *Sexual Subversions*, Allen and Unwin, Sydney.

Grosz, E. (1994), *Volatile Bodies*, Allen and Unwin, St. Leonards, New South Wales.

Grosz, E. (1995), *Space, Time, and Perversion*, Routledge, London.

Gupta, A. and Ferguson, J. (1997), *Anthropological Locations*, University of California Press, Berkeley.

Gurevich, A.Y. (1969), 'Space and Time in the Weltmodel of the Old Scandinavian Peoples', *Medieval Scandinavia*, Vol. 2, pp. 42-53.

Hall , D. and Kinnaird, V. (1994), 'A note on women travellers', in D. Hall and V. Kinnaird (eds), *Tourism: A Gender Analysis*, Wiley, Chichester.

Haraway, D. (1988), 'Situated knowledge: The science question in feminism and the privilege of partial perspective', *Feminist Studies*, Vol.14, pp. 575-99.

Haraway, D. (1991), *Simians, Cyborgs and Women*, Routledge, London.

Harding, S. (1986), *The Science Question in Feminism*, Open University Press, Milton Keynes.

Harley, J.B. (1996), 'Deconstructing the Map', in J. Agnew et al, *Human Geography. An Essential Anthology*, Blackwell, Oxford.

Heidegger, M. (1971), *Poetry, Language, Thought*, Penguin, New York.

Hirsch, E. and O'Hanlon (1995) *The Anthropology of Landscape. Perspectives on Place and Space*, Clarendon Press, Oxford.

Holmes, R. (1987), 'Introduction', in M. Wollstonecraft and W. Godwin: *A Short Residence in Sweden, Norway, and Denmark*, And *Memoirs of the Author of 'The Rights of Woman'*, edited by R. Holmes, London, Penguin.

Holland, N. and Huntington, P. (2001) *Feminist Interpretations of Heidegger*. The Pennsylvania State University Press, Univ. Park, Pennsylvania.

Højrup, T. (1977), *Det glemte folk. Livsformer og centraldirigering*, Institut for europeisk folkelivsgranskning/Statens byggeforskningsinstitut, København.

How, A. (1995), *The Habermas-Gadamer Debate and the Nature of the Social:* Back to Bedrock, Avebury, Aldershot.

Ingold, T. (1993), 'Globes and spheres. The topology of environmentalism', in K. Milton (ed.), *Environmentalism: the view from anthropology,* ASA Monographs 32, Routledge, London.

Ingold, T. (2000), *The Perception of the Environment: Essays on Livelihood, Dwelling and Skill,* London, Routledge.

Irigaray, L. (1985), *Speculum of the Other Women,* Cornell University Press, Ithaca NY.

Irigaray, L. (1991), *Marine Lover of Friedrich Nietzsche,* Columbia University Press, New York.

Irigaray, L. (1993a), *An Ethics of Sexual Difference,* The Athlone Press, London.

Irigaray, L. (1993b), *Sexes and Genealogies,* Columbia University Press, New York.

Irigaray, L. (1996), *I Love to You. Sketch of a Possible Felicity in History,* Routledge, New York.

Irigaray, L. (1999), *The Forgetting of Air,* University of Texas Press, Austin.

Irigaray, L. (2002), *The Way of Love,* Continuum, London.

Jackson, P. (1989), *Maps of Meaning,* Routledge, London.

Jacobs, J.M. (1994), ''Shake 'im this country': the mapping of the Aboriginal sacred in Australia – the case of Coronation Hill', in P. Jackson and J. Penrose (eds), *Constructions of Race, Place and Nation,* Minnesota University Press, Minneapolis.

Jacobsen, J.K. (1983), *Moderne turisme: en sosiologisk analyse av sentrale trekk i turistenes handlingsmønstre,* Institutt for sosiologi, Universitetet i Oslo, Oslo.

Jacobsen, J.K. (1997), 'North Cape – the making of an attraction', *Annals of Tourism Research,* Vol. 24, pp. 341-356.

Jager, B. (1971), 'Horizontality and Verticality. A Phenomenological Exploration into Lived Space', in A. Giorgi et al, *Duquesne Studies in Phenomenological Psychology Vol. I,* Duquesne University Press, Pittsburgh.

Jameson, F. (1984), 'Postmodernism, or, the Cultural Logic of Late Capitalism', *New Left Review,* Vol. 146, pp. 53-92.

Jasen, P. (1995), *Wild Things. Nature, Culture and Tourism in Ontario, 1790-1914,* University of Toronto Press, Toronto.

Jung, C.G. (1995) *Memories, Dreams, Reflections,* Fontana Press, London.

Kaplan, C. (1987), 'Deterritorializations: The rewriting of home and exile in western feminist discourse', in *Cultural Critique,* Vol. 6, pp. 187-98.

Karjalainen, P.T. (2003) 'On geobiography', in V. Sarapik and K. Tüür (eds.), *Place and Location. Studies in Environmental Aesthetics and Semiotics III,* Estonian Academy of Arts, pp. 87-92.

Karjalainen, P.T. (2000), 'Earth Writing as Humane Art', in K. Lehari and V. Sapik (eds.) *Place and Location. Studies in Environmental Aesthetics and Semiotics I,* Estonian Academy of Arts, pp. 21-27.

Keith, M. and Pile, S. (1993), 'Introduction', in M. Keith and S. Pile (eds), *Place and the Politics of Identity,* Routledge, London.

Keller, E.F. (1985), *Reflections on Gender and Science,* Yale University Press, New Haven.

Keller, E.F. and Grontkowski, C.R. (1993), 'The Mind's Eye', in S. Harding and M.B. Hintakka (eds), *Disovering Reality,* D. Reidel, Dordrecht.

Kirby, K. (1996a), *Indifferent Boundaries. Spatial Concepts of Human Subjectivity,* The Guilford Press, New York.

Kirby, K. (1996b), 'Re:Mapping subjectivity. Cartographic vision and the limits of politics', in N. Duncan, *BodySpace*, Routledge, London.

Koskela, H. (1999), *Fear, Control and Space: Geographies of Gender, Fear of Violence, and Video Surveillance*, The Geographical Institute of the University of Helsinki Publications A 137, University of Helsinki, Helsinki.

Kristeva, J. (1984), *Revolution in Poetic Language*, Columbia University Press, New York.

Kristeva, J. (1986a), 'Women's Time', in T. Moi (ed), *The Kristeva Reader*, Blackwell, Oxford.

Kristeva, J. (1986b), 'The System and the Speaking Subject', in T. Moi (ed), *The Kristeva Reader*, Blackwell, Oxford.

Kristeva, J. (1987), *Tales of Love*, Columbia University Press, New York.

Kristeva, J. (1991), *Strangers to Ourselves*, Harvester Wheatsheaf, New York.

Kristeva, J. (1995), *New Maladies of the Soul*, Columbia University Press, New York.

Kvale, S. (1996), InterViews, Sage, London.

Lakoff, G, and Johnson, M. (1980), *Metaphors we Live by*, University of Chicago Press, Chicago.

Lanfant, M.-Fr., Alcock, J.B. and Bruner, E. (1994), *International Tourism. Identity and Change*, Sage, London.

Lash, S. and Urry, J. (1994), *Economies of Signs and Space*, Sage, London.

Lauter, E. (1984), *Women as Mythmakers*, Indiana University Press, Bloomington.

Lefebvre, H. (1991), *The Production of Space*, Blackwell, Oxford.

Lehtinen, A. (1991), *Northern Natures. A study of the forest question emerging within the timber-line conflict in Finland*, Helsinki, Geographical Society of Finland, Reprint from Fennia, Vol. 169, pp. 57-169.

Ley, D. (1980), *Geography without Man: a Humanistic Perspective*, School of Geography Research Paper 24, Oxford University, Oxford.

Ley, D. and Duncan, J. (1993), *Place/Culture/Representation*, Routledge, London.

Low, S. and Lawrence-Zuniga, D. (2003) *The Anthropology of Space and Place: Locating Culture,* Blackwell, Oxford.

Lowenthal, D. (1985), *The Past is a Foreign Country*, Cambridge University Press, Cambridge.

MacCannell, D. (1976), *The Tourist. A New Theory of the Leisure Class*, Shocken Books, New York.

Malpas, J. (1994), 'A Taste of Madeleine: Notes Towards a Philosophy of Place', *International Philosophical Quarterly*, Vol 34, pp. 433-451.

Malpas, J. (1998), 'Finding Place: Spatiality, Locality, and Subjectivity', in A. Light and J.M. Smith (eds), *Philosophy and Geography III. Philosophies of Place*, Rowman and Littlefield, Lanham.

Massey, D. and Allen, J. (1984), *Geography Matters!*, Cambridge University Press, Cambridge.

Massey, D. (1994), *Space, Place and Gender*, Polity Press, Cambridge.

McDowell, L. and Massey, D. (1984), 'A Woman's Place?' in D. Massey and J. Allen (eds), *Geography Matters!*, Cambridge University Press, Cambridge.

McDowell, L. (1992), 'Doing Gender: Feminism, Feminists and Research Methods in

Human Geography', *Transactions of the Institute of British Geographers*, vol 17, pp. 399-416.

Mills, S. (1991), *Discourses of Difference: An Analysis of Women's Travel Writing and Colonialism*, Routledge, London.

Mills, S. (2000), 'Written on the landscape: Mary Wollstonecraft', in A. Gilroy (ed.) *Romantic Geographies*, Manchester University Press, Manchester.

Morris, M. (1993), *Maiden Voyages: The Writings of Women Travellers*, Vintage Books, New York.

Mortensen, E. (1994), *The Feminine and Nihilism: Luce Irigaray with Nietzsche and Heidegger*, Scandinavian University Press, Oslo.

Mulvey, L. (1989), *Visual and Other Pleasures*, Macmillan, Basingstoke.

Myrhaug, M.-L. (1997), *I modergudinnens fotspor*, Pax, Oslo.

Nash, C. (1996), 'Reclaiming Vision: Looking at Landscape and the Body', *Gender, Place and Culture*, Vol. 3, pp. 149-169.

Nash, D. (1977), 'Tourism as a form of imperialism', in V. Smith (ed.) *Hosts and Guests. The Anthropology of Tourism*, University of Philadelphia Press, Philadelphia.

Nast, H. and Kobayashi, A. (1996), 'Re-corporealizing vision', in N. Duncan (ed.), *BodySpace*, Routledge, London.

Nast, H. and Blum, V. (1998), 'Where's the difference?: The Heterosexualization of Alterity in Henri Lefebvre and Jaques Lacan', *Environment & Planning D: Society & Space*, Vol. 14, pp. 559-580.

Nast, H. and Blum, V. (2000), 'Jacques Lacan's Two-dimensional Subjectivity', in N. Thrift and M. Crang (eds), *Thinking Space*, Routledge, London.

Nesmith, C. and Radcliffe, S.A. (1993) '(Re)mapping Mother Earth: A Geographical Perspective on Environmental Feminisms', *Environment & Planning D: Society & Space*, Vol. 11, pp. 379-94.

Nielsen, J.M. (1990), *Feminist Research Methods. Exemplary Readings in the Social Sciences*, Westview Press, Boulder.

Norberg-Schultz, C. (1980) *Genius Loci. Towards a Phenomenology of Architecture*, Academy Editions, London.

Norris, J. and Wall, G. (1994), 'Gender and Tourism', *Progress in Tourism, Recreation and Hospitality Management*, Vol. 6, pp. 57-77.

Norwood, V. and Monk, J. (1987), *The Desert is no Lady: Southwestern Landscapes in Women's Writing and Art*, Yale University Press, New Haven, Conn.

Oelschlaeger, M. (1997), 'Geography in a Time of Cultural Crisis: Helping Philosophy find its Place', *Ecumene*, Vol. 4, pp. 373-88.

Okely, J. (1996), *Own or Other Culture*, Routledge, London.

Olwig, K.F. and Hastrup, K. (1997), *Siting Culture. The Shifting Anthropological Object*, Routledge, London.

Olwig, K. (1993), 'Sexual Cosmology: Nation and Landscape at the Conceptual Interstices of Nature and Culture; or, What does Landscape Really Mean?', in B. Bender (ed), *Landscape: Politics and Perspective*, Berg Publishers, Oxford.

Olwig, K. (1996), 'Reinventing Common Nature: Yosemite and Mount Rushmore – a Meandering Tale of a Double Nature', in W. Cronon (ed), *Uncommon Ground.*

Rethinking the Human Place in Nature, W.W. Norton and Company, New York.

Olwig, K. (2001), 'Landscape as a Contested Topos of Place, Community and Self', in S. Hoelscher, P.C. Adams and K.E. Till (eds), *Textures of Place: Geographies of Imagination, Experience, and Paradox*, University of Minnesota Press, Minneapolis.

Olwig, K. (2002a), 'Landscape, Place and the State of Progress', in D.R. Sack (ed), *Progress: Geographical Essay*, Johns Hopkins University Press, Baltimore.

Olwig, K. (2002b), *Landscape, Nature and the Body Politic: From Britain's Renaissance to America's New World*, University of Wisconsin Press, Madison.

Pickles, J. (1984), *Phenomenology, Science, and Geography*, Cambridge University Press, Cambridge.

Pile, S. (1996), *The Body and the City: Psychoanalysis, Space and Subjectivity*, Routledge, London.

Pile, S. and Thrift, N. (1995), *Mapping the Subject. Geographies of Cultural Transformation*, Routledge, London.

Plumwood, V. (1993), *Feminism and the Mastery of Nature*, Routledge, London.

Plumwood, V. (2002), *Environmental Culture: The Ecological Crisis of Reason*, Routledge, London.

Pratt, M.L. (1992), *Imperial Eyes: travel writing and transculturation*, Routledge. London.

Pratt, G. (1993), 'Commentary: Spatial metaphors and speaking positions', *Environment & Planning D: Society & Space*, Vol. 10, pp. 241-244.

Relph, E. (1976), *Place and Placelessness*, Pion, London.

Reusch, H. (1895), *Folk og natur i Finnmarken*, A.W.Brøggers Bogtrykkeri, Kristiania.

Richter, L. (1994), 'Exploring the political role of gender in tourism research', in E. Theobald (ed.), *Global Tourism – The Next Decade*, Butterworth/Heinemann, Oxford.

Robinson, J. (1994), *Unsuitable for Ladies. An Anthology of Women Travellers*, Oxford University Press, Oxford.

Rodman, M. (1992), 'Empowering Place: Multilocality and Multivocality', in *American Anthropologist*, vol. 94, pp. 640-656.

Rojek, C. (1985), *Capitalism and Leisure Theory*, Tavistock, London.

Rojek, C. (1995), *Decentring leisure: Rethinking Leisure Theory*, Sage, London.

Rose, G. (1993), *Feminism and Geography*, Polity Press, Cambridge.

Ryall, A. and Veiteberg, J. (1991), *En kvinnelig oppdagelsesreisende i det unge Norge. Catharine Hermine Kølle*, Pax, Oslo.

Salomonsen, J. (1999), *Riter. Overgangsriter i vår tid*, Pax, Oslo.

Schiøtz, E.H. (1971), *Utlendingers reiser i Norge. Itineraria Norvegica*, Universitetsforlaget, Oslo.

Schurmer-Smith, P. and Hannam, K. (1994), *Worlds of Desire: Realms of Power*, Edward Arnold, London.

Schwartz-Salant, N. (1995) *Jung on Alchemy*. Princeton University Press, Princeton.

Scott, J. (1988), 'Deconstructing Equality-Versus-Difference. The Uses of Poststructuralist Theory for Feminism', *Feminist Studies*, Vol. 14, pp. 33-50.

Seamon, D. and Mugerauer, R. (1985), *Dwelling, Place and Environment*, Columbia University Press, New York.

Seamon, D. (1985), 'Reconciling old and new worlds: The dwelling-journey relationship as portrayed in Wilhelm Moberg's Emigrant novels', in D. Seamon and R. Mugerauer (eds), *Dwelling, Place and Environment*, Columbia University Press, New York.

Shands, K.W. (1998), '(Em)bracing space', *NORA*, Vol 6, pp. 21-30.

Shields, R. (1991), *Places on the Margin*, Routledge, London.

Simonsen, K. (1996), 'What kind of space in what kind of social theory?', *Progress in Human Geography*, Vol. 20, pp. 494-512.

Skavhaug, K. (1990), *North Cape: Famous Voyages from the Time of the Vikings to 1800*, Nordkapplitteratur/Nordkappmuseet. Honningvåg.

Smith, A. (1996), *Julia Kristeva. Readings of Exile and Estrangement*, Macmillan. London.

Smith, N. and Catz, C. (1993), 'Grounding Metaphor. Towards a Spatialized Politics', in M. Keith and S. Pile (eds), *Place and the Politics of Identity*, Routledge, London.

Smith, V. (1977), *Hosts and Guests. The Anthropology of Tourism*, University of Pennsylvania Press, Philadelphia.

Smith, V. (1992), 'Introduction', in V. Smith (ed), Pilgrimage in Tourism: The quest in guest, *Annals of Tourism Research*, Vol. 19, pp. 1-9.

Soja, E. (1989), *Postmodern Geographies*, Verso, New York.

Squire, S. (1994), 'Gender and tourism experiences. Assessing women's shared meanings for Beatrix Potter', *Leisure Studies*, Vol. 13, pp. 195-209.

Steedman, C. (1995a), 'Maps and Polar Regions', in S. Pile and N. Thrift (eds), *Mapping the Subject*, London, Routledge.

Steedman, C. (1995b), *Strange Dislocations. Childhood and the Idea of Human Interiority. 1780-1930*, Virago Press London.

Steinsland, G. (1997), *Eros og død i norrøne myter*, Universitetsforlaget, Oslo.

Svanquist, B. K. (2000a), *Naturumgänge ur et individperspektiv*, Karlstad University Studies 2000:9, Institutionen för samhällsvetenskap och Gruppen för Regionalvetenskaplig Forskning, Karlstad.

Svanquist, B. K. (2000b), 'Naturumgänge ur et individperspektiv', *Nordisk Samhällsgeografisk Tidskrift*, nr 31, pp. 37-57.

Swayn, M. N. (1997), *Gender in Tourism, Annals of Tourism Research*, Vol. 22, nr. 2.

Taylor, C. (1989), *Sources of the Self*, Cambridge University Press, Cambridge.

Thrift, N. (1999), 'Steps to an Ecology of Place.' in D. Massey, J. Allen and P. Sarre (eds), *Human Geography Today*, Polity Press, London.

Thrift, N. and Crang, M. (2000), *Thinking Space*, Routledge, London.

Tilley, C. (1993), *A Phenomenology of Landscape: Places, Paths and Monuments*, Berg, Oxford.

Tuan, Y.-F. (1974), *Topophilia. A study of environmental perception, attitudes, and values*, Prentice-Hall, Englewood Cliffs.

Tuan, Y.-F. (1977), *Space and Place: The Perspective of Experience*, Edward Arnold, London.

Turner, V. (1967), *Forest of Symbols*, Cornell University Press, Ithaca.

Turner, V. (1974), *Dramas, Fields, and Metaphors: Symbolic action in society*, Cornell University Press, Ithaca.

Urry, J. (1990), *The Tourist Gaze: Leisure and Travel in Contemporary Societies*, Sage, London.

Van den Abbeele, G. (1992), *Travel as Metaphor: From Montaigne to Rousseau*, University of Minnesota Press, Minneapolis.

Veijola, S. and Jokinen, E. (1994), 'The body in tourism', *Theory, Culture & Society*, Vol. 11, pp. 125-151.

Von Franz, M. L. (1995), *Creation Myths*, Shambala, Boston.

Warren, K. J. (1997), *Ecofeminism*, Indiana University Press, Bloomington.

Weiner, J. F. (1991), *The Empty Place. Poetry, Space and Being among the Foi of Papua New Guinea*, Indiana University Press, Bloomington.

Whitford, M. (1991), *Philosophy in the Feminine*, Routledge, London.

Wolf, D. L. (1996), *Feminist Dilemmas in Fieldwork*, Westview Press, Boulder.

Wolff, J. (1994), *Resident Alien. Feminist Cultural Criticism*, Polity Press, London.

Wollstonecraft, M. and Godwin, W. (1796/1987), *A Short Residence in Sweden, Norway, and Denmark. And Memoirs of the Author of 'The Rights of Woman'*, Edited with an introduction and notes by Richard Holmes, Penguin, London.

Yaeger, P. (1995), 'Toward a Female Sublime', in B. C. Freeman (ed), *The Feminine Sublime*, University of California Press, Berkeley.

Other references

Nordkapp Reiseliv AS (1997), Brochure.

The Land of the Midnight Sun, and North Cape, Brochure, Thomas Cook & Son, London, 1890.

Cook's Tourist's Handbook. Norway, Sweden, and Denmark, 1891, Thomas Cook & Son, London, 1891.

Cooks Tours in Norway, Sweden and Denmark. Brochure, Thomas Cook & Son, London, 1892.

Cook's Excursionist and Tourist Adviser, 1 May 1866, 12 June 1875, 29 June 1875, 9 December 1875, 8 March 1876, 4 April 1876, 1 May 1876, 12 July 1876, 11 September 1876, 19 May 1883.

Index

For Product Safety Concerns and Information please contact our EU representative GPSR@taylorandfrancis.com Taylor & Francis Verlag GmbH, Kaufingerstraße 24, 80331 München, Germany

Batch number: 08158427

Printed by Printforce, the Netherlands